# Expected in Heaven

# Expected in Heaven
## *The Story*

VERA GRIMMIUS/DELEEUW

XULON PRESS

Xulon Press
2301 Lucien Way #415
Maitland, FL 32751
407.339.4217
www.xulonpress.com

Unless otherwise indicated, Scripture quotations taken from the Holy Bible, New International Version (NIV). Copyright © 1973, 1978, 1984, 2011 by Biblica, Inc.™. Used by permission. All rights reserved.

Paperback ISBN-13: 978-1-6628-4162-0
Ebook ISBN-13: 978-1-6628-4163-7

# Acknowledgements:

I want to give special thanks to people who helped and encouraged me write this story: my niece, Shelly Schoo, who went above and beyond in guiding me. We spent many hours on Zoom discussing and going over details; my daughters, Sharmae Flores and Rochelle DeGroot, who also helped by reading the manuscript and giving helpful advice during the writing process; a special thank you to my granddaughter, Jessica Grimmius, who drew the front cover picture, and my grandson, Roman Grimmius, who did the artistic layout for the front cover. A special thanks also to Tricia Boss who was the photographer of original picture on cover.

Finally, I will never forget the one who inspired me to write in the first place, my dear husband of forty-eight years, Tom Grimmius. This book is dedicated to his memory, along with the memory of two other men who played a very important part in my life, John Grimmius and John DeLeeuw. John DeLeeuw inspired me to finish this project and I owe him much gratitude.

# Contents

Prologue . . . . . . . . . . . . . . . . . . . . . . . . . . . . . . . . . . . . . ix

Part I . . . . . . . . . . . . . . . . . . . . . . . . . . . . . . . . . . . . . . . . 1

Chapter 1 – The Early Years . . . . . . . . . . . . . . . . . . . . . . 3

Chapter 2 – The Call . . . . . . . . . . . . . . . . . . . . . . . . . . . .25

Chapter 3 – War and Life . . . . . . . . . . . . . . . . . . . . . . . .31

Chapter 4 – A Construction Business . . . . . . . . . . . . . . . .43

Chapter 5 – The Idaho Move . . . . . . . . . . . . . . . . . . . . . .49

Chapter 6 – An Unexpected Event. . . . . . . . . . . . . . . . . . .58

Chapter 7 – Hopeful . . . . . . . . . . . . . . . . . . . . . . . . . . . .65

Chapter 8 – California. . . . . . . . . . . . . . . . . . . . . . . . . . .74

Chapter 9 – Raising Children . . . . . . . . . . . . . . . . . . . . . .82

Part II . . . . . . . . . . . . . . . . . . . . . . . . . . . . . . . . . . . . .95

Chapter 10 – Vesta . . . . . . . . . . . . . . . . . . . . . . . . . . . . .97

Chapter 11 – Babysitting . . . . . . . . . . . . . . . . . . . . . . . .102

Chapter 12 – High School. . . . . . . . . . . . . . . . . . . . . . . 110

Chapter 13 – Falling in Love. . . . . . . . . . . . . . . . . . . . . .123

Chapter 14 – Love and Marriage. . . . . . . . . . . . . . . . . . .132

Chapter 15 – Raising a Family and Life Changes . . . . . . . 138

Chapter 16 – A Surprise from God . . . . . . . . . . . . . . . . .152

Chapter 17 – A Sad Time . . . . . . . . . . . . . . . . . . . . . . . 160

Chapter 18 – The Good Life Mixed with Trial . . . . . . . . . . .173

Chapter 19 – Country Living. . . . . . . . . . . . . . . . . . . . . . .187

Chapter 20 – Running Businesses . . . . . . . . . . . . . . . . . . 198

Chapter 21 – Years of Plenty and Years of Learning. . . . . .205

Chapter 22 – Business Ventures and High
      School/College . . . . . . . . . . . . . . . . . . . . . . . . .223

Chapter 23 – More Life Changes . . . . . . . . . . . . . . . . . . .241

Chapter 24 – Grandchildren. . . . . . . . . . . . . . . . . . . . . . . 248

Chapter 25 – Handling Life Changes . . . . . . . . . . . . . . . . 260

Chapter 26 – More Babies . . . . . . . . . . . . . . . . . . . . . . . .275

Chapter 27 – Wedding Celebration. . . . . . . . . . . . . . . . . 280

Chapter 28 – The Year of Armageddon. . . . . . . . . . . . . . . 288

Chapter 29 – More of Life and Love . . . . . . . . . . . . . . . . .294

Chapter 30 – Trip of a Lifetime: Israel . . . . . . . . . . . . . . . 300

Chapter 31 – A Half-Marathon . . . . . . . . . . . . . . . . . . . .309

Chapter 32 – A Year of Wonderful Memories . . . . . . . . 318

Chapter 33 – Challenging Days . . . . . . . . . . . . . . . . . . . .326

Chapter 34 – Expected in Heaven . . . . . . . . . . . . . . . . . .339

Postscript. . . . . . . . . . . . . . . . . . . . . . . . . . . . . . . . . . . . .352

# Prologue

There was a spiritual turning point for Vesta as she went off to class, only looking to spend time with her friend and fill her social calendar. She loved people, but, to her surprise, God's plan for Vesta (Schuil) DeVee did not include nurturing her friendship with Cheryl or growing her social life. Instead, He wanted Vesta to grow closer to Him. He wanted her to realize where she came from and was going, not for herself but for Him. In the end, it was to help her see what it meant to be expected—really expected. (Let's start at the beginning.)

Part I

## CHAPTER 1

# The Early Years

The year was 1933 and considered one of the worst years of the Great Depression. Franklin D. Roosevelt was president and working hard to keep the financial markets from collapsing further by having the banks take a holiday and close for almost nine days. Many cities had long food lines, and across the country, one in four people were unemployed. The country's troubles were overwhelming, but two teenage girls living in a small country town in northern Michigan were unaffected. They lived in a place where everyone grew most of their own food and traded with each other so that no one went hungry. They didn't notice the trouble elsewhere. Instead, they were like most teens, with their minds focused on their own families and community.

It was almost time for the Young People's meeting at the McBain Christian Reformed church that evening, so Mag and Johanna were discussing what to wear. "What do you think, Jo, does this look okay?" Mag asked with a worried sigh.

"Of course, you look adorable, as always. The guys are sure to notice you first." Jo laughed as she knew her big sis worried far more than needed.

It was late spring, so they decided to wear summer dresses. Mag was fifteen while Johanna was fourteen, and they enjoyed doing all the things young girls did at this age. Most of all, they loved talking about the boys they were interested in. Later that year, they would turn sixteen and fifteen, making them feel very mature.

Johanna loved life, and although she wished she had more schooling, she enjoyed the family she worked for and made a good living cleaning their home and caring for their children. In her community, the Young People's meeting was the highlight of the week; it was one of the few occasions they spent time with people their own age. A main joy of the meeting, for young women like Mag and Jo, was watching couples get together.

Johanna liked many of the local boys, but none of them caught her eye. After discussing God's Word with their pastor, they had refreshments, which gave them the opportunity to get better acquainted with the boys. Time flew by for Jo and Mag, who loved to talk to as many people as they could. They would offer to help with cleanup and were often some of the last to leave. As they headed home, the girls would walk slowly down the road while the boys, who could drive, would follow them in their cars.

When a boy saw a girl, he was interested in, he would ask if she and her friends needed a ride home. In this small country community, there was no danger of accepting rides that these young people were aware of. They all knew each other and their families. The young men knew better than to leave anyone alone. Everyone was sure to have a ride by the end of the evening.

This was Frank Schuil's first time at the McBain Young People's meeting. His regular church was about five miles to the north. When Johanna Van Til arrived, Frank could not keep his eyes off her and was eager to ask her to ride with him. He was beginning to wonder if he would get the chance. She and her older sister seemed to know everyone. Then he saw her coming out the door just as he was heading to his car with his friends.

"Hi there," Frank said, trying to sound confident. "Would you like us to take you home?"

Johanna took one look at Frank and said, "No, I don't even know you." She was playing hard to get since she had noticed him earlier in the evening. She did like his handsome face and sweet nature as she watched him talk with his friends. She also noticed when he looked her way a few times. It thrilled her that he offered her a ride. However, Johanna was telling the truth and wanted to get to know him before accepting a ride in his car.

After Johanna's rejection, Frank was scared to death and decided to forget about her, despite how sad it made him feel.

However, God had other plans for Frank and Johanna. A few months later, Frank and Johanna met again at the wedding of mutual friends. After several games young people played on such occasions, Frank realized that maybe Johanna was interested in him after all. One of the favorite games young people played at weddings was "Farmer in the Dell." Johanna realized she had scared Frank when she turned him down for the ride. She was determined to encourage him at this wedding. Every time she was chosen, she then chose Frank. It wasn't long after the wedding that they started dating.

Johanna and Frank realized they loved being together and found every excuse to be around each other. Frank soon discovered that Johanna was much braver than she first appeared. Frank wanted to kiss Jo badly, but he had no idea how to proceed and was somewhat anxious that he might offend her. One evening, Frank tried to say goodnight to her, once again, without kissing her. When Johanna realized he was leaving, she grabbed his face with her hands and planted a kiss on his lips. Frank never forgot that moment and loved her more deeply than ever for it. After dating for some time, Johanna turned seventeen in November 1935. At eighteen, Frank felt ready to ask this beautiful woman to marry him. Unfortunately, Frank's father, John, had other plans and told the entire Schuil family they were moving to California.

*Oh no*, Frank thought. *I can't live here without my family and no steady income of my own.*

Frank was right, and Jackie, Frank's youngest sister, later wrote in her diary about their move to California.

> *In 1936, during the Great Depression, my dad sold the farm, auctioned off all but bare necessities, and bought a new Ford with the proceeds. All of us kids piled in the back seat. We pulled a trailer with household necessities hitched behind and struck out for California. This was long before the U-Haul days and was an old-fashioned open-top trailer. We made pretty good time and stopped at auto courts, now known as motels, for the nights. We drove through big cities where everyone lived close together in neat little houses. We saw huge cacti in the Arizona Desert and drove on a wonderful new highway, Route 66. I was only five, so this was a great adventure.*

*We settled in the San Fernando Valley. Life was great there—no smog—oranges, walnuts, and other goodies for the picking—not too many people. There were several Christian Reformed families settled in the area, some directly from Holland and no church. My Dad, John, was instrumental in getting a church built in Glendale, California. He was the main contractor. My brothers, Frank and Jim, also worked on it along with other volunteers, and in no time, we had a lovely church and recreation hall that our religious and social life centered around. This was only the first of my dad's moves.*

It took a year of Frank writing love letters to Johanna for his father to realize that Frank couldn't get his mind off Johanna.

One afternoon, Frank's father asked him if they should send Johanna a one-way train ticket to California. He knew of someone who needed a live-in nanny and thought this would give Frank and Johanna a chance to decide if they wanted to marry.

Frank was thrilled. It took some persuading on Johanna's part, but since she was clearly in love, her parents realized they needed to let their daughter choose to stay or leave.

After a year together in California, Frank and Johanna Schuil were married on March 31, 1938. Johanna had turned nineteen in November, and Frank was twenty. They started their married life in California but decided to return to Michigan since they missed their family and friends back home. Another reason to return was that they were expecting their first child, and Johanna's pa had offered Frank a job on his farm. Matthew Phillip, their first son, was born on November 21, 1938. They were pleased to discover so early in marriage that Johanna became pregnant without difficulty and that childbearing was easy for her.

Initially, Frank felt it would work to come back to their home-town in Michigan and help Johanna's pa, Henry Van Til, run the family farm in the small town of Vogel Center. Johanna's siblings were out of the house except for her youngest sister Hattie. Therefore, here they were, trying to help her pa lighten his load.

It seemed like a wonderful idea to Johanna to be home, close to family again, but it wasn't meant to be. Frank and her father could not agree on anything. They argued from dawn to dusk. Johanna's father struggled with health issues and wanted help on the farm, but it was a poor potato farm, where they barely scratched out a living.

Johanna cherished her memories of growing up here with her seven siblings. They never had extras, but somehow, there was always enough food to eat. Chickens helped keep meat and eggs on the table. Johanna's parents knew how to barter with the neighbors, and their children learned at a young age how to make extra money. Johanna's ma, Margaret, knew how to make a dollar stretch further than anyone. Henry and Margaret taught their children the value of money by allowing them to make their own choices on spending some of the money they earned.

To help make peace between her father and husband, Johanna pleaded with Frank, "Please just try to reason with him. I know you want to try some different crops, but he has worked this ground for so long. You know it's hard for him to change."

"'Reason'—he is not one to reason with!" Frank shouted.

"Shh, he'll hear you."

"You know I'm tired . . . I just think we should head back to California. My parents have a place we can rent behind their home, and there are some good building jobs there. Everyone thinks California is the place to be." Frank responded more quietly.

"Frank, do you really want to go back to your folks? You know how your father is so controlling, and your mother, well, she doesn't exactly love me. I'm never quite good enough in her eyes."

"Oh, come on, honey, you are good enough for me, that's for sure. I just can't stay here when your dad won't be reasonable. I can't earn my keep or begin to raise our family on a worthless potato crop."

"Let's sleep on it and pray about it. I believe God will lead us to know what we should do." Johanna's words quieted Frank, and he relaxed. They knew that, together, with God, they could make a good decision.

Johanna spent long hours praying and poring over scripture that gave her peace Frank couldn't explain. He was sure with their prayers and by searching God's Word, they would make the right decision.

That's how, during their second year of marriage, Johanna agreed to return to California. Johanna saw the relief on her ma's face when she shared this decision with her. They left Michigan in summer 1939 with promises to write and hoping to see each other again soon.

On the road back to California, Johanna realized another baby was on the way. Imagine her surprise as their son, Matthew, was barely seven months old, and someone told her that if she nursed him, she didn't need to worry about getting pregnant.

*Well, someone didn't know what they were talking about,* Johanna thought. *This is going to be a long trip. Thankfully, my Frank is a good driver, but will our car make it all the way to California?*

Just as Matthew settled down for a nap, they heard a loud **bang**! Frank swore and pulled over to see what he feared . . . a flat tire. Tires were expensive. Again, Frank and Johanna prayed as they drove slowly on a thin spare to the next gas station. Somehow, they drove the entire five miles and, with some hammering to the rim and another used tire, they were on their way.

Another problem during the trip was the cost of gas. They barely had enough money to make the trip, so they would drive a stretch of highway until the tank was nearly empty before they stopped for gas. Frank never forgot this time in his life when he felt so helpless to take care of his family. Later in life, Frank never let his tank go below half-empty, and he made sure his tires were brand new or in great condition before any cross-country trip.

Somehow, they made it to Burbank, a small town in Southern California. In those days, there were no freeways, and the area consisted of small farms with a few cows and chickens dotting the countryside. Frank's parents owned one such farm on five acres. A few years later, they sold all five acres for a few hundred dollars. How were they to know that several years after that, the farm would be sold for a few thousand dollars per acre? Interestingly, Frank's parents never settled in one place long enough to benefit from their investments. Behind their home was a chicken coup that was renovated into a small house. This small house became the home of Johanna, Frank, and little Matthew. Johanna tried to make the house cozy, but no matter how hard she scrubbed, there was a lingering odor that never quite went away.

California was a good place for Frank to find a job and, soon, he found steady work in a supermarket. Unfortunately, Frank's father was very controlling. Since Frank and Johanna didn't pay rent for their house, Frank's father insisted he had the right to Frank's entire paycheck.

*When will I be able to live my own life?* Frank wondered bitterly. *I should have listened to Johanna and stayed in Michigan. But then, I would have to listen to her dad. I don't know which is worse.*

In addition to worries over how to handle their fathers, most of the world was at war. Somehow, the US had managed to stay out of it at that point. Frank was concerned the US would get involved soon. Frank could be called to war, but having a child kept him lower on the draft list.

Despite their worries, Johanna, his dear wife, was pregnant again. Her pregnancy went quickly and, for the most part, she felt great. Although she did her best to eat well, Johanna was naturally thin because she was in constant motion. Since she was pregnant, she couldn't nurse and was thankful that their first child, Matthew, was an easy baby and a good eater.

It was a beautiful Easter Sunday, March 24, 1940. Johanna knew her baby was due soon, but she wanted to enjoy the special day. Frank hopped out of bed and gave her a romantic kiss. She never tired of his endless affection. She rose slowly, planning to get herself ready after she took care of Matthew. The first sharp pain hit Johanna while Matthew was squealing with joy in his bath. She took a few deep breaths, decided to quickly dress Matthew, and relax before getting herself ready. Matthew was extra squirmy that morning, but she managed to dress and feed him in between contractions.

*Hmmm*, Johanna thought. *Should I tell Frank or wait a bit to make sure it's the real thing?*

Just then, a big contraction came. Johanna decided to have her mother-in-law call the doctor since Frank was in the bathroom. Just as another contraction hit, Johanna grabbed Matthew and made a mad dash for the front house. John, Frank's father, took one look at Johanna and made a beeline for the door. Frank's mother, Janice, immediately panicked. Johanna wasn't the panicky type, so she consoled her mother-in-law between contractions as Matthew played happily nearby. Thankfully, Frank burst through the door. He told his mother to hurry and get some warm water ready while he whisked Johanna into bed. Finally, Johanna relaxed as her Frank managed the chaos. They called the doctor, but Johanna knew this baby wasn't waiting for him. She told Frank she felt her baby's head, and he went into mechanic mode. Frank called for all the items he saw the doctor use when Johanna gave birth to Matthew. He was a quick learner and not afraid to take over in urgent situations. Johanna was so thankful for his abilities and knew these gifts would always serve them well.

"Hurry!" screamed Janice. "The cord is around the baby's neck."

"Mom, hush. It's alright."

"Johanna, deep breath; you are doing great. Rest if you need to. Remember, with Matthew, your body pushed when it needed to," Frank whispered soothingly.

Another contraction and Johanna pushed out a beautiful baby girl who was screaming her head off. Frank worked quickly to wrap his new daughter in blankets and remove the umbilical cord. This wasn't easy since it was wrapped around the baby's neck three times. Tying and cutting the cord was even more frightening, but Frank kept his head as he carefully tied and then cut it.

Thankfully, the doctor arrived just in time to finish the task of afterbirth and check Johanna's vital signs. Baby Sara Lynn didn't seem to like her bath and had been screaming most of her short life. Frank wondered to himself if this screaming was a hint of Sara's future personality.

Johanna regained her strength quickly since Sara's birth took less than an hour, and returned to her life of caring for her children. She found that the days went by quickly with little ones in the house.

Before Johanna knew it, they were celebrating Sara's first birthday. She hired a photographer to take pictures of Matthew and Sara. She also decided to treat both children by having some friends and their mothers over for some homemade cake and ice cream.

It was March 24, 1941. World War II, as it had become known, was raging in Europe, and the US was doing its best to stay out of the conflict. Johanna hated reading about so many people dying and hearing the stories about concentration camps that were unbelievable.

*Could people really do such things to other human beings?* Johanna wondered. She reflected further and thought about what people did to each other in biblical times. Thinking of Jesus, and what was done to Him, Johanna sadly realized that yes, they could do those terrible things.

Earlier that year, in January 1941, Johanna lost her mother, Margaret Van Til. It happened suddenly. One day, she collapsed from a heart attack. Johanna's younger sister, Hattie, fourteen at the time, was the only one with her when it happened.

Hattie phoned Johanna, sobbing, and as she talked to her, she cried, "I'm sure I will die too. Ma made such a terrible noise in her throat and chest. I was so afraid and didn't know what to do. I know I will have nightmares about it forever!"

Johanna comforted her younger sister by sharing her beliefs about who God was and how He would take care of Hattie. They prayed and cried together. Johanna suggested that Hattie see if a friend could come and stay with her until she felt better. It seemed to help Hattie. Afterward, Johanna called her other sisters. They cried and prayed together, thinking of ways they could help Hattie and their father recover from the shock of their mother's sudden death.

The months flew by despite these trials. Johanna and Frank loved their children who grew rapidly. The picture Johanna had of Matthew and Sara made her chuckle every time she saw it. The photographer did such a great job capturing their personalities with Matthew trying his best to love on Sara, but Sara would have nothing to do with it. The pictures, a group of three, were adorable. Johanna knew she would cherish them for years to come.

On December 7, 1941, it was Saturday night; the house was clean, and the baths were taken. Frank's shoes were polished, and his shirt ironed. Johanna's suit jacket and skirt were ready to wear. Her hair was up in pin curls. They always looked forward to attending church on Sunday and, after the morning service, having a roast beef dinner along with a time of rest before attending the evening service. Frank and Johanna loved their church and their friends at the Sun Valley Christian Reformed Church. They only missed if one of the family was sick. This Sunday church turned out to be more important than usual. When they arrived home, the world was hearing the dreadful news of the Pearl Harbor bombing when more than 2000 men perished as their ships sank in the harbor. The attack destroyed America's main fleet and left the country vulnerable to invasion. Frank and Johanna felt the shock with the rest of the nation.

In the months following the attack, the US rallied quickly. Many men enlisted, and many more were drafted. Shipbuilding was accelerated to replace the losses from Pearl Harbor. Factories manufactured planes so quickly that they needed extra help from women. A clever advertising campaign inspired women to answer the call. The campaign, "Rosie the Riveter," used the logo "WE CAN DO IT," and encouraged women to join the fight for their country. Johanna was deeply moved by recent events and noticed a large road sign calling for women to become "Rosies." She decided to talk with Frank and her mother-in-law about becoming a riveter.

"I don't know," Frank said hesitantly. "You've never done anything with tools or worked on engines before. Do you think you would enjoy that kind of work?"

Frank's mother, to Johanna's surprise, ended up being the most supportive. She offered to babysit the children and she was sure Johanna could learn whatever was needed to do the job. It was settled, and Johanna was off to be a riveter for three days a week. She loved this time in her life. She met a wide variety of women, and when they could hear one another, enjoyed having an adult conversation. California was filled with people from so many backgrounds—in contrast to her home-town in Michigan, where everyone grew up with a Christian influence and were mostly of Dutch ancestry.

As Matthew and Sara grew, Frank became restless in their cramped living quarters and tired of giving his paycheck to his father every week. They were also concerned that more men were needed for the war effort. Older men were being called, even those who were married with children. One evening after the children were tucked in their beds, Johanna felt it was time to have a heart-to-heart time with Frank.

"Frank, how is work going?" Johanna began.

"It's okay, but to tell you the truth, I have no interest in getting the promotion they're planning to give me," Frank sighed.

"Why not?" Johanna asked, although she was pretty sure she already knew the answer.

"It's so hard to be interested in more pay when I know my dad expects to take it all," Frank stated. "To be honest, we might have an even bigger problem since California seems to be calling older men to the service more quickly than other states. I'm not sure why that is, but I'm worried about it."

In the end, Frank's dad decided for them. All of them sold the homes to move to Nevada and see what construction work was available there. Johanna kept an open mind and agreed to move to support her husband's dreams and God's will. They arrived in Nevada and soon found the place that, according to Frank's father and brother, was booming with lots of new construction.

"Who on earth would want to settle in this God-forsaken place." Johanna wondered as they drove into Nevada. She kept this to herself as there was no changing Frank's mind when he thought it right to follow his family. She decided to wait for God to move, leading where He wanted them to be.

They settled on living in Fallon, Nevada. When they left California, Johanna suspected she might be pregnant. When she did the calculation, she was shocked to discover she was already four months along. After telling Frank, she found a doctor and a hospital, since she didn't want her husband to deliver this baby too. Unfortunately, soon after they arrived in Fallon, construction work became scarce. Frank and Johanna knew they needed to stay in Fallon until after their baby was born. They hoped that the money Frank made over the last few months would cover expenses until they moved on. In the end, Frank's father came to their rescue and loaned them the money they needed on the promise Frank would work it off at the first chance he got.

Johanna's last month of pregnancy flew by. She packed her hospital bag especially early since she wanted to make sure she got to the hospital on time. Since Nevada is mostly desert, December 5, 1942, was a warm day but, in contrast, the nights were cold. While she shivered, Johanna felt a sharp pain and knew she needed to go to the hospital. She looked at the clock, and it was 10 p.m., and Frank was fast asleep.

"Frank, wake up!" Johanna shouted. "It's time. The baby is ready, and we better not wait too long this time." Thankfully, friends from their church lived nearby and came right over to stay with Matthew and Sara.

"Hurry, Frank, I'm having another contraction and can feel the baby coming!" Johanna screamed as they sped to the hospital.

Frank quickly parked by the front doors of the hospital and said, "Hang on, honey. We're here. I'm not looking for a parking space. That's it, lean on me. I have you—we just need to get up those stairs." Frank did his best to stay calm for Johanna's sake.

The nurses tried to check them in, but Johanna suddenly screamed, squatted down, and out came their son. There was a lot of chaos until everyone realized what had happened. During all the confusion, Johanna simply lay down on the floor and waited with her little one in her arms. After the surprised staff got things under control, Frank and Johanna named their new baby Stephen Allen and soon discovered he was perfectly healthy. For years to come, however, his siblings teased Stephen that he had problems from falling on his head when he was born, even though he didn't actually fall on his head. Frank had somehow managed to catch Stephen as Johanna squatted.

Johanna delivered her babies so quickly and easily that she recovered remarkably well. Just before Christmas 1942, she was ready to move back to California as Frank's whole family decided they should try to find work in California again. Before they moved, his parents purchased a group of homes in the Long Beach area. Travel wasn't easy with two young children and one infant. Sara could be a handful when Matthew teased her, and Frank ran out of patience when the noise level was high. Frank would threaten the children by swinging his hand over the back seat all while watching the road. Matthew and Sara were quick and knew how to avoid Frank's hand, but they had their warning and usually calmed down. Thankfully, baby Stephen slept for most of the trip, only crying when he was hungry. Everyone was relieved and happy when they finally arrived in Long Beach.

After arriving in California, Frank was able to get work in construction with his father and brothers. However, the threat of being drafted was heavy on Frank's mind. Frank's younger brothers both considered enlisting. Frank's youngest brother, Paul, joined the Merchant Marines and was part of the war effort but didn't see battle. His other brother Jim didn't enlist and wasn't drafted either.

About halfway through 1943, Johanna received news that Hattie, her youngest sister, was ill with leukemia. Johanna could hardly believe her little sister would have to endure her fear of dying. Hattie had just turned fifteen in December 1942. At the time, there was no known cure for leukemia; the doctors could only offer blood transfusions to extend Hattie's life a little longer.

It was July 30, 1943, when Hattie wrote to her dear sister Johanna.

*Dear Sis and family,*

*This is Friday forenoon, and I'm still in bed. I feel fine, but I have a little fever yet at night, so I must stay in bed. The doc was over yesterday and gave me another iron shot. I have had three of them now. I can eat like everything. Gerald was out picking huckleberries yesterday afternoon. He got sixteen quarts. Anna Mae is here today to help Mag. Everybody comes and brings me something. I got a nice box of candy of Mrs. Tom TeBoss.*

*Hattie*

This was the last time Johanna heard from Hattie. On Aug 30, 1943, at the age of fifteen, after being sick for only two and a half months, she went home to the Lord.

With three little ones at home, Johanna couldn't travel back to Michigan for the funeral. This broke her heart. To regain her strength to carry on, she found a quiet place to spend time with her Lord. After reading many Bible passages, Johanna's strength was renewed. God's Word gave her hope and peace, but her tears still flowed from time to time.

November came quickly, and more bad news came from her family in Michigan. Her father had taken a turn for the worse, and her eldest brother, Fredrick, was sick. Soon, another letter arrived from Fredrick, who was thirty-seven years old and had a wife and five children.

He wrote:

*Dear Sister, Brother, and family,*

*Well, I thought I better drop you a line, although it will not be an encouraging letter. On the 26th of August, I went to Ann Arbor, and the 26th of September, I came home. I had seven transfusions at the time. I stayed home a month and went back for a checkup, and I gained weight and color, and my blood was holding its own, although it could have been a lot better. And on the 13th of November, I became a lot weaker because I didn't have enough blood. So, I went with Clarence Bolt on Saturday eve, the 13th of November, and got there on Sunday morning and stayed until the 26th of November. Now, I have been home a couple of days, and when I sit and lay down, I can't hardly believe that I have such a fatal sickness.*

*I had four transfusions while I was there the last time. But I think the next time I will go to Cadillac hospital for my transfusions. It is easier to get blood donors to come to Cadillac than to Ann Arbor. They told me the only thing they can do for me is transfusions.*

*In Ann Arbor, they wouldn't tell me the name of this sickness, and our family doctor, Dr. Selzer of Marion, hesitated to tell me the seriousness of it, although I did find out. It is called Leuka Leukemia. I don't know if I have those words spelled right. The doctors in Ann Arbor said there were a lot of different kinds of leukemia, and the fatal reports I get are from around here.*

*I lack mostly red cells and some white cells, and I have too many of another kind of white cells. And they are produced in the morrow of the bone. They don't dare to give me X-ray treatments because I have too many white cells. But there is also a warring member in my blood stream, which kills the cells. I am not positive on that last statement.*

*Of course, there is an Almighty God who rules and overrules everything. And I have learned to pray, even in this sickness, "Thy will be done."*

*Dad has been sick, but his lung trouble is about over, although his heart is quite weak. I don't think he is out of danger yet. Jake and Jennie Bronkhorse are so busy they haven't time to go and see him. They were here for a minute this noon after I told them they better go and see him. But they didn't have time during the week, and after church it gets dark too quickly. Well, this is Sunday evening, Jake and Jennie did go after church to see Dad after all.*

*Sister Mag was over about 5:30 p.m. and said Dad had encephalitis. It is the inflammation of the lining of the brain. He is not conscious. And he has also lost control of his urine. I don't think he will live much longer.*

*And so goes this life. While I was in the hospital, Hattie died and this last time, Mr. Bolt died and Dad got sick. So, we are having our sorrows.*

*Well, I will close with love.*

*From,*

*Fredrick and Merrilyn*

Johanna's father died before the letter from her brother arrived, and Fredrick died on December 27, 1943. Johanna and her siblings felt like Job, wondering who would be next. Johanna knew she would never have made it through this without her Lord and Savior. Her faith had always been important to her, but now it was everything.

Johanna didn't understand how anyone could face life without God. She did realize that with everything happening in the world, people talked less about being atheists.

The war raged on, and men died daily. It made Johanna's heart ache for all of the wives and mothers in mourning. After losing four of her family members, and three so close together in time, she could identify with them a little more closely. Sadly, she had only attended her father's funeral but was able to see

Fredrick before he passed away. Her heart longed to go back to Michigan, but she wanted it to be at the right time, God's time, for another move.

Her sister Mag knew Johanna wanted to return to Michigan; what she didn't know was that Frank was anxious to return as well. He still worried he could be drafted. With three children at home now, he didn't want to leave Johanna alone with that burden.

Frank contacted a friend in Michigan who knew of an opening on a dairy farm in Rockford. He asked if Frank was interested in the job, and Frank told him it sounded great. His friend also found a rental home in the area for Frank and Johanna's growing family. They moved back to Michigan in early spring 1944. Frank was the dairy foreman. This suited him well since he was good with people. He was also skilled at fixing machinery, which allowed John, the owner of the farm, to enjoy his freedom and retirement.

John felt fortunate to have such a good man in Frank. It gave him confidence knowing that he was honest and great with the farm crew and could fix anything that broke down.

For the first time in her married life, Johanna began to feel settled. Matthew had finished first grade and seemed happy at his new school in Rockford. It was the beginning of summer, and Johanna loved the warm weather. She felt happy and content, even though she had suffered a great deal the previous year. She had her family close, and her children were healthy and strong. She knew they were in a great place to raise the children.

Frank came home one day excited. It seemed that something important happened in France; a battle they called D-Day, and there was hope that the war would end soon. To Johanna, D-Day appeared only to cause a lot of men to lose their lives, and she feared that many mothers and wives would be left grieving and alone. She tried to comfort herself with the knowledge that they had three healthy children and hoped they didn't need to worry about the ominous-looking envelope the postman delivered a few days later. She waited anxiously for Frank to come home, and she stood nervously looking on as he opened it. It was only a request that Frank check in and confirm that his family status was unchanged. It didn't appear to ask him to report for duty, but with so many killed in battle, more family men were called to the frontlines.

Frank and Johanna prayed hard that night for all the sorrow caused by this horrendous war, not only at home but also in Europe, Japan, and all over the world. It was hard to believe some of the reports they heard of concentration camps killing the Jewish people just because they were Jews. They heard stories of entire Jewish families held captive and killed. It was more than Johanna could bear. She wondered if the world could endure much more and if Jesus would come soon. She prayed that God's people, the Jews, would be saved the way Romans 11 talked about.

CHAPTER 2

# The Call

Another year went by, and the war continued. Johanna was thankful that many of her family were not called to serve since she didn't think she could handle more death after recently losing four of her close family members.

Frank worked hard at the dairy but still dreamed of getting back into construction. Matthew, Sara, and Stephen were a handful and kept Johanna's days full. Now that they lived away from Frank's parents, they kept Frank's paychecks, and Johanna became the household bookkeeper.

Johanna was only allowed to attend school until eighth grade, but Frank was forced to quit after sixth grade. Many people like Johanna and Frank's parents felt that making a living was far more important than attending school after a certain age. They also believed that making a living took the strength of the body more than the strength of the mind. Johanna loved school and was upset she had to quit, but for women, it was considered more important to stay at home and take care of the children. She begged and begged, but Johanna's father couldn't understand why she could possibly need more schooling. Now Johanna was using her math skills to manage their family expenses and help Frank save a little from each paycheck. She hoped to surprise him one day with enough savings to start the "Frank Schuil" construction company.

Unfortunately, that day wasn't meant to be quite yet. A fore-boding-looking letter had arrived from the state department. The war wasn't over, although the allies seemed to be winning and Berlin was to be invaded. So, when Johanna saw the letter, her heart sank. She wanted to open it but knew she needed to wait for Frank. When he arrived after a long day of working in cold weather, Frank was a bit on edge. Johanna fed the family dinner and then put the children to bed.

Finally, they had time to sit together and discuss the day. Johanna took a deep breath and said, "Frank, I waited until after dinner so we could see what this letter would say together."

As she handed the letter to him, Frank had a concerned look on his face and said,

"Wow! I thought I didn't need to worry—I guess it doesn't pay to get too comfortable."

Frank squeezed Johanna's hand and then opened the letter. To their dismay, the letter called Frank into service for the US Armed Forces. He was told to report the following day. Johanna cried. Even though she prayed through the afternoon for strength, she was afraid. Frank held her tight and let her cry as tears fell from his eyes as well. They had heard the stories of so many losing their lives and men coming home from the war with major injuries. Others they knew had changed, seemingly overnight, from being happy, confident men to silent, nervous men with no will to live. Naturally, Johanna and Frank sup-ported their country in this war. Yet, it was difficult when one personally was going to battle.

After a long night of prayer, Johanna made Frank his favorite breakfast of scrambled eggs, bacon, and buttermilk pancakes. They kissed long and hard, and she sent him off while the children were still eating their pancakes. It was a long day for Johanna after Frank left. Instead of worrying, she realized she should thank the dear Lord she had some extra money saved from being so frugal with Frank's paychecks. So many women needed to work when their husbands went off to war, but because of their savings, Johanna could probably stay at home with her children while he was away.

Frank returned home much sooner than Johanna expected. Frank had his papers, and he needed to report for duty the following week. He had a few days to get everything in order and let his employer know he would be gone for at least two years unless the war ended before then. It was May 1, 1945, and a beautiful spring morning, but neither Frank nor Johanna could enjoy it. Neither listened to the news coming out of Europe that day since they were caught up in their own worries. They had a lot of preparations to make, and Frank would leave in five days for who knew how long. He felt sadness and the pressure of how to help his wife and children. He was thankful they had relatives nearby and a boss who reassured him that his job would be waiting for him when he returned.

May 6 came too quickly, and Johanna held Frank extra-long that morning until, finally, Frank groaned, "You have to let me go, honey. I don't want to leave, but I must. We must trust God to take care of us." After saying a prayer together, they parted with tears and lots of hugs for each other and the children.

Frank rode the bus to the Army base in Grand Rapids, Michigan. As they approached the base, things looked a little strange. There was loud cheering coming from the base and what appeared to be a celebration. Frank was so sad about having to leave his family; celebrating seemed ridiculous.

When they arrived and hopped off the bus, Frank asked the first men he saw what was going on.

"Where have you been? Haven't you been listening to the news lately?" one man asked Frank.

"No, I've been too busy getting ready to come here. What is going on?" Frank asked again.

"Why, the war is as good as over! We don't even have to report any more since most of us were already too old or had too many kids to support. The Army is more than happy to send us right back home."

Frank could hardly believe his ears. He couldn't wait to get home and surprise Johanna with the news. In the meantime, he wasn't sure what he had to do, so he waited with the cheering men. Finally, someone got on the loudspeaker and said, "Men, thank you for reporting today. I have good news for each of you who came out. I'll read a list of names, so you'll know if you are officially released from duty. It is an amazing day. The allies have won the war! Tomorrow, Germany will officially surrender."

On his way back home, Frank could hardly contain his excitement and couldn't wait to see Johanna respond to the news. The bus ride seemed to take forever, so when they finally arrived at Rockford, Frank decided to run home instead of trying to call Johanna. After all, three miles wasn't that far. When Frank arrived home, he burst through the front door, completely out of breath, just as Johanna was getting the children up from their naps. The sound of Frank's shouting scared her, and poor little Stephen burst into tears from Johanna's jump as she was holding him.

*Oh, my Lord*, thought Johanna. *What in heaven's name is going on? Is that Frank? It sounds like him, but it can't be. I hope he didn't get lost or go to the wrong place.*

Before Johanna had another second to think, there Frank stood, looking so handsome with his curly black hair, shining blue eyes, and the biggest smile she'd seen in a long time. He wrapped his arms around her and lifted both Johanna and Stephen high in the air, planting kisses on both of them.

"IT'S OVER! IT'S OVER!" Frank kept repeating.

"What's over?" Johanna shouted.

"THE WAR. IT'S OVER!" Frank shouted back. He danced happily with the children and Johanna, who could hardly believe her ears.

As the news came on the radio, everyone around the world cheered. Later, when people realized the terrible atrocities that had been committed during the war, especially to the Jewish people and all the suffering that took place, tears flowed. Frank and Johanna never forgot watching so many people suffer in one way or another. The newspapers showed gruesome pictures of concentration camps with corpses everywhere and some strewn along the road. It was almost too much for Johanna to handle.

Frank spent a lot of time reading the newspaper and listening to the radio while Johanna spent her time praying and studying her Bible. She loved attending the women's group at their church and sharing in God's Word with others. She also enjoyed serving with her ladies' groups at church.

There were opportunities to send money to help missionaries and the poor around the world and locally. Although money was tight, God always provided for their needs, and both Frank and Johanna were determined to share what little they had. The pictures of wartime poverty were imprinted on their minds.

CHAPTER 3

# War and Life

It was June 5, 1945, and the war in Europe had officially ended on May 8, 1945, with the allies signing peace agreements. Frank loved America and was thankful the war had not taken place on US soil or created suffering as it had in Europe. Yet he feared that the US could be invaded next. As he read through the peace agreements, the people in charge seemed to feel the same way. In the agreements, they placed the US in strategic locations, such as Germany to help ensure our protection.

Frank worried most about the conflict with Japan as there were many people of Japanese descent in the country, albeit in controlled housing areas. He didn't like that the war was officially over but there still seemed to be conflicts and wondered how they would end or if he would be called to fight.

It was a time, which would later be called the baby boom years when many men returned from war. The US economy was strong, and people had hope that they would see better times. Frank wondered how Japan would impact the world since its ruler was no better than Hitler and also wanted to rule the world. Frank had a bad feeling about it, but deep down, hoped he was wrong, and all would be well.

As with most summer days in Michigan, August 6, 1945, started out humid with a threat of rain in the air. Johanna decided to visit a nearby lake and pack a picnic lunch. The children were excited. After they arrived at the lake and did some swimming, they sat on a blanket and had a lunch of egg salad sandwiches, apples, and fresh-baked chocolate chip cookies. Johanna was thankful the rain had stayed away but she could hear thunder in the distance. She knew she needed to pack up her crew and head home. They made it home just before the downpour. After the rain, Frank arrived home from his job on the dairy farm. Johanna was proud of her handsome husband, and after putting the children down for some quiet time, she enjoyed a warm hug from him. They talked of their hope that one day soon, they would have enough money saved to finally start their own construction company.

The next day, the newspaper headlines announced that an atomic bomb was dropped during the night on Hiroshima.

*Oh, Lord God*, Frank thought. *I want the war to end, but this is frightening.*

As they listened to the radio, the news of the bombing continually worsened—so many people had died and were injured. Frank and Johanna mourned that so many died to bring peace to the world. They spent time praying together for the people of Japan and those who dropped the bomb. Just when they thought things couldn't get worse, a few days later, on August 9, 1945, there was a report of a second bomb that was dropped on Nagasaki. Also, the city of Manchukuo was invaded by the Soviet Union. The Japanese leaders knew they were beaten by these events and immediately surrendered. Frank couldn't believe what he read and the devastation he saw in the newspaper. Since the Japanese were no longer considered a threat to America, the Japanese Americans were finally released and allowed to return home. Frank and Johanna wondered if life would ever be normal again for anyone.

Life did continue, and some things faded from their memories. However, no one forgot how terrible the Holocaust was for the Jews or the destruction caused by the atomic bombs. Books were written by people who survived Hitler's death camps, memorials were built, and movies were made to keep the truth of the war's atrocities in front of future generations. It was a time in history that significantly impacted the future. One would think it would have helped people become closer to God, but instead, many turned away from God during this time and looked more to material gain.

Johanna wanted to keep the right perspective on life. Along with Frank, they knew they had to live for God and always put Him first. They never missed Sunday worship or taking the children to Sunday school and youth groups. These practices helped all of them grow in their faith. They never missed family devotions and tried to teach the children the importance of loving God's Word by asking them to repeat the last word Frank read each evening. The children learned to listen closely so as not to miss the word. It helped Johanna to listen carefully, and she watched with pleasure as her determined children competed to be the first to repeat the last word of the Bible reading.

Every summer, the entire family attended two weeks of church camp; this was one of their favorite annual events. It included camping in cabins, lots of games at the lake, singing around the campfire, and special speakers for the adults while the kids enjoyed great Bible lessons with crafts. Frank and Johanna loved being camp counselors, and the boys begged to be in Frank's cabin, as he told the best nighttime stories. Frank shared his hunting and fishing adventures and stories about living in different states. His repertoire was filled with exciting escapades, and he knew just how to build up the listeners' excitement right through to the very end of the tale.

The young boys would always beg for more stories, but Frank would have to say, "We need energy for tomorrow, boys. Lights off for now. Tomorrow is another day."

By this time in the life of the Schuil family, Frank had left the dairy farm in Rockford and moved to the Fremont area, where he found a job in construction. Around the same time, Frank's dad and brothers realized that going back home to Michigan could prove to be a good move for them also. So, with their families, they moved to the Fremont area too. Frank and Johanna were already settled into their life in Michigan, so they no longer needed to answer to Frank's father. This helped improve relations between the families and, once again, the cousins enjoyed each other. Playing together was particularly easy since they all lived close on a wooded lane between the towns of Newaygo and Fremont.

Johanna continued to care for the children and manage their finances. Matthew turned seven that November and enjoyed school more than he ever thought he would. Sara would turn six the following March, and kindergarten filled her days with joy. Stephen, who would turn three on December 5, was full of energy and ran around the house while his siblings were at school. Johanna was thrilled to do the bookkeeping, feeling like a secretary in her own home. Her days were filled with washing, cooking, and cleaning, but, thankfully, she was done with diapers and bottles as her babies had grown up.

Johanna did worry about getting pregnant again since no birth control method seemed to work particularly well for her. However, she reasoned that there could be worse things than having four children. Johanna knew that time helped parents forget how much work it was to care for a newborn, and they only remembered the joy babies brought.

That year, for Christmas, they were able to buy the children some special gifts. Michigan, never short on snow in the winter, meant that sleds were not only a wonderful gift for the children but also a practical one. Their home was on a hill and had a great trail for sledding in the backyard, so they would be entertained for hours. With their natural athletic abilities, Johanna knew that Matthew and Sara would master sledding in no time. For Stephen, Johanna decided to buy a tricycle that seemed more age-appropriate for him than a sled.

The holidays came and went, and Johanna was right about the gifts she had chosen for the children. Every chance they got, they bundled up to play with the sleds, sharing rides with little Stephen and pushing him around on his tricycle. The snow had been heavy that December and the road to their home was extremely icy, especially at night. The icy roads concerned Frank whenever Johanna drove to her weekly ladies' Bible study. She hated missing her Bible study and would sweet-talk Frank until he could not refuse to let her go. No harm was done, she reasoned. The church was only two miles away.

During one of her Bible studies, the ladies were having such a great time that they failed to notice the snow coming down. As they were leaving, Johanna realized she better hurry and hoped the road wasn't too icy. She reached the road to her house safely but still needed to make it up a steep hill. Johanna said a prayer just as the car started sliding and, before she knew what happened, she was in the ditch. She slightly injured her side during the slide into the ditch. She said a prayer of thanks after she realized nothing was broken.

"Oh, for goodness sake. My Frank is not going to like this at all." Johanna shouted out loud to God. "How are we going to get out of this one, God? I know I can't walk up the dark and slippery hill without breaking any bones. I trust You, Lord, to keep me warm and send a rescuer. Thank You, Lord, for what You'll do even before I know Your answer."

With her prayer complete, Johanna decided to sit tight and wrap herself in the blanket she kept in the car in the winter. She was sure Frank would soon realize that she wasn't home and would call a friend to see if she had already left the church. She readied herself for Frank's "I told you so," as it was sure to come. Johanna didn't have to wait long; she soon saw Frank's pickup drive slowly down the road. He almost missed seeing her since her car was barely visible from the road. Johanna had managed to climb out of the car and, in the almost waist-deep snow, frantically waved with both arms. Just as Frank was about to pass, he caught sight of her waving.

"Oh, thank You, Lord," Frank prayed.

Frank had been worried sick, as he had watched the storm develop over the last two hours. When Johanna was late coming home, he checked with friends who were already home. After talking with them, he knew then it was time to search for her on the road. After letting Matthew know where he was going, Frank jumped into his pickup. He was so relieved to find Johanna unharmed that it almost made him cry. Frank worried easily, so he had imagined all kinds of horrific scenarios. All he could do was jump out of his truck, scoop her into his arms, give her a big kiss, and take her home. Frank was so relieved that he just wanted to get her chilled body in bed as quickly as possible. It was probably on that very late December night of 1945 that Vesta Kay was conceived.

During the winter of 1946, Frank kept busy fixing farm equipment and doing building repairs on the side. He was a self-taught mechanic who learned by taking old motors apart and putting them back together again. The good economy, along with Frank being a noble, dependable employee, helped his frugal wife save more money.

Once again, Johanna's pregnancy was easy for her; she didn't even suffer from morning sickness. For her, giving birth was a breeze. Johanna knew she was blessed and made sure she took time every day to praise her Lord.

Of course, there were occasional struggles in her marriage, particularly since Frank had not learned how to manage money. This was because any money Frank earned as a child was turned over to his father.

*How can children learn the value of a dollar unless they're allowed to decide how to spend and save what they earn?* Johanna wondered. *I am glad that my parents allowed us to decide how we spent what we earned as children. It's the best time to learn from your mistakes. Oh, I wish Frank would learn how to manage money better and be more careful with it.*

In the meantime, Frank was busy justifying his purchase of a beautiful new Ford Sedan. After all, given the amount of money he brought home those days, the car was very affordable. He was sure Johanna could figure out how to pay for it and stay within their budget. Frank hoped she wouldn't worry about making the $700 down payment and paying $25 a month for the next three years. Regardless, it was too late now; he'd signed the paperwork before he discussed the details with her. As Frank drove up in the new car, from the look on Johanna's face, he knew he was in trouble.

"Frank, how could you? You used more than half of our savings to buy that car. I need you to be more careful. I know we're doing well, but that does not mean we can spend needlessly. Our car was running just fine. Now here we are in debt again." Johanna's temper rose.

Frank shouted back using words he later regretted since the children were nearby. He knew he was being a terrible example by arguing with his wife. Frank hated being angry with her, but his love for nice cars made it hard for him to do the right thing. Frank didn't realize what he put his family through when he prioritized driving a fancy new car and using the best hunting and fishing gear.

"Doesn't every man deserve some of the niceties in this world?" Frank reasoned. This weakness continued to be a problem for Frank. It took years for him to realize how much work it was for Johanna to stretch the household dollars because she understood there was no changing his spending habits.

Johanna also knew she needed to be forgiving and a bit more flexible with their money. It was new for her to have a good amount in their savings account, and it worried her to spend too quickly or too much.

The cold winter days were finally behind them, and the sun began to shine more often between the rainy days of spring. The children became antsy for school to be over. Even Johanna had spring fever. It felt good to hang the clothes outside instead of next to the furnace in the basement, and Sara and Matthew started to help around the house and yard.

As summer arrived, it brought days of learning to plant flowers and other plants in the garden. Johanna always loved a fresh garden but never had the space to plant one. Now, with

Frank's help, they planted tomatoes and a few berry bushes. She and the children also loved to hunt for wild huckleberries and used them to bake fresh berry pie, a special treat for the entire family.

During the summer, the children would often run to their cousins' house to play. This gave Johanna a much-needed break and time to concentrate on the household books. She kept track of their savings and Frank's earnings from both his construction job and part-time farm work.

They still dreamed of having a construction business of their own. Johanna prayed that God would clear the way for their business if it was His will. She knew it would be a big endeavor.

It was the first of August in 1946; the children were getting ready to go back to school. The summer passed quickly, and Johanna had difficulty feeling comfortable. She was already eight months pregnant and was due around September 20. As she felt a strong kick from the baby, she thought to herself that her baby couldn't come too soon. She was ready to sit on her doctor's doorstep if that's what it took to be certain all went well with the delivery. She prayed about it often and talked to her doctor, so he knew what to expect.

Johanna allowed the children to play with their cousins on a day that was perfect for baseball. Sara and Matthew had their balls, gloves, and bats ready and four-year-old Stephen in tow.

During the game, no one noticed when Stephen and his cousin Glenny, who was also four, decided to go off and play on their own. The older children enjoyed a great game of baseball, but Glenny and Stephen were too young to play with them. As the little boys took off down the road, they noticed the mailman filling the mailboxes. Neither boy wanted to admit whose idea it was, but they ended up running down the road, taking the mail out of the boxes, and throwing them into the trees. They thought it was a great game, having no idea that it was a federal offense to steal mail. Since they weren't very discreet when they scattered the mail, a sheriff, who happened to be driving by at the time, noticed the trail of mail. By the time he caught up to the boys, they had created quite a mess. That evening, the two little boys went to bed with sore bottoms, while the older children were given a good scolding for not watching their little brothers more closely. Frank and Johanna, embarrassed, just shook their heads. Johanna realized that no matter how busy she was, she needed to keep a closer eye on her children in the future.

September 21, 1946, dawned a balmy, sunny day. Johanna was thankful for weekends during her pregnancy to have Frank home. He knew how to take charge if the doctor couldn't make it in time. Johanna felt her first contraction just before lunch and immediately notified her doctor, alerted Frank, and called her sister-in-law, Lucy, who would watch the children. After three more sharp pains and just as the doctor entered the house, her water broke. Frank, the doctor, and his nurse moved quickly, putting Johanna in the bed covered with plastic and sheets. Vesta Kay, like the rest of Johanna's children, was born in no time. The birth happened so quickly that stitches weren't needed, and there wasn't even time for pain medicine. Mother and baby were resting quietly, so Frank thought he'd get in a quick nap too. Then suddenly, there was a loud knock at the back door.

*For Pete's sake*, Frank thought. *What is this about? Don't they know we just had a baby?*

At the door stood Lucy with Stephen in her arms. He had swallowed a nickel and wasn't breathing. They jumped into the car, leaving Frank's mother and Sara to stay with Johanna. Frank and Lucy sped to the hospital while Frank held Stephen upside down, praying that his face would stop turning blue. Just as they pulled up to the hospital, the nickel flew out of Stephen's mouth, and he coughed, gasping for air. Frank was so relieved he just hugged his little, brown-eyed boy until Stephen squirmed to get free.

"We must not tell Johanna about this until things settle down a bit," said Frank.

Lucy agreed, but she realized that Frank was more frazzled than Johanna would be if she knew about the incident. Nevertheless, she agreed that, for now, it would be best to keep her worry-free. She was so relieved that Stephen's life was spared, especially since she felt awful for not watching him closely enough, but who would expect a four-year-old try to eat a nickel?

As Vesta grew, she was as quiet as the other children were noisy, and they all fought to hold her and get her attention. She was content to play alone and often talked to dolls, dogs, cats, and sometimes the invisible girl. When Johanna asked one day, "Who are you talking to, Vesta?" she replied matter-of-factly, "Oh, just the girl."

All of Frank and Johanna's children were very different, not only in personality but also in appearance. Matthew had blond hair with blue eyes while Stephen was dark with brown eyes and hair. Vesta was as blond as Sara was dark. It was hard to tell they were sisters. Frank doted on his girls and was proud of his boys, always hugging and kissing them as babies. Since Johanna and Frank were not hugged much after they were toddlers, they didn't hug their children much either. Their children still felt loved and, in fact, would be embarrassed if they saw other parents hug their children in public.

In later years, Frank realized he missed out on having a close relationship with his sons. He regretted not spending more time teaching his boys to hunt and fish. He realized he wasn't patient when teaching these activities to his sons and pre-ferred to hunt and fish by himself. In the end, he missed his chance with the boys since, outside of hunting and fishing, he never learned to play other sports or swim and was often busy working.

To have another baby in the house was a joy for Frank. He never expected to be this involved with his fourth child, but Vesta was easy to love, and it always surprised him how much she seemed to need him. She was afraid of strangers and clung to him in crowds, which made him want to protect her even more. Johanna tried to get some professional photos of her, but Vesta cried at the sight of the photographer and his large camera. As the children grew and Vesta was toddling around, Frank invested in a movie camera. Johanna was a little annoyed with Frank's frivolous purchase until she saw the movies he made. She realized the movie camera captured precious memories that could be saved for years and admitted that maybe the camera wasn't such a bad use of their money after all.

## CHAPTER 4
# A Construction Business

I t was summer 1948 when Frank and Johanna established the Schuil Construction Company. Frank purchased a pickup and the necessary tools. He hired four employees, and they built custom homes, did remodeling work, and worked on commercial buildings. That first year, business was so good that they began constructing a home of their own. They worked on it slowly to make sure they could always pay their employees. Johanna enjoyed selecting flooring, fixtures, paint colors, and all the other things that were needed to build a new home.

With all of her daily responsibilities, Frank and Johanna decided it was time to find a bookkeeper to help Johanna. With Matthew being ten and Sara, eight, the kids helped with doing dishes and folding clothes. Although everyone wanted to take care of and entertain almost two-year-old Vesta, Sara usually won her attention. Johanna was relieved when Vesta learned to carefully climb up and down the stairs.

Johanna remembered the day she saw six-year-old Sara carrying infant Vesta down the stairs. "She was crying, Mom" was Sara's answer to why she picked up Vesta to bring her down the stairs. Thankfully, Sara was agile and handled the job better than Johanna thought she would. Johanna also appreciated that Sara learned quickly and chores, like changing diapers, were easy for her. She knew just how to hold the diaper and pin, so she didn't prick Vesta by mistake. If anyone was pricked, it was Sara.

In summer 1949, Frank continued to be busy with his new business, but he still loved taking his family to the local 4th of July celebration and fishing with his brothers. Johanna and Frank always belonged to a church family, so they also had a large group of friends and family who lived nearby. Enjoying picnics with family and friends was a favorite summer pastime, and they continued to go to church camp every summer.

Church camp was something they looked forward to, well, everyone except Vesta. It was hard for her to be separated from her mother for any length of time. In fact, it took poor Vesta until junior high to relax when she was separated from her mom. Not surprisingly, in her pre-school years, she was often seen in public, anxiously clinging to either Frank or Johanna.

Both Frank and Johanna were raised to follow God and His ways. They loved reading the Bible with their children. Whenever they sat down, they prayed before and after the meal, thanking God for His provisions. Frank wanted to set a good example for his kids but praying aloud in front of others made him nervous. Johanna encouraged him unsuccessfully until she wrote prayers for him to memorize. Frank used these prayers for the next fifty years at their meals. He understood the importance of God's Word and wanted his children to hear it daily.

Frank read a few chapters of the Bible daily to his family year after year, reading through it from cover to cover. In those days, most Christians read and studied the King James Version of the Bible. It was easy to memorize and very poetic. The children learned many verses at both Sunday school and Christian school. They didn't always understand everything in the Bible, but as it says in Hebrews 4:12, "God's word is sharper than a two-edged sword penetrating even dividing the soul." What Frank felt so inadequate to teach, he hoped that hearing God's Word every day would touch the hearts of his children. Every night before bedtime, Frank got on his knees and poured the rest of his inadequacies before the Lord.

The children had a great time running around on their big country lot, riding bikes, and playing ball—baseball, a favorite of Matthew, Sara, and Stephen. Sara never wanting to be out-done and would race on foot or bike with the boys. She knew how to catch, hit, and throw a ball with the best of them. Matthew could be annoying and treated her like a boy by punching her in the arm. Of course, Sara quickly learned to fight back to protect herself.

While Vesta's siblings played in the yard, Vesta was always in the house with her mother. Vesta loved being indoors so much that Johanna couldn't help calling her a little house plant. Staying indoors had its drawbacks; while her siblings were learning all kinds of sports, she didn't learn any. Finally, when Vesta was sixteen, she learned to ride a bike, and at twenty-one, she learned to swim.

The seasons went by quickly when life was busy. With so many trees in Michigan, autumn was full of color. As the leaves fell, Johanna noticed their savings fell too. She knew business slowed in winter, and at the end of the year, taxes were due. Frank always complained about the amount of money they paid Uncle Sam. He never quite understood how the tax system worked when one owned his own business. It didn't seem fair to pay taxes and then more for one's employees.

Frank would often argue with Johanna as if she could change the entire tax system.

The following year, they owed taxes to the government and began receiving warning letters. Johanna managed to pay them before too many penalties were added. She prayed that the following year would be easier.

Business picked up that spring, but the winter was longer than usual, so Frank and his crew couldn't work outside until the end of May. To make things worse, snow started to fall again in early November. Johanna worried that another short season would make it difficult for them to pay taxes. Thankfully, Frank had made some tough financial decisions by laying two employees off and selling their new home.

Unfortunately, the debt still loomed over them since the cost to build their house meant they barely broke even on the sale, and there were so many expenses with a family to care for and a business to run. Johanna worked through numbers in detail, knowing she had to speak with Frank about what to do or sell next. One evening, they finally had a chance to talk.

"Frank, we need to figure out how we can make it through the next year. Money is tight, and we must pay taxes soon. Maybe my family can loan us some money until we have enough work to cover all our expenses," Johanna reasoned.

"Honey, I know money is tight, but if we held off paying the taxes, we would have plenty to get through the year," Frank replied, hopefully.

"That's not a good idea, Frank, but I'll check to see if we can get an extension. Our bookkeeper will know what needs to be done. Though, I would rather pay our taxes and owe my family than owe the government. Is there any chance you'd reconsider?"

"NO, and don't ask again!" Frank's temper flared, and Johanna knew the discussion was over. There was no use arguing with him when it came to owing her family money. It puzzled Johanna as to why Frank could owe everything and anything to his family, but her family could not loan them money. Johanna believed it had to do with his pride. She felt Frank wanted to paint a picture of "all is well" for her family. She worried that pride could become a thorn in her dear Frank's side that only God could remove.

Unfortunately, the bookkeeper wasn't much help. He thought they could get an extension on their taxes, but he was wrong. Before Frank and Johanna had a chance to figure out what to do next, there were men at the door telling them they owed back taxes. The only choice they had at this point was to file for bankruptcy. When people declared bankruptcy back then, the government had no pity, and all of their possessions were sold at auction. The Schuil family was only allowed to leave with the clothes on their back.

Frank had purchased a beautiful accordion for Sara a few months before, and he was determined to keep it. He didn't tell Johanna but hid it from the auctioneer until he had a chance to put it in the trunk of the car. When Johanna discovered what Frank had done, she felt a little guilty, but at the same time, she was glad they had it. Sara squealed with delight when she saw her accordion in the trunk. Many years later, she still enjoyed playing it from time to time.

For the next three weeks, the family lived with Johanna's sister Mag's family. The children attended school in Vogel Center. Matthew was in seventh grade and Sara in sixth. Poor Stephen struggled with both reading and math and was held back two grades. In those days, dyslexia wasn't well understood, and children like Stephen failed their classes instead of getting extra help. He was back in second grade while Vesta started kindergarten. Johanna hoped they could stay in Vogel Center, but since Frank's family had left Michigan a year earlier, Frank's father wanted the family to join them in Idaho. They convinced Frank that Grangeville, Idaho, was the ideal place for them to settle down.

## CHAPTER 5
# The Idaho Move

I t was October 1950, and Johanna couldn't believe they were driving to Idaho with only the clothes on their backs. The children had started their school year in Michigan when they were living with her sister Mag. Now the children would continue at the Grangeville, Idaho, public school as soon as they were settled. She tried to be thankful, but this was one of the worst things she had ever endured.

Johanna had to admit that under these circumstances, many men would have suffered a nervous breakdown. Not her Frank; he was stubborn but stronger from their experience. She counted her blessings; four healthy children who survived chickenpox, measles, mumps, and whooping cough, not to mention several bouts of the flu and colds. Johanna also caught whooping cough after which she had a weakness for coughing. Thankfully, Frank managed to stay healthy through it all. They were particularly fortunate that none of the children, like so many others at the time, contracted polio. The year was 1950, and her children continued their schooling just as winter was starting in Idaho.

Back in Michigan, Johanna's brothers and sisters tried to help Frank financially, but he wouldn't accept it. Years later, all of the children remembered the feelings they had when looking out the car window as they drove away from their home and wondering why men were selling their toys, clothes, and furniture. They didn't fully understand how they had a car to drive to their dad's family in Idaho. The travel was hard since they only had enough money to stop for one night and the food, they bought at grocery stores along the way.

They were so glad to arrive in Fenn, a town outside of Grangeville, until they saw the "house" Grandpa Schuil had waiting for them. As Matt jumped out of the car, he thought, *You can't be serious! This isn't a house*. Vesta was so tired, but as she looked around, she discovered that there was very little furniture to rest on. Sara was already feeling the pressure of being the new kid in town. While Stephen was grumpy and tired, he was glad to be free to run around a little. The home was an old schoolhouse with a big center room equipped with blackboards but no chalk and small rooms around the outer edge.

"Frank, really? Where should the children sleep?" Johanna complained as she felt the stress of both traveling and losing all of their possessions.

Finally, Frank's brothers and dad arrived with mattresses, and Frank's mother, always a great cook, brought over a nice meal that they all enjoyed. With full stomachs, Frank, Johanna, and the children felt refreshed and grateful for a place to sleep. There were only two twin beds for the four children to share. The girls had no problem squeezing together, but the boys fought awhile before they ran out of energy and fell sound asleep, one boy at one end and the other at the other end. Johanna smiled at the boys as she turned out their light.

Johanna held in her tears until she heard Frank's deep breathing. She quietly rose to fall on her knees and cry before the Lord. She opened her Bible and began reading Jeremiah 29 about the Israelites making a mess of their lives and ending up in captivity. Johanna also felt captive in Fenn until she read verse eleven.

"God told them He had a plan for them to prosper them and not to harm them, plans to give them hope and a future."

"Really, God?" Johanna sighed. "Could you mean my family and me?"

Johanna had never felt God's presence so strongly. As she continued reading, she found more promises of restoration from God for Israel. She felt like a wayward child of God who was given new hope. She and Frank had been through so much, and all Johanna did was complain. She resolved to support and encourage Frank so that, together with God's help, they could overcome their trials. She slept well after God calmed her heart and filled her with hope.

The family lived in Fenn for only two months when they moved to a home in Grangeville, where they were closer to the children's school. The home they rented wasn't the prettiest house on the street, Johanna thought, but at least it was an actual house and not a school building.

The children became acquainted with and made some good friends. The town was small, so everyone seemed to know everyone. Since Matt loved sports, he searched for friends to play ball games with. Sara loved riding horses and was delighted that there always seemed to be an extra horse available on Saturdays when the girls would go riding. Matt and Sara both knew how to make friends easily, as did Stephen.

Stephen seemed to enjoy his cousins the most. They were all boys close to his age. Vesta had friends as well, even though she was quite shy. Idaho wasn't her favorite place, probably because she was afraid of many of the things that were popular there, like horses and sports.

This area supposedly had less snow than where they came from in Michigan. However, Johanna wondered about this claim when the snow flurries started upon their arrival in October.

"Oh, this is just a fluke and will pass soon," claimed her father-in-law.

"This town is growing, and construction is going gangbusters," another declaration of her in-laws, which Johanna doubted was true.

As Johanna explored the area, she saw no signs of construction. It appeared to be a simple farming community in northern Idaho, situated between mountains and rivers. The area was ideal for hunting and fishing, however, which was her in-law's top priority. Family came second for them unless you wanted small-town country living. It wasn't that Johanna didn't like small towns; she just knew jobs could be scarce.

Johanna knew God had a plan for her, so she exercised patience. As she suspected, construction work in the area was scarce. Thankfully, their cost of living was low since Frank's father owned the house they lived in.

Frank helped renovate the house so his father could eventually sell it, but Johanna wasn't sure repairs would help since it was a real eyesore. She didn't complain because she was thankful for a roof over her head. Instead, Johanna focused on keeping it clean and praying for better days.

Things started looking up when Frank found a steady job at the local sawmill. However, when the snow set in at the beginning of December, Frank realized that, although he enjoyed hunting and fishing so close to home, Idaho wasn't the right choice for his family. The town was small, and there was no Christian school for the children.

The boys were doing well as was Sara, who couldn't get enough of riding horses. However, Johanna wasn't a cowgirl by any stretch of the imagination, and neither was little Vesta. They were girly girls who needed to live in a bigger city. A week before, Vesta almost had a heart attack when she saw a horse try to bite another horse but grabbed Sara's leg instead. Sara, being as tough as she was, gave the horse a quick swat, and he let her go. Since the skin wasn't broken, Sara recovered quickly and was excited to have horse teeth marks to show off at school.

Frank couldn't help but smile to himself when he saw poor Vesta's pale face after the horse bit Sara. Vesta was so sensitive and rarely did anything wrong. When Frank did punish her, all he needed to do was look her way, and she would immediately burst into tears. Frank never forgot the day his brother's family invited Vesta over for the afternoon. Frank and Johanna lived differently than his brother's family and worried about allowing Vesta to visit them alone. Sure enough, they took Vesta along with their children to the first Disney movie, which played at the theater downtown. Frank and Johanna were both extremely upset when they found out.

"How dare they do that!" Johanna yelled at Frank. "They know we don't approve of going to the movies.

Frank tried to calm her down by promising to talk to his brother about it. Johanna just replied angrily, "It would do no good, so just skip it!"

Frank realized Johanna was right, so in the end, Vesta had to bear the brunt of Johanna's wrath, an experience Vesta never forgot.

"Vesta, why didn't you tell them to bring you home?" Johanna scolded.

"I did, Mommy, but they said it would be fine. I'm sorry, Mommy. I should have tried harder," Vesta cried.

What made Vesta cry even harder was that she really wanted to go to the movies. If she had realized how guilty and sick to her stomach she would feel afterward, Vesta would have fought much harder to have them take her home. It turned out she didn't even like "Snow White" that much. The witch was far too spooky!

The end of 1951 drew near, and the Schuil family had lived in Idaho almost a year by then. Frank and Johanna found out they were expecting another child. Hoping for a fresh start, Frank talked to his father about moving back to California after the baby came. Frank also asked him about possibly managing the rental homes his father owned in Long Beach. At that time, his father wasn't very open to the idea, so Frank decided to bide his time and wait for a better opportunity to speak with him.

Winter passed with more heavy snow that began in October, and now, in the middle of February, there was no sign of it letting up. Johanna sighed as she hung clothes in the basement and dreamed of California weather. She was about four months away from delivering her fifth child, and her hips felt every stair she climbed, especially when it was cold.

It was Saturday, and the children were having a shouting match upstairs. "What now?" Johanna quietly asked herself. "Sara, please come down here! I need your help to hang some clothes," Jo shouted, in hopes of getting the children away from one another.

Miraculously, Sara came dashing down the stairs. Just then, she also heard Frank's booming voice and the boys scattering across the floor. "Oh, thank the Lord! Frank is home," Johanna said as she smiled to herself.

The Schuil family made it through the tough winter and somehow managed to pay their bills and keep food on the table. It was exciting for Jo and the kids to see the sun in March, so they all bounded outside to play. That evening, as was their tradition, when their schoolwork was finished, they read for a while and played games before heading off to bed.

June did not come soon enough. The children were so happy to be free from schoolwork and glad warm weather had returned. Jo decided it was time to start her three older children in swim lessons. She noticed they could go to the park not far from their home. Through the YMCA, there were free lessons for children at the park's public pool. They could even walk there since the park was a couple of blocks from their home, just up a small hill.

Matthew and Sara arrived at the pool with Stephen in tow, and they were asked questions about their swimming abilities. Sara realized that if she could swim across the deep end of the pool, she would be in a more advanced class. When asked, Sara lied, "Sure, I know how to swim across the pool."

"Ok," said the instructor. "Jump in and show me."

*Well*, thought Sara, *here goes nothing*. In she jumped, and after watching the other kids, managed a decent breaststroke while taking a few breaths in between.

Matthew gaped at her, wondering, *How in the world? I didn't know Sara could swim! Hm, maybe I should try too*. But, alas, fear got the best of him after he could not copy what the others were doing. Much to his embarrassment, he ended up in Stephen's class, who caught on to swimming quite quickly and passed him up. "Well, shit, I'm good at other sports! So, what if I can't do this!" Matthew remarked to Sara and Stephen on the way home that day. After that, Matthew decided to quit the lessons and see if he could find some odd jobs that summer.

Vesta was very content to stay home that day and play with her new white kitten. She had no desire to learn to swim, and Johanna did not push her when tears filled Vesta's eyes as her mother suggested them.

June 16, 1952, was a warm summer day, and Sara and Stephen had completed their first two weeks of swimming lessons. That morning, Jo's first labor pain came. Jo knew she had to let Frank know quickly and get the children off to their cousin's house. This baby would be delivered at home with the doctor coming to them. Their bedroom was ready, and the doctor was called.

Thomas Allen did not take much longer to enter the world than Jo's other children. Everyone loved helping with this little blonde, blue-eyed baby boy. They all thought he was just adorable. Johanna recovered quickly as she had so many willing hands to love on Thomas and keep him entertained.

Sara had done so well in her swim class she begged to continue learning that summer as more advanced classes were offered. One day, she came home very excited. "Mom, guess what?! The final class is a junior life-saving class. They said I could do it since I passed all the other classes with flying colors! Can I do that too, Mom?"

"Well, I suppose it won't hurt to know about life-saving. That is quite an honor to be chosen for the class, Sara." Johanna was proud of her brave daughter, who wasn't afraid to take risks.

Sara excelled in learning how to pull her instructors to the side of the pool as they pretended to drown for the class. They were taught basic CPR and other life-saving techniques. They became strong swimmers and learned to hold their breath longer under water. Sara enjoyed the athletic challenges. It was a summer experience she wouldn't soon forget.

## CHAPTER 6
# An Unexpected Event

For Frank and Johanna, living close to either of their families was difficult. Frank's brothers, Jim, and Paul, who both loved to hunt and fish as much as Frank, also drank a bit too much alcohol for Johanna's taste. Frank and Johanna decided early in marriage that their home would be alcohol-free since both had family members who were alcoholics. Frank's brothers didn't drink excessively, but Johanna disliked the idea of them offering beer to her husband while they hunted. Frank knew how to handle his brothers, so he didn't mind saying no to them when they offered him a drink. However, the one thing Frank hated saying no to was hunting or fishing trip invitations. Frank would sweet-talk Johanna until she gave in if he wanted to go hunting or fishing with his brothers.

It was early fall 1952, and deer hunting season was about to open. Frank tried to charm Johanna into letting him join his brothers on a hunting trip, but with money so tight and another baby to feed, "sweet-talking" wouldn't work this time.

"Come on, Frank!" Jim shouted, "Don't tell me you are going to miss this. Johanna will be fine. I know she has another little one to care for, but Mom is close by and so are our wives. She will be fine. Don't worry. You've been working hard, and you deserve some fun; you know you like hunting as much as we do."

"I'm sorry. I just can't this time. You guys go and shoot an extra deer for me," Frank replied sadly. He was worried about Johanna and didn't want to upset her needlessly. Their family had gone through so much since the move, and she had her hands full with the four older children and now a baby.

Paul and Jim packed their pickup with camping supplies. They also loaded their horses in their trailer, saying goodbye to their families, and left without Frank. They had their red plaid shirts with them so that no one would shoot them by mistake, and they made sure the ice chest had some extra beer since, away from family, they had a little more freedom. Between the two of them, they had eight children. Paul had three children with his wife Lucy, while Jim and his wife, Adeline, already had five. Needless to say, the Schuils were a prolific family.

The men drove the back roads for about two hours when Jim spotted their campsite. They were joining a group of friends with young families who were ranchers or farmers from the area. Jim and Paul pulled up and started unloading their horses and gear. They could have easily been mistaken for two handsome cowboys out of a Western movie.

"Howdy, great place you guys found! We have some burgers to share tonight," Jim shouted as he pulled the pickup between some evergreens.

The campsite was an ideal place for the hunters. Soon, the burgers were sizzling in a frying pan over the fire. They planned to hunt for deer the next day. With full stomachs and several beers downed, they were ready for a good night's sleep. They set the alarm for three a.m. and were soon fast asleep.

"Wake up, let's get going," shouted Paul. "It sounds like the woods are alive with animals. I can't wait to try out my new rifle."

"Man, I shouldn't have drunk that last beer. I'm tired, but okay, I'm coming, I'm coming," moaned Jim.

The men packed their gear and headed up the mountain where there would be more deer.

"Can't we go a little faster, Paul?" Jim challenged.

"What's your hurry?" Paul replied. "These curves make me sick when I take them too fast."

"You'll be okay. I made us get a late start, and we need to make up some time.

Just a few more miles, and we'll be in the perfect spot," Jim said.

The men unloaded their horses and spent the day quietly riding through the forest. They saw a few deer but nothing they could get in their rifle sights. Maybe the next day would be better. They still needed to go fishing for their dinner. At the river, they ran into their friends who had already caught plenty for their evening meal.

The week went by quickly. They enjoyed the peace and serenity of the mountains and the comradery that came with hunting with their friends. On their last night, everyone ate and drank in celebration of shooting two bears and three deer between them. They were excited that there was plenty of fresh meat to share with their families. Since it was their last night, the men decided to live it up since there was enough beer for each of them to have two more. Although Jim and Paul had a two-hour drive home that night, it was only 7 p.m., so they had plenty of time to celebrate with their friends before they left. At 9 p.m., they headed out so they wouldn't worry their wives, who were expecting them home that night.

They loaded up their trailer with the horses and other gear and finally left about 10 p.m. Paul drove since Jim was a little tipsy. Jim was glad his younger brother was driving since Paul was a cautious driver.

"Maybe pick up some speed . . ." Jim wasn't able to finish his sentence as a split-second later, the pickup hit a bear in the road. The pickup slid out of control and rolled down the mountain. Paul was thrown from the truck, and then everything went black. Jim also flew through the air before hitting his head on a rock and blacking out.

It was dark, and Jim felt a strange sensation on his face. "Am I dreaming?" Jim asked himself.

As he became more aware of his surroundings, he realized one of the horses was standing nearby. He tried to jump up but realized he could hardly move. That was when he noticed the blood.

"Where am I?" Jim wondered, "Why can't I move? Where did this blood come from?"

Jim had to think hard to remember why he was in the woods. Then he searched for his pocket watch to find out what time it was.

*Oh good, it's here. Maybe the time will help me remember,* Jim thought.

He started saying his name, age, and his wife and family members' names, hoping that would help. He couldn't see his pocket watch's hands in the dark, so he wasn't sure if it was late night or early morning. He looked around, realizing he was on a steep slope.

"Maybe I can crawl up this hill," Jim said to himself. His horse was still standing nearby. Jim knew that his horse was young and on the wild side, but he didn't have many options but to try to get her attention. Jim called the horse softly, "Come here girl. It's okay. Let me have your harness. Do you think you can pull me up the hill?"

After what felt like hours, with the horse's help, Jim found the road. It seemed to be a remote spot, so he tried unsuccessfully to pull himself up on his horse. At that point, Jim decided to send the horse off, hoping it would somehow alert someone that he and Paul were in trouble.

"Thanks, girl, for all you've done. Go home if you can find the way. Ye-ha!" Jim shouted as loudly as his weak voice allowed.

After sending the horse away, Jim passed out. About an hour later, he woke again, disorientated and unsure of where to turn. It occurred to him that he could die, and he had no idea where his brother Paul was.

"Maybe it's time to pray, God," Jim said with a shaky voice. "How to begin? I'm a rather young man and don't always do right by You. I believe You care about me, and right now, I don't know where to go. Please, God, can You show me?" Jim passed out again, but this time, when he came to, he noticed a light in the distance.

"I think I need to crawl toward that light."

Jim remembered the training from his days in the military and did the Army crawl toward that light. A cabin seemed to appear out of nowhere, and Jim crawled up the steps and onto the porch. Later, his doctors said it was a miracle he even survived his injuries, much less made it up the steps and let the people inside know he was there. Jim knew God had guided him to the house since while he was passed out, God took him by the hand and said, "You have to live a while longer."

"I will always follow You, Lord, the best I can," Jim answered in his spirit.

The entire family was devastated by the news that Paul was found dead on the mountain after the accident. Paul was a young father and husband who left behind a wife and three children. His wife, Lucy, could not stop crying. She had no skills and was scared. She was so angry with God and didn't believe it fair that she was the one to lose her husband. At the funeral, she was forced to listen to the promises of God, which she barely believed anymore. Soon after the funeral, Lucy decided to leave Idaho and return to California. Her parents lived there, and she knew they could help her.

Johanna helped Frank with his grief since she had experienced so many deaths in her own family. She also helped him work through the guilt he felt from not being with his younger brothers to help with the driving. Johanna also felt some guilt because she was thankful that Frank was living and healthy. They held each other closer that night, knowing that it could have been Frank in the graveyard. They thanked God for life and prayed for poor Lucy. They worried about both her material needs and her spiritual well-being. She seemed to be struggling so much with God's place in her life.

Frank was thankful for his brother Jim's recovery. About three months after the accident, Jim was up and about on crutches, and a few months later, he was walking on his own. Although Jim always had a limp after the accident, the doctors marveled at his recovery. Originally, they told Jim that he would be in a wheelchair for the rest of his life. Jim realized God had done much more for him than he first believed. The accident and recovery affected Jim in ways he didn't even realize, but his children did.

## CHAPTER 7
# Hopeful

The Schuil household needed more space since all four of their older children shared a bedroom. Little Thomas was also growing quickly and would need to share a room with Matthew and Stephen. To accommodate their growing family, the Schuils moved to a bigger home in Grangeville. The house even had an indoor bathroom and three bedrooms. With more space and a bathroom, Johanna didn't want to be ungrateful, but the house was another neighborhood eyesore. Every time she drove up to it, she asked forgiveness for her disappointment in the structure they called home. She constantly reminded herself that in Hebrews 11:9–10, Sarah and Abraham lived in tents, looking forward to a home whose builder was God. She decided it was time she looked more at what God wanted her to be than what she wanted to be.

In fall 1953, Thomas was sixteen months and showing signs of wit and intelligence. The older siblings enjoyed his antics and gave him lots of attention. Vesta started second grade. Vesta was very shy, so school wasn't her favorite place. Fortunately, the school in Grangeville was small, which helped her adjust. Matthew was in his first year of high school, Sara was in eighth grade, and Stephen was beginning fourth grade. Winter came early that year, which made construction work difficult to find but, somehow, the Schuil family kept food on the table.

Frank decided it was time to seriously discuss with his father the idea of moving his family back to California. He hated moving his dear Johanna again but felt she might be more than ready to leave Idaho. They both loved the California weather, and Johanna was quick to make new friends. Frank also knew Johanna wanted the children to attend a Christian school, and there was a good one in Bellflower, California.

The first chance he got; he approached his father.

"What do you think, Dad, of me moving back to California and taking care of your rental homes in Long Beach?" Frank asked. "Since work is hard to come by here, I think it may be time for us to leave when summer comes. The lumber millwork is good but doesn't pay enough to support a family with five children. Construction has slowed down, and people don't have extra to spend on repairs, so they do it themselves. I believe California offers better employment options for me."

Frank's dad thought a few minutes as he was never much of a talker, "Well, son, the beauty of this country is hard to beat, and the hunting and fishing is great. It's hard for me to have you go after losing Paul. I'd like you to give Idaho another chance."

"Well, Dad, give it some thought. I know you miss Paul, but I have a family to provide for. I don't think this is the best place to raise our family. I'll talk to Johanna and will talk to you again," said Frank, trying to hide the annoyance from his voice.

Frank left his dad cutting wood and headed home. It wasn't much of a home—almost a shack compared to the house he had built for them in Michigan. In many ways, Frank was glad he never lived in that house; it would have made living in the Grangeville house even more difficult. He knew he would need to be persistent with his dad and get his family out of Idaho soon. He wasn't going to give up.

Unexpectedly, help came for Frank when his sister Hannah visited from California. She came to provide extra support for their parents after their brother Paul's death. Their parents were extremely upset at the funeral, and when Paul's wife and children abruptly left Idaho, it was almost more than their parents could bear.

Hannah took Frank aside and said, "I think you need to leave Idaho. There is so much opportunity in California right now. I'll talk to Mom and Dad for you and encourage them to let you go. I know that will be difficult for them, but you have a wife and five children to consider."

The two of them strategized about how to best talk with their parents and then started planning a trip to California. They decided Frank and Johanna should come together to look at their dad's houses in Long Beach and find work for Frank. They also discussed having their youngest sister, Jackie, stay with Frank and Johanna's children while they were gone. Frank was thrilled to have Hannah's support for their move to California and knew she looked forward to having family nearby.

Johanna welcomed the children home from school as they took off their winter coats and boots on the back porch.

"STOP IT!" Sara yelled. "You stop it," Matthew whined in reply, mimicking a girl's voice, which made Sara even madder.

When Stephen tried to walk around the corner, he became fair game for Matthew's teasing. "Hey, where do you think you're going, stooge head? You have to wait until I'm good and ready if I need you to hang my coat and clean my boots."

Sara saw her chance to hit Matthew and run but she wasn't quick enough for his kick.

*Man, that hurt*, thought Sara, but there was no way she would cry. Instead, she slugged him again, causing him to curse. It was too late before Matthew realized that Johanna was standing within earshot. His mother quickly pulled him by the ear to the bathroom and washed his mouth out with soap. Stephen snickered in the background the entire time.

*Next time, I'll get you good*, thought Matthew.

Finally, Johanna settled the kids down, reading in different areas of the house or doing homework. Vesta was the only one who didn't like to tease and fight. Most of the time, they protected her, but if any of her siblings tried to tease her, she would burst into tears. Her older siblings were another story. They seemed to get pleasure out of screaming at each other and calling each other names. "Lord in heaven," Johanna prayed, "help me learn how to discipline these children you've given me. I feel so inadequate."

While she contemplated, Johanna began to prepare dinner for the family. Sara finished her homework quickly and watched little Tommy. Johanna was so focused on her cooking that she didn't hear Frank sneak in through the back door. She nearly jumped out of her skin when he wrapped his arms around her from behind. It was always much easier when Frank was home and helped with the children. One stern word from him, and everyone jumped to attention. Johanna wished she had that much control over them.

When dinner was ready, the family sat down and folded their hands in prayer, thanking God for a good day and the food on their table. Dinner conversation was a joy for Johanna; her family loved to eat, and there was something about food that calmed everyone's spirit. For this meal, they had mashed potatoes and gravy with fried chicken and green beans. She also made Frank's favorite salad—lettuce with cut apple chunks and sliced bananas mixed with a dressing of miracle whip and crushed pineapple. Finally, there was a surprise of homemade vanilla pudding for dessert. Frank marveled at Johanna's ability to stretch the food budget and how she always managed to prepare a feast for the family.

When they finished eating, it was time to read the Word of God. They were reading through Genesis again. The kids loved Genesis because it was full of exciting stories. Genesis included the creation story and Adam and Eve with the serpent, which usually made the children ask how a snake could talk. The story of Noah and the Flood was another favorite, along with the stories of Abraham and his children. The book of Genesis ended with the story of Joseph, which most of the family agreed was the best of all. Frank always read the Bible after dinner as his father had done when he was growing up. It usually took two to three years to finish the entire Bible if they read a chapter or two every evening. Frank continued to test their listening skills by having them repeat the last word he read.

After the dishes were clean and all the children were in bed, Johanna noticed that Frank wasn't asleep in his chair. *I wonder what is on his mind*, she thought since Johanna was normally the night owl while Frank always fell asleep early. That night, Johanna could tell something was up, so she sat down near him and waited.

Frank looked at her from behind his newspaper and said, "What do you think about moving back to California? I know this is kind of sudden, but it has been on my mind for some time. I don't think there is a future here for us, and I'd like to get the children back in a Christian school. I talked with my sister Hannah today, and she thinks it's time for us to move back, and she was going to help persuade Dad as well. I know this will be hard—another move and all, but . . ."

Johanna could hardly wait to interrupt, "It's okay, Frank. I'm with you all the way. Whatever you decide. I don't think this is the best place for our children to grow up, and I know there will be more opportunities for you in California. What about your dad, how do you think he will feel about us moving given the recent loss of your brother Paul?"

"That's one of the issues he shared earlier when I tried to discuss moving with him," Frank said quietly. "I told him I would talk to you and get back to him. I know he wants us to stay, but he also realizes it would be better if we leave. He just needs time to heal from the loss of his son."

"Oh, honey," Johanna said wisely, "he will never get over the grief of losing a child, but he will get stronger in his faith and closer to God as time goes on. Let's pray together right now for God to lead us and comfort him."

Together, Frank and Johanna got on their knees and prayed for the Lord to open doors for their move. They claimed verses from the psalms that talk about God giving them the desire of their hearts. They felt this move would be a good one, but they wanted His direction as so many things in the past few years had gone wrong for them. They both felt comforted after their time together with the Lord and each other.

A few days later, the door opened wide for Frank and Johanna to move to California. Serendipitously, all of the tenants moved out of the Schuil's rental homes at the same time. Also, Frank's mother, Janice, was thrilled to learn that he wanted to move and take care of the property in California. There were three homes on a two-acre parcel in Long Beach. They had purchased it several years earlier and hoped the rentals would be a nice source of income for them.

*All those rentals have been a constant source of trouble*, thought Janice. She was certain Frank would take care of the properties and make all the much-needed repairs.

With his mother's support and his sister Hannah cheering them on, Frank and Johanna got ready to make the trip. It was the middle of November, and although it was cold and rainy, the roads were clear as they drove to California. The houses in Long Beach were in decent shape, so the next hurdle was to find a job for Frank. Hannah introduced Frank to the owner of a furniture store who needed help, and he hired Frank on the spot. Frank asked if he would hold the job until after Christmas so they'd have some time to settle in and the children wouldn't miss any school. Both Johanna and Frank forgot how much they loved the weather in California. They missed it so much that when they arrived back in Idaho, they immediately started packing.

While they were in California, a wonderful thing happened to Frank's dad, John. Upon Frank's return to Idaho, John told Frank the story. It made the move to California a lot less painful for John.

The day they arrived home, his father was anxious to talk to Frank. John asked Frank to meet in his garage, where John was repairing a pickup. As they looked under the hood together,

Frank guessed his dad was going to ask him about a problem with the engine but instead he started talking about Frank's brother Paul. Frank was surprised but tried to act calm, not knowing what his father was about to discuss with him.

"You know Frank, if you died tonight, I wouldn't worry about where you would be," John stated slowly. "In fact, I wouldn't give it a second thought, but when Paul died, that was my greatest fear, and I suppose it made me mourn for him even more. When his wife and kids left too, I missed Paul even more and worried for his soul. To tell you the truth, I worried he didn't love God and wasn't covered by Jesus's forgiveness. I worried so much that I prayed earnestly about it, asking God if my son was in heaven or not. "

"Well, Dad," Frank asked slowly. "Are you still concerned, or do you feel at peace about it now?"

His father replied, "An amazing thing happened to me the other night, something that never happened before. It was more than a dream—almost a vision. It felt so real. Even when I woke up, I knew it was real. God showed me that Paul was with Him in heaven. I saw them both so clearly. I knew the one man was Jesus and the other, my Paul. Frank, I can't tell you the amazing peace it gave me. It also assured me that God will take care of you and your family, and I don't have to worry anymore. As you know, I tend to interfere with my children's lives because I think I know better. You'll understand this when your children grow up. Anyway, I want you to know that if you decide to move to California, you go with my blessing."

"Thanks, Dad! That is indeed an amazing experience. I can only imagine how comforting that was and rejoice with you and Mom. I can't wait to tell Johanna about it, and I promise to do the best job I can to take care of your homes in California.

Everything fell into place for us to make the move. A job is waiting for me, and we want to leave during Christmas break. I was hoping that would be okay with you, Dad."

"You are a good man, Frank, and I know God has good things in store for you. I'll be praying everything goes well, and if you need money for house repairs, let me know."

The weeks before Christmas break passed so quickly that Johanna worried she wouldn't finish her packing. The Schuil family didn't have much to pack yet; with five children, it was surprising how much they needed to bring with them. Frank rented a trailer that was full in no time. Finally, they said their goodbyes.

As much as Janice supported the move, she would miss her eldest son and his family terribly. She worried this move would be their last and that there would be a good chance he would never live close to them again. After their goodbyes were over, Janice went inside and had a good cry.

John had his struggles in letting Frank go as well. Although he told Frank to go, deep down, he wished he could stay. Frank was his favorite son, which made him feel guilty because he didn't want to be like Isaac with his son Esau. In the biblical story of favoritism, the father ends up losing his son. He was so proud of Frank and what a good man he was that he hoped to keep him close. Now he was doing his best to give him over to God.

## CHAPTER 8
# California

During the winter, White Bird Hill was the first difficult area to travel while pulling a trailer. Thankfully, the snow that had fallen earlier in the month was mostly melted. Frank was a good driver but not always patient, particularly with a car full of rowdy, happy children. They were all excited about the move but could be difficult to calm down in a car.

The trip included one stop in Winnemucca, Nevada, thanks to the money Frank's mother gave them for a hotel and some extra food. It was a blessing for all of them to have a good night's rest. They arrived in Long Beach on the eve of December 20, 1954.

When they arrived in Long Beach, they quickly set up in the main house to make it their new home. They grabbed the mattresses and bedding that were tucked away in easy-to-access places that first night.

Frank planned to rent or even sell the other two houses immediately, although his father wanted to sell all three, if possible. Frank knew he needed to talk to his father about keeping the big house until he could afford to buy a place of his own.

"Dad, give me some time," Frank reasoned. "These houses need repairs and a little paint before they can sell anyway. I'm sure I can rent the other two houses soon. Some of the neighbors have friends who may be interested. If possible, Dad, could you give me about two years to save up and buy a place of my own for my family."

John agreed to wait for Frank to fix up the houses. Two years would go by quickly, and it would be better to have the houses in good shape before they were sold.

Frank's job at the furniture store went well. He discovered his gift for persuading people to buy nice things there. Maybe it was because he loved nice things himself or because he enjoyed talking to people. Whichever it was, Frank's boss, Manny, liked having him on the floor selling to customers. Since Frank could repair most items that came in damaged, he also helped Manny save money on return shipping charges.

With Frank working at the store, he and Johanna were able to fill their house with much-needed furniture and their first TV set. Although the TV set was free and Manny warned Frank it was a junk item, Frank took it home. Vesta occasionally sat in front of it, pretending to watch and dreaming of the day it would work. Sara and Matthew were involved in sports after school, so they weren't as anxious to watch the TV as Vesta. Stephen would beg Vesta to play board games, which helped them both get their minds off the broken TV.

As an experienced mechanic, Frank tried to fix it. No matter how many times he opened it up and changed out parts, only a few fuzzy lines appeared on the screen. Finally, Frank decided it was a piece of junk, so he cut the wood apart to see if he could at least use that for something else.

One day at the store, Manny surprised Frank when he said, "Frank, here is a TV that works. It has a small screen, but I thought you and your family might enjoy it."

Frank was so excited, "Thanks, Manny. I'll let you know what the family thinks! My kids will want to watch all the shows they hear their friends talking about."

That same night, the excitement in the Schuil house was palpable. Everyone raced through dinner and the dishes. No one even argued about who was doing what; the dishes simply disappeared into the cupboards, all clean and dry.

Johanna got into the act and surprised everyone with some popcorn made by shaking a pan of kernels in oil across a stovetop burner. When the corn stopped popping, melted butter and salt were added. Frank and Johanna enjoyed the evening as much as the children; all of them laughing until their stomachs hurt while watching the *I Love Lucy* show.

Although Frank liked his job at the furniture store and got along famously with his boss, he knew he needed to look for a better-paying job. His children were growing up, and Christian school tuition was expensive. Wonderful people from the church helped to pay their tuition, but Frank wanted to take over responsibility for it. That evening while the children were doing homework, Frank had the opportunity to talk it over with Johanna.

"Johanna, honey, you know we need a better income. I was thinking of taking a day to drive around and see what kind of construction work might be available," Frank said thoughtfully.

"Good idea, Frank. Manny can only pay so much, and it isn't enough for our family. I know you don't want to depend on help from your father or people from our church for our entire lives. Let's get on our knees and ask God to lead us to just the right place," said Johanna, who was always ready to bring their trials to the Lord.

Frank knew Johanna was right, so together, they asked their God for direction. They were certain God cared about them, and they trusted Him to guide their lives. They were, however, both surprised when the very next day, a neighbor mentioned that her husband was looking for a good construction man. Her husband owned a construction company and had more work than he could handle. He'd spent a long time trying to hire a man he could trust. Johanna knew her Frank was trustworthy, and his skills fit the job qualifications perfectly. She couldn't wait to tell Frank how God already seemed to have answered their prayers.

When Frank walked through the door that evening, he could see the excitement on Johanna's face.

"What is it, Johanna? You look like you're going to burst," laughed Frank as he swooped her into his arms and planted a kiss on her lips.

"Frank, stop this minute," Johanna giggled. "I have some wonderful news."

"It can't be as wonderful as 'I love you,' can it?" Frank whispered in her ear.

"Ok, ok, you win. Do you want to hear or not?" asked Johanna impatiently.

"Fine, so what is the news?" Frank surrendered with a mischievous smile on his face.

"My goodness, you made me forget how I was going to tell you. SO, here it is—I think you got a construction job," Johanna blurted out with pleasure.

Frank was stunned. This was the last thing he expected Johanna to say. She didn't even have a car to go out and look for a job for him. How in the world?

Johanna read his mind and said, "Frank, it is our neighbors. The ones with the lovely home we always admire. I met her today as I was out strolling with Tommy. We got to talking, and one thing led to another, and she mentioned that her husband owned a construction company and was looking to hire a good man he could trust."

Frank could hardly believe how quickly God had answered their prayers. What a lucky coincidence that Johanna just happened to meet that neighbor on her walk. Then he realized that wasn't luck, it was God. Just as Acts 17 says, God chooses the exact places He has in mind for one to live.

*Thank You, Lord, for what You will do with this opportunity for me*, thought Frank.

God opened the door for Frank to work in construction once again. He left the job at the furniture store quickly since a relative of Manny, who needed work, had moved to town recently. Manny hated losing Frank but knew the construction job was a great fit for Frank with much better pay. A few days later, Frank started his job with the Harry Bench Construction Company.

California was booming, and as a result, so was construction. Although he could have done well, Frank wasn't ready to open his own company. Johanna knew it was fear of failure that held him back. Frank was happy to let someone else worry about paying the employees and taxes. He was glad he didn't need to be concerned about expenses and could have Johanna take care of their household finances.

One year passed quickly. It was 1955, and an opportunity came up to sell his father's rental houses and buy a home of their own. Frank could hardly believe he would be entirely debt-free and prayed he would never need to be bailed out by his father again. Johanna had saved the $1,000 needed for the down payment. While Frank's employer, Harry, trusted Frank and Johanna so much that he loaned them the remaining $15,000 needed to buy the house.

They moved to a lovely home on Pepperwood Street off of Lakewood Boulevard. When Vesta, who was nine years old at the time, saw the house, she fell in love with its wraparound porch and the two small palm trees and short hedge that lined the sidewalk leading up to the porch.

It was a three-bedroom home with a nice-sized bathroom and large living room. Sara shared a room with Vesta while Matthew and Stephen had the other room. Baby Tommy slept in his crib until he was big enough for a small bed in the boys' room. Space was tight, but no one seemed to mind.

Since California had so many warm days, the boys spent most of their time in the large backyard. The outside space was ideal for playing basketball in the driveway and baseball in the long yard with the neighbors. Johanna marveled at how fast her children were growing up. She could hardly believe Matthew was sixteen, with Sara fifteen and Stephen thirteen. There were three teens in her home, no wonder it felt a little chaotic at times. Thomas was three now but still a bit of a handful. His siblings grew tired of his antics, which they no longer viewed as cute. Johanna knew this, too, would pass, and she tried to handle life with prayer and God's Word.

Johanna was thrilled because it was a wonderful place for her family to thrive. She loved Southern California and its mild year-round weather. She never missed the season changes when her hip or back would ache in colder climates. With her children growing up, Johanna thought about getting a job to help with the expenses that grew with them. She loved getting out of the house and decided to talk to Frank about looking for a job.

The next morning before the children were awake, she saw her opportunity. "Frank, honey," Johanna ventured, "What would you think if I worked a few days a week at Woolworths? I was shopping there the other day and was told by a sales clerk they needed extra help. I'd love to help bring in a little extra money. Our growing boys eat more and more, and there are extra school expenses with Matthew and Sara loving sports the way they do." Johanna paused to see Frank's reaction. He had a thoughtful look on his face, so she ventured forward, "What do you think? Should I apply?"

Frank knew Johanna had a lot of talent, but he felt bad that he couldn't support the family alone. He decided that she should do what she thought was best for her. However, Frank cautioned, "Honey, if it gets too much for you, know that I don't want you to overdo it just because you want a little extra money."

It was settled, and Johanna went that very day to apply at Woolworths. If three-year-old Tommy hadn't been with her, she would have been put to work immediately. Johanna worked late afternoons and evenings for about one year at Woolworths before having another miscarriage. Her first one happened shortly after they moved from Idaho to California. This was the second one in two years. It made Johanna realize she wasn't as strong as she liked to think, and Frank and Johanna agreed it was time for her to quit her job.

Johanna realized it was hard for her to take care of her busy family, even though the children were a big help. Sara expertly cleaned the house and was also a wiz at sewing. If she tired of her clothing, she would ask Johanna to bring fabric from the store so she could sew a new skirt and blouse for herself. Vesta and Stephen did the dishes every night, and Sara also helped with preparing the meals. Matthew was less involved at home because he was busy with his junior year studies, sports, and working with Frank on Saturdays to earn money to pay for college.

Frank worked hard but still loved to get away occasionally to hunt, fish, and forget about his responsibilities. Harry continued giving Frank more and more responsibility. He could see that Frank got along well with the men; they respected him and would listen to his ideas. So, Harry promoted Frank to foreman. Frank appreciated the extra pay but he felt the stress of the added responsibility.

Although Frank wanted to go hunting, he knew the hunting license was expensive, and they didn't have extra money to spare. Johanna was also wary about Frank going hunting ever since his brothers had their accident. In the end, Frank decided to make the trip because he needed a break, and his boss was willing to give him a few days off.

CHAPTER 9

# Raising Children

Frank was raised in an era when parents often pursued their own passions without involving their children. As a result, he didn't realize how his sons were interested in hunting and fishing with him. Even if he did bring them along, he could barely afford one license, let alone three. Although he deeply loved his children, he never knew how to truly express it. As he aged, it baffled Frank that two of his sons always welcomed Frank and Johanna at their homes but rarely visited their parents in Lakewood.

Frank also didn't realize how much his sons needed his attention while they were growing up. Growing up in rural Michigan, Frank spent his free time helping with the farm, feeding the animals, and milking the cows. There was never time for playing sports or swimming. In contrast, his sons lived in a Southern California suburban neighborhood, a completely different world. They were active and full of mischief; they loved playing baseball, swimming, and racing around on their bikes. For Frank, his main source of entertainment as a child was hunting and fishing, which his parents strongly encouraged since it put food on the table.

One thing Frank loved doing with his family was taking road trips. As the kids got older, it became difficult to take everyone on a trip in the same car. One day, he thought about this dilemma and suddenly had a great idea. Now that Matt had his driver's license and Sara was fifteen, they could visit their grandparents in Grangeville, which was about a twenty-five-hour drive. His parents and siblings would love to see the two of them. Matthew had a nice car they could drive. It wasn't brand new, but Frank made sure it was in good running order with reliable tires before they left. Johanna was a little skeptical about her children taking such a long trip on their own. At the same time, she knew that she and Frank had traveled further with much less.

By July 12, 1955, Frank was able to give Matthew the time off to take the trip. Sara and Matt were excited to go on this adventure. They didn't have enough money to stop at a motel but were confident that twenty-five hours of driving in one stretch was no big deal. Before they headed out, they packed food and brought a little money along to pay for snacks and gas.

Sara and Matthew drove with their windows down to feel the breeze of that warm July day. Matthew was thrilled to take his little black '41 Chevy Coup with its aqua and white interior on the trip. He had worked hard doing grunt work for his dad the previous summer to buy it. Now they would put it to the test on a strenuous road trip through mountain passes and long valley stretches. They began their journey late in the afternoon blasting the latest Elvis hit, "Rock Around the Clock," on the car radio. They headed out on Route 66 toward Victorville to catch the 95 in Nevada.

They continued their journey by taking the route to Nevada, leaving California behind. As the sun set, they made their way through a small town on the road leading toward Las Vegas. A police officer and his wife noticed this very young couple and decided to pull them over for questioning.

Like most teenage girls, Sara had packed for every occasion. Back then, girls wore full net, stick-out slips under gathered skirts. Sara brought her slip along and insisted she hang it in the back by the window so it wouldn't get smashed in a suitcase.

Matthew was embarrassed by the slip but figured the only people who would see it were their cousins before she put it in a closet. Neither of them realized how much it looked like part of a wedding dress.

Sara stayed put while Matthew opened the door to talk with the officer. All the officer said was, "You need to come with me, please." Sara wanted to object, but Matthew was saying okay, and before they knew it, they were at the local police station. *Well, at least we aren't being kidnapped*, Sara thought.

Neither Sara nor Matthew could imagine why the police wanted to talk to them. Before they had time to think, they were taken to separate rooms.

"What is your name, and where did you come from?" asked one officer. "Who are your parents; what is your mother's maiden name? How old are you? Where does your father work?" Sara was so annoyed. She answered the questions one by one, and, finally, one of the men asked, "Are you eloping?"

Sara was ready to scream. "Are you kidding? That's my brother. We're going to visit our grandparents in Grangeville, Idaho. We're not ELOPING!"

She tried to be patient, but patience wasn't one of Sara's virtues. She didn't realize the impression she and Matthew made with their cute car and her slip hanging in the window. Sara was as dark as Matthew was light. She had big brown eyes while Matthew was blond and blue-eyed. They didn't even look related, let alone like brother and sister. Finally, after being questioned for almost two hours, the officers believed them and decided to let them go. The officers were surprised that their parents trusted their teenage children to travel that far alone.

On their way out, Sara was madder than a hornet and ready to complain about how poorly they were treated. Matthew saw the look in Sara's eyes and knew he had to get her to the car, or they would surely be arrested for something else.

"It's okay, Sara. Come on, let's just go!"

"But we should not have been treated that way. I'm so mad about how long they kept us here!" Sara yelled over her shoulder as Matthew practically dragged her into the car, worried the officers would find another reason to detain them.

The drive ahead was long but their experience with the police kept them wide awake. They had so much to talk about and soon realized they were laughing hard at how funny and ridiculous it was.

"Stop," Sara giggled. "I'm going to pee."

It was now very late, and their goal was to drive straight to Idaho. Highway 95 was extremely boring and the longest leg of the journey. They soon ran out of both conversation and radio reception. Sara asked, "Hey, Matt, are you okay? Could I take a nap?"

"Sure, no problem. I'm wide awake." Matthew said confidently.

About an hour later, Sara awoke to a rolling feeling and realized they were off the road. "Matthew! Wake up! You are off the road!" Sara screamed.

Thankfully, a trucker noticed them swerving and was able to help them get their car out of the ditch. "You kids be careful now. This is a long stretch of road. You going to be alright?"

Sara spoke boldly, "Yes I'm wide awake now, so I'll drive, and my brother can get some sleep."

They waved goodbye to the trucker when Matthew asked, "Are you sure you want to drive? You don't even have your license."

"I know, but you can help me get started, and, well, how hard can it be? Besides, look around; there are no people or police, hopefully," Sara replied. After a few lessons on how to start and shift, off they went with only a couple of jerks and giggles. Matthew promptly fell back to sleep while Sara drove, staying wide awake.

About two hours later, Sara noticed the gas tank was running low. After fifteen minutes of poking him, she finally woke Matthew and said, "Matt, we're almost out of gas. I'm going to pull into that small station at the bottom of this hill. I'm not sure I know how to stop though." As she spoke, she was stepping on the brake, and they flew past the gas tank.

"Sara, what are you doing? Put your foot on the clutch too, now!" Matthew yelled. From there, Matthew backed up the car, pumped their gas, and took over driving.

They made it through the next day without too many incidents. Matthew made sure he ate enough snacks, and they took turns driving and napping as long as they felt they were safe. This far north, the sun did not set till almost 10 p.m., which helped, but now it was night again. They decided, this time, they needed to talk to each other to stay awake.

Before they knew it, they were on White Bird Hill, the only road entering Grangeville from the south. It had a steep grade with many switchbacks. Although cars and trucks were smaller in the 1950s, this road was particularly narrow. It was 2 a.m. and pitch black as they began the drive up. There were no street-lights, so they used their brights. Just as they came around the fourth switchback, there was a truck on the other side of the road, so Matthew quickly dimmed his brights. Suddenly, his lights went out completely.

"OH SHIT!" Matthew yelled, knowing he used a word his mom hated, but he could not help himself in the moment. Somehow (with God's help and protection, Johanna said later), they made it safely to their uncle Jim's house. He promptly took them to town for breakfast and had a new alternator put in the car. At this point, Matthew and Sara were down to their last dollar, so their grandparents and uncle helped them out with some expenses and gave them some extra money when it was time to return home.

During their visit, Sara helped Adeline around the house to thank her aunt and uncle for their hospitality. She cleaned the kitchen counters and got on her hands and knees to scour the large tile floor. She also helped with the wash because, with six children in the house, there was always more laundry to be done.

During the trip, Matthew and Sara also saw some of their old school friends and had the chance to do some fishing and ride horses. All in all, they enjoyed visiting their grandparents, uncles, aunts, and cousins in Idaho. Fortunately, they made their trip home in record time without any police encounters or car problems.

Their adventure with the police served them well for years to come. Sara used the story for her speech class, calling it "The Day I was Arrested for Eloping." During the speech, she had the entire class spellbound and, of course, earned an A for her effort. Matthew used the story to entertain friends, knowing that not many people were taken to the police station during their road trips.

Most parents would not have sent two teenagers on such a long trip on their own, but Frank and Johanna had traveled so much in their early marriage that they didn't think twice about it. Although Matthew could be difficult at times, Sara was extremely brave and dealt with him well. Her bravery, however, could get her in trouble at times.

Later that same summer, Sara and her friends decided to go to Huntington Beach, which was about twenty miles away. They packed lunches and had just enough money for the roundtrip bus ride. Soon, they were enjoying the sun and waves.

"Wow," exclaimed Janet. "This water is so cold." The ocean water in Southern California was usually around sixty-eight degrees, but that day, it was only sixty-five. After their first swim, the girls relaxed on the beach and warmed up.

"Hey, is that John and Larry over there? You know, the cute guys in our geometry class?" asked Carol as she poured baby oil over her body. "Wait, it looks like a couple more guys are with them. Let's go over to say 'Hi.'"

The girls had a blast flirting with the guys. They were some of the cutest, most popular boys in school. It was noon when they started getting hungry, so the girls pulled out their lunches. The boys were hungry too but not at all prepared, so Riley asked, "Do any of you happen to have some extra cash? We're hungry too but didn't plan to stay this long. When we ran into you cute ladies, we just had to stay. So, any chance you can help us out?"

The girls looked at each other sheepishly, but before they had time to discuss it, Janet offered the boys their bus money. After lunch, they continued having a great time except for one embarrassing moment when Rachel ran into the water. A wave hit her, pulling her strapless bathing suit down and giving the boys a full-frontal view of her naked. Rachel quickly dove under the water, struggling to pull up her suit and fighting the waves at the same time.

Soon, everyone realized it was time to head home. At this point, the girls had to admit to the boys that their lunch was paid for with the girls' bus fare. Riley responded chivalrously with, "No worries, girls, we'll get you home."

They packed up their beach gear, walked to the road, and started to hitchhike. Since there were eight of them, they needed to catch a ride with at least two cars. It was growing darker, and finally, a car stopped. Since there was only enough room for the girls, the boys were left behind. The boys ended up walking almost six miles before they were picked up by someone going their way and who could drop them close to home.

When Frank came home from work that evening, he was surprised that Sara wasn't home from the beach. He called Janet's parents, and Janet wasn't home either. Janet's father came to the Schuil's house to discuss what they should do next. They decided to call the police and have them check on the buses coming from Huntington Beach. Just as they were dialing the phone, a strange car pulled up, and out piled the girls.

At this moment, Frank realized that, for good or bad, Sara was fearless. He was torn between being relieved that she was safe, albeit slightly sunburned, and wanting to wallop her good. He was learning how much there was to worry about when teenage girls were involved and thought to himself, *I'll be glad when a good man comes along so I can marry my girls off.*

Frank decided early on that to help his sons do better in the world, he would teach them to work hard and focus on their education. Since he only had a sixth-grade education, this decision created a conflict for Frank. Often, instead of simply encouraging his sons to focus on their schoolwork, he ended up arguing with them. When this happened, Frank would wonder, *Don't they see how important education is for their future? That it is their chance to better themselves and avoid backbreaking work for the rest of their lives?*

During their arguments, Matthew would constantly resist, not because he didn't agree with his father, but because he loved to disagree with him in general. As Matthew grew up, he became more agreeable and learned how to make his father proud.

Frank loved to watch Matthew play basketball and baseball. From working in construction with his dad during the summer, Matthew knew he wanted to get a desk job after college and used the money he earned to pay his own way through Calvin College in Michigan, which filled Frank with pride and joy.

The year was 1958, and Matthew was attending his first year of college while Sara was in her senior year of high school. Matthew worked hard for his grades, but for Sara, making good grades was easy. Despite her success in school and, much to

Johanna's disappointment, Frank saw no reason to encourage his daughters to attend college.

One evening, Sara asked, "Dad, what would you think if Peter asked for my hand in marriage?"

Johanna was afraid this might happen, but she was still unprepared for the question. Even though Sara was a senior and had been dating Peter Velder since they were in eighth grade, Johanna had high hopes for her daughter.

"No, Sara, you both need to wait a bit, and with your good grades, what about going to college for a year or two before getting married?" Johanna responded. "Peter is only a year older than you and needs more time to mature. Waiting would be best for both of you in the long run. Don't you agree, Frank?"

Frank quickly replied, "Johanna, honey, there is no point in sending Sara to college and spending all that money; for what, so she grows up a bit? That's the most ridiculous thing I've ever heard. Besides, Peter's family has a dairy business where he loves working."

Sara didn't mean to cause an argument, so she decided to sneak out of the room and see what Vesta was doing. Maybe she would find another time to talk to her dad about getting married to Peter. *College, blah,* Sara thought. *I'd rather have my own home and family. It's hard enough to be away from Peter since his family moved to Chino. I'm not taking any chances of losing him to some other girl by going to college.*

In the end, Sara got her way since her father saw no need for his girls to go to college. She had, after all, found a good man who was from a strong Christian family and had a good future in front of him.

Early in the same year, Frank received one of the biggest surprises of his marriage to Johanna. When she approached him one evening, looking dismayed, he wondered if he would be scolded again about Sara and Peter's engagement. Instead, Johanna blurted out, "I think I'm pregnant."

"What! How can that be? I thought we were being so careful."

"I did too, Frank, but the doctor said that sometimes when a woman approaches menopause, it is easier for her to get pregnant."

"So, you already went to the doctor?" Frank asked.

"Well no, but I talked to them on the phone and told them my symptoms. I have an appointment next week and have already missed two cycles."

"I can't believe this. You're thirty-nine, and I'm forty. It's been six years, and you've had two miscarriages since Thomas was born." Frank uttered as the news slowly sunk in.

"I know, I feel the same way, and we don't know if I'll miscarry again. To be honest, this pregnancy feels more solid than the last few. We may want to start preparing to be parents again."

*What will our kids think?* Frank felt some nervousness that his older children might be shocked that Frank and Johanna still enjoyed sex at their age. *They don't realize that our bodies age but our minds don't. Admittedly, it will be a little embarrassing but I'd love being a new father again,* thought Frank.

Frank and Johanna confirmed with their doctor that she was pregnant, and by the third month, they decided it was time to tell the children. Sara's wedding was coming up in August, and Matthew would be returning home from college for the summer soon.

The conversations with their children and friends went just as Frank and Johanna suspected they would. Many people were thrilled for them, others seemed a little embarrassed, and some were quite shocked. Their children were mostly shocked! They called Matthew at college and, although he was a little surprised at first, he was happy for his parents. Vesta was excited, and Sara decided to sew her mom a pretty lace smock since Johanna would be quite pregnant at her wedding. All the children made it through their own dramas, and soon, the discussion turned to the critical topic of whether the baby would be a boy or a girl.

The day of Sara's wedding arrived, and Vesta (who was a candle lighter) could hardly contain her excitement and nervousness. She was sure that her candle would blow out while she was walking down the aisle since she was scared to death to light a match. On the day of the wedding, she thought she might faint, but after the first candle was lit, she breathed normally again. Thomas was the ring bearer with a sweet cousin, Jenny, being the flower girl. Matthew and Stephen were groomsmen and thrilled to be part of the wedding party.

Everything went smoothly, and the family enjoyed all the delights of this first family wedding. Sara and Peter loved it as well and were excited to leave on their honeymoon. Sara could scarcely believe she was married and with both parents being fully supportive. It was an exciting and thankful time for her and Peter. On their first night, they stayed at a nice hotel in Southern California. At eighteen and nineteen, they didn't have much money, so they decided to take a road trip to Idaho to visit their relatives. In Idaho, Sara's grandparents, John and Janice Schuil, were thrilled to have the newlyweds stay with them. Both Peter and Sara enjoyed visiting the family plus the hiking, fishing, and swimming they did during the trip.

After the wedding, Matthew returned to Michigan for his second year at Calvin College. Frank was so proud that his oldest son attended college and was doing so well there. Matthew liked being back where he grew up and hoped to find a good Christian wife at Calvin. He also looked forward to being eligible for an office job when he finished his degree. Although Matthew earned a lot of money over the summer digging ditches on his Dad's construction sites, it was hard, backbreaking work. He gained a new respect for his dad after watching him manage a crew of tough construction workers and was particularly impressed by how much they respected Frank. Despite this, Frank and Matthew had a hard time seeing eye-to-eye on a lot of topics—whether it was politics or how they believed the modern-day church should be run. Matthew inherited his stubborn streak from his grandfather and dad, so even though he cared for them deeply, he seldom expressed that love openly.

Part II

CHAPTER 10

# Vesta

I t was 1958, Dwight Eisenhower was in his second term as president, and the country was in the Cold War with the Soviet Union. After atomic bombs were used at the end of World War II, the Cold War started because many people worried that the bombs would be used again to destroy more people, economies, and countries. At that time, the two most powerful countries in the world were the United States and the Soviet Union. Many Americans believed that the communist governments of the Soviet Union, China, and some smaller countries in Eastern Europe and Asia threatened America's freedom.

In one particular country, Vietnam, the communist regime, led in the north while the southern part fought to remain a democracy. Many television shows and spy movies were made about fighting communism, and the conflict in Vietnam became a concern in the US and the rest of the free world. All of this occurred just as Vesta became a young woman.

Vesta was excited that Johanna's pregnancy was going by quickly and they would soon have a new baby in the house. Johanna was eager as well but wondered how they would find the money to buy all the things a new baby needed. Her prayers were answered when the ladies of the church surprised her with a baby shower. The shower reminded Frank and Johanna how grateful they were for their church family. They had grown to love Bethany Christian Reformed Church. Johanna and Frank thanked God for bringing them to this place where their family could thrive.

It was 7:00 a.m. on the morning of December 16, 1958, when Vesta woke up to the sound of her father talking in an enthusiastic voice. She listened quietly since it was rare for Frank to be home at this time of the day.

Vesta held her breath when she heard her father say, "Johanna's doing great, but it was a long night. I think she was nervous about becoming a mother again at forty and that something could be wrong with our baby. The doctor kept telling her to relax. They tried to keep me out of the delivery room, but they gave in when I said, 'NO WAY. I've seen every one of my children born and even delivered one myself.' I know it helped Johanna that I was there, but I must admit, I was a little worried myself. I never saw your mother get so stressed out, she's usually cool as a cucumber birthing her babies. In the past, she never had time to feel a lot of pain because she had all of you so quickly. Three hours seemed like forever to both of us, but it's over now, and Johanna and the baby are doing great. I better go now and get the kids ready for school, bye Sara."

Vesta was about to burst, so she ran out to see her dad. She jumped up and down, begging him to tell her whether she had a new brother or sister! She desperately wanted a baby sister, and her dad kept telling her the odds were on her side since every other child they had was a girl. Although this was good reasoning, Vesta knew it wasn't foolproof as her mother told her not to assume but wait and see what God would give. Vesta loved baby boys too, but her brother Thomas was a handful, and a sister would be a nice change. As her father stood there smiling, Vesta hoped God would give her the desire of her heart, a new baby sister.

"So, Dad, what did Mom have?" Vesta shouted. By this time, Thomas and Stephen were in the room trying to figure out what all the commotion was about.

Frank couldn't stand it any longer, "It's a GIRL," he yelled happily.

The boys weren't nearly as thrilled about their new baby sister, and given Frank's lack of culinary ability, were more concerned about who was fixing breakfast. After some cold cereal and toast, the next challenge was preparing their lunches. Thankfully, Johanna taught the children well, and they knew how to fix their lunches. Frank had a hunch that the boys grabbed a few more cookies than Johanna would have allowed, but that day, he reasoned, was a day for celebrating.

As soon as the baby, Rachel Marie, came home from the hospital, Vesta took care of her whenever Johanna was busy. Soon, she became a second mother to her. In addition to taking care of Rachel, Vesta quickly learned how to iron, fold clothes, change diapers, wash out dirty diapers, and clean the house. People might say the Schuils were overworking such a young girl, but Vesta, who was twelve at the time, loved it. She enjoyed cooking and cleaning, and Vesta loved Rachel as if she was her own child. Vesta realized how much she loved homemaking, dreaming of the day a special guy would come into her life so she could have children and a home of her own.

One of Vesta's favorite things to do was spend time with Sara and Peter, who were expecting a baby of their own. Everyone laughed at the fact that Johanna would be a mother and a grandmother only ten short months apart. Vesta was thrilled that she would have another baby to play and help with.

Before long, Denise Renee was born on October 7, 1959, the following year. She was a happy baby with a head full of hair. Vesta first believed that Rachel was much cuter than Denise. What she didn't realize at thirteen was that she was biased, just like any mother who thinks her baby is the cutest. It didn't take long for her to love both babies as Denise practically became Vesta's second child. Vesta spent many weekends with Sara and Peter, particularly since they appreciated her babysitting to give them a chance to have some date nights.

Vesta loved spending time with her sister and looked forward to doing everything Sara planned for them. Sara especially enjoyed going to the movies with Vesta and, afterward, they'd go out for a hot fudge sundae. Vesta worked hard and didn't expect much, but Sara loved to buy gifts for her.

During afternoons in the late 1950s, old movies were shown on TV. About once a week, Sara did the ironing while she watched the movies. This was before polyester made ironing clothes obsolete. Vesta loved watching movies while Sara ironed since Johanna didn't allow anyone to watch TV during the day.

People would often mistake thirteen-year-old Vesta for a six-teen or even eighteen-year-old. She had long blond hair and green eyes but didn't think she was nearly as beautiful as Sara with her sparkling brown eyes and all-around good looks. Vesta accidentally discovered that she was more attractive than she realized. She and some friends were playing softball in the street when a car full of teenage boys came around the corner. Everyone moved to let the car pass. One of the boys saw Vesta and couldn't stop staring. "Hey, baby" was all he managed to say. He continued to stare until they were out of sight. Although she never saw that boy again, Vesta was sure she turned ten shades of red, and the softball game lost its appeal since all she could do was dream about boys who might be interested in her.

Vesta was a dreamer at heart and would mostly fantasize about boys and becoming an actress. The first acting role she tried out for was in a school play. She was devastated when she wasn't chosen, but another teacher challenged her to memorize a speech and enter a contest. Vesta loved the speech contest and realized that even when life didn't go the way she believed it should, she could look for other opportunities to develop her talents and have fun doing it.

# CHAPTER 11

## Babysitting

V esta spent many happy days helping with her baby sister. She loved playing with Rachel and fixing her hair. With all that Vesta learned from being an older sister and aunt, Vesta was a highly sought-after babysitter. Of course, she believed that the cutest baby girls were Rachel and Denise. During the summer, Vesta loved staying at Sara and Peter's house and was thankful when her sister asked her to stay and her Mom let her go.

Much of Vesta's early teenage years were spent learning from her mom and Sara about what made their babies happy and how to care for them. In the summertime, she often babysat for a family down the street, the Crenshaws. Vesta enjoyed the benefits of earning her own spending money. With four children, the job was challenging, but the mother loved having her babysit because Vesta was trustworthy, and her parents were nearby in case of an emergency. Thankfully, the oldest daughter, Terri, helped Vesta keep her three younger brothers under control. They constantly tested the limits, and Vesta wasn't always sure how to handle them.

One Saturday night, Vesta and Terri planned to put the boys to bed and have Terri pretend to sleep too. They didn't want the boys to be jealous that Terri got to stay up later than they did.

"Are you sure we have to go to bed at eight?" Steven yelled.

"I have to go to the bathroom. Michael kicked me!" cried the youngest, Timmy.

"I did not! Timmy's such a baby, he just got in the way of my foot," Michael yelled.

All the boys were cute with their curly hair, big brown eyes, and long eyelashes. Timmy was the cutest with his darling baby features. Vesta didn't understand how they could be so cute and still be such a handful.

"Okay, it's time to settle down. Please stop hitting each other and take turns using the bathroom." Vesta used her calmest voice, hoping she sounded in control.

With all the chaos, it usually took at least an hour to get the boys settled down. When it was finally quiet, Terri would come around the corner with a smile on her face. Vesta and Terri could relax and watch a TV movie with the popcorn and snacks her mom had left for them.

One such evening just as they settled in, an earth-shattering noise came from the boys' room. Before Vesta and Terri made it down the hall, all three boys burst from the room crying.

*Well, at least they're alive*, Vesta thought.

A strange cloud of smoke, with a terrible smell, came from the room, and the boys could barely open their eyes.

"What on earth happened?" Vesta asked. "What is that smoke?" Vesta was surprised at how calm she felt in this situation. As she grew older, she realized it was a gift that God gave her—the ability to think clearly when there was chaos all around her.

The boys all talked at once. Finally, Steven admitted, "We found a silver tube on the window ledge, we dropped it, and it exploded."

"Can you get it for me?" Vesta asked. She was not sure if it was a good idea to get the tube but did not know of another way to solve the mystery.

"I think so," Michael said, being the brave one of the bunch. He walked back into the smoke-filled room and returned with the silver tube and his eyes full of tears.

At this point, Vesta had no choice but to call their mother. She didn't know where the smoke came from and seeing the silver tube didn't help. On her drive home, their mother realized what happened.

"It was the tear-gas gun that I keep in my purse when I work late at night. I had it on the ledge of my bedroom window but forgot about it when we traded rooms with the boys," she explained to Vesta.

Turning to the boys, she shouted "I had to leave work for this! You boys shouldn't have even seen the tube since it was hidden behind two nails. You are in big trouble and will have to answer to your father for this!"

Although it came with its challenges, babysitting helped Vesta pay for extras in her pre-teen and early teen years. She also came to realize how fortunate she was to have good parents and the presence of God in their home. After babysitting for many families who lived in a variety of situations, some quite dysfunctional, even at her young age, she knew when something didn't feel quite right. After she arrived back from babysitting in homes where there was no belief in God, she found a noticeably different atmosphere in her home. It wasn't until much later that Vesta realized the lack of God's presence caused the difference.

This became even more clear one summer when Vesta spent ten days babysitting four children whose parents took a trip. Vesta was already an experienced babysitter and wasn't far from her family in case of any emergencies. It was surprising that the parents were willing to leave their children with a thirteen-year-old. She was relieved when the job was over. As hard as Vesta tried, the house was in constant chaos with stacks of laundry and junk everywhere. She encouraged the kids to put their things away, but since they wouldn't help, Vesta did her best to keep everything organized. She was pleasantly surprised when the parents returned and sang her praises about how nice the house looked. Vesta appreciated the big paycheck, but quickly said her goodbyes and vowed never to babysit for this family again.

Not all of Vesta's babysitting jobs were difficult. She often watched the children of her favorite neighbors, who had a lovely home and sweet children. Others, also from their church, left delicious baked goods for Vesta. They were so good that she had to be very careful not to eat them all. Another neighbor Vesta babysat for, Ben, and his wife, Louise, protected her like she was their daughter, telling Vesta that if Mr. Crenshaw had too much to drink and tried anything strange while walking her home after babysitting, she should shout for Ben, and he would rescue her. Thankfully, Vesta never needed to yell for him since she was generally well-known and respected in the neighborhood. Ben and his wife were dear friends of her parents, and their children were the age of Rachel. Later, Rachel became very close friends with their daughters.

During her junior high years, Vesta enjoyed school much more than she did in grade school. One reason was that she met her three soul sisters: Diana, Janie, and Caroline. They were all fun-loving girls from loving families and, together with Vesta, attended the Christian schools in Bellflower and Artesia. The four girls were different in size, shape, and family background but had many of the same interests. Junior high girls could be hard on each other, so if two of her friends were staying overnight with each other, they often discussed the flaws of the other two. Deep down, Vesta knew this wasn't a nice thing to do, but at times, she couldn't resist it. Gossiping with friends was fun, and it never occurred to Vesta that she might be discussed when she wasn't present. It's how people often think, "Surely they can't find anything wrong with me? After all, I'm so nice."

Slumber parties were a favorite of Vesta and her friends. Vesta loved to go to slumber parties but didn't like how she felt afterward. She always felt like she had the flu and needed to sleep it off. In the end, slumber parties were so much fun that Vesta decided that "flu feeling" was worth it. The girls would listen to Elvis Presley and the latest music of Fabian, Frankie Avalon, The Beach Boys, and many more. Since they weren't taught to dance in their Christian school or at home, they tried doing the stomp and twist or would just jump around.

At the time, the church considered movies a tool of the devil and taught that dancing was too suggestive to boys. As the church evolved, Vesta's parents were not as strict as they had been in the past about movies and dancing. Also, since television was now a regular part of their family life, her father saw that movies weren't that different from his favorite shows like

Gunsmoke, Bonanza, and Cheyenne, and dancing was part of *The Lawrence Welk Show*, which Frank and Johanna watched every Saturday night.

For Vesta, she would often daydream about boys and all the handsome TV stars. She hoped that a TV star might fall in love with her. When church became too boring, Vesta found that dreaming of boys was a wonderful distraction and helped the service pass quickly. At their slumber parties, she learned she wasn't alone in dreaming of boys; her girlfriends all went crazy over the same handsome movie stars and rock-and-roll stars as Vesta. They also agreed that the guys in their seventh-grade class were less appealing than the eighth-grade boys who were definitely more desirable.

Although they had limited knowledge of the subject, the girls discussed what it would be like to kiss a boy, but the first time they heard the term "French kiss," they had no idea what it referred to. When Vesta asked her brother Stephen about it, he explained that French kissing was kissing with one's tongue, and Vesta was sure she misunderstood him. As soon as Stephen realized Vesta was confused, he couldn't resist asking her if her first kiss was going to be a French kiss. Her answer was "Of course, NOT! How gross."

Caroline was Vesta's closest friend in junior high, and she often spent Friday nights at Caroline's home. Since they were eight years old, both Caroline and Vesta had been skating the side-walks. Therefore, they loved going to the roller-skating rink together on Fridays. Skating was a good way to spend time with boys without having the pressure of a real date, especially since whenever it was time for the couples' skate, Caroline and Vesta were usually asked to skate. It was thrilling to hold hands with a boy during the couples' skate, even though both Vesta and the boys' hands were a little clammy. They had great fun, and Vesta appreciated Caroline's mom driving them to and from the rink. Since it never occurred to them to leave the skating rink, they always felt safe being at the rink unsupervised.

Despite having a group of great, loyal friends in junior high, it was still a difficult time for Vesta. She struggled academically while her friends seemed to get As and Bs without much effort. Vesta would study half the night and still end up with a C- or D+. She also matured faster than her friends. When it was time for the class picture, Vesta realized she was the tallest in her class because the inconsiderate photographer put her in the back row with the boys. She was horrified. Then there was the problem of required showers after PE since Vesta was the only one in her class with breasts. Her friends weren't much help (they may have been envious) since they loved teasing her with birthday cards that showed women with big boobs.

Another difficult time that Vesta never forgot was when everyone in her entire class was going steady except her (this isn't an exaggeration, the entire class was paired up). After breaking up with her "boyfriend," her friend Janie tried to cheer her up by saying, "I shouldn't have gone steady with Larry. It was dumb; you didn't miss anything, Vesta. In fact, you are the lucky one."

The only good thing about that situation was it didn't last long. At that age, some of the boy-girl relationships broke up in as little as two days. In the end, Vesta felt bad that she wasn't asked to go steady by anyone but decided to go on enjoying her life anyway.

Eighth-grade graduation arrived, and Johanna surprised Vesta with a shopping trip for a graduation dress. They bought the most beautiful dress Vesta had ever owned. It was yellow chiffon with a taffeta under the fabric. It had big, puffy sleeves and netting that made the skirt flair out perfectly. They also bought her spike-heeled shoes. Even though they made Vesta afraid she might fall during the ceremony, she loved them so much she decided not to worry. On graduation evening, her father was bursting with pride, and Vesta was thankful she was graduating despite struggling with her grades.

## CHAPTER 12
# High School

The year was 1960, and they were all celebrating Labor Day with friends of the Schuil family. Frank and Johanna loved to have barbeques with friends. Their children grew up appreciating these fun gatherings.

*How can summer be over?* Vesta wondered. *School is already starting again. I've never been more nervous in my entire life.*

"Mom, did you wash my blouse? I want to wear my favorite outfit on Monday. I'll make sure my nylons are ready. I've heard that the upperclassmen like to make fun of freshmen, especially during Freshmen Orientation. Can we go to the store so I can pick up some makeup and deodorant?" Vesta asked, trying not to sound overly concerned. Johanna smiled to herself, enjoying that Vesta shared her feelings so freely. She couldn't recall her other children being so open with her during their teen years.

Now that Sara was married, the two of them shared more since their baby girls were close in age. Life continued to be busy for Johanna, with Matthew in his senior year of college and Sara a young wife and mother. Stephen was still in high school but was working hard at becoming an entrepreneur.

Johanna was sorry to watch Stephen struggle at school but didn't know how to help him. He was already behind since being held back two grades in grade school. Frank often yelled at Stephen, which didn't help, but Johanna felt helpless to prevent that from happening. Frank wanted all his boys to go to college. Johanna suspected that Stephen would never go to college, but she knew he would be successful as he had a knack for making money.

Then there was Tommy. Tommy had no problem with his schoolwork, but Johanna noticed how he would scream as loud as he could if Stephen teased him. She also noticed his sly smile when Frank lost his temper and came at Stephen with his strong hands. Most of the time, Stephen dodged his dad pretty well, but one time, the bathroom door took the brunt of Frank's powerful swing. Thankfully, since Frank was a carpenter, he was able to quickly repair it.

Vesta was Johanna's strongest ally when it came to getting Frank's temper under control. She wasn't afraid to speak up and tell her dad to "STOP" when he went off in a rage. Johanna was also grateful that Vesta could manage baby Rachel so well. Reflecting on her life during this time, Johanna wondered if she had paid enough attention to her precious middle daughter. She hoped that Vesta would do well in high school and go on to college.

As Vesta finished preparing for her first day of high school, she knew her goals weren't aligned with Johanna's. Vesta loved her mother deeply but also loved her sister Sara and admired her as a mother. She saw Sara's life of marriage with little Denise as the perfect life. Vesta often dreamed about who she would fall in love with and marry. One of the things Vesta looked forward to most in high school was dating.

Vesta constantly pestered her mother with the question, "Can I start dating when I'm fourteen like Sara did?"

Every time, Johanna responded, "How do you know anyone will ask you?"

Vesta didn't know if anyone would ask her on a date, but if someone did, she wanted to say yes with her parent's blessing.

In the end, being a high school freshman was as frightening as Vesta expected but in ways that she never anticipated. For example, the lockers assigned to the freshman girls were located right below the senior boys' lockers. *Who on earth planned this?* Vesta wondered. Although she enjoyed looking at the most gorgeous guys she'd ever seen in her life, it wasn't easy reaching over them to get her books and still be on time for class. As the year progressed, Vesta noticed that getting to her books wasn't that difficult, and the senior boys seemed to like how the freshman girls were quite nice-looking.

Vesta continued to struggle with her grades. Many years later, she discovered that her preferred learning style was visual. Unfortunately, when Vesta was young, especially in grade school and junior high, almost every subject was taught using verbal techniques, and she had to either sink or swim in that learning environment.

Things improved for Vesta in high school because she could choose classes from pre-college, secretarial, or bookkeeping tracks. Since Vesta felt she wasn't college-bound, she chose to focus on bookkeeping. It turned out to be the best choice for her, something she didn't fully appreciate at the time. Years later, she came to realize that even when she was not that sensible, God had His hand on her life.

Vesta excelled in her typing and office machine classes. At the time, everyone believed that typing was something only secretaries needed to know how to do. No one anticipated how important typing skills would be for everyone just a few decades later.

Vesta's freshman year kept her life full, and she got her wish to date at fourteen. First, there was "Twirp Week"—a funny name for a certain time when the girls asked the boys out on dates. Vesta and her friends discussed in detail who they wanted to ask out to make sure that none of them asked the same boy. Twirp Week was how she and most of her friends went out on their first dates. Most of her group settled on asking out sophomore boys since they decided no one in their class was worth dating. They also considered the junior guys who were quite cute. They all knew that the gorgeous senior guys were out of their league.

During her high school years, Vesta often visited her sister Sara. They enjoyed each other's company, and Vesta loved having a confidant, in addition to her mother, to share her high school adventures. Sara liked hearing Vesta's stories since they brought back her high-school memories. Sara was impressed with how the Christian school had improved and grown and was happy that Vesta could attend high school at its new campus.

One big improvement since Sara had attended was the music department. The choir had a new, young director that Vesta needed to audition with to join. On the day of her audition, Vesta was a nervous wreck, but she won a spot in the choir. She was excited but surprised when, after being a soprano for her entire life, she found out that she would be singing alto. At first, Vesta was worried about singing alto, but she had a friend in the choir who was a strong alto. Vesta just followed her lead.

One thing Vesta hadn't realized when she visited Sara in Chino was how many other teens lived there with their dairy families. One Sunday evening at church, when Vesta was visiting Sara, she didn't notice that guys were checking her out.

"Who's that good-looking girl with Peter and Sara?" one guy asked.

Another, trying to sound like he knew her, "It's her sister. I think she's twenty or so."

"Maybe even twenty-one," another guy piped in. Although none of them was sure of her age, they never would have guessed she was only a freshman in high school. Most of them were seniors or had graduated and were working on their family's dairy farm. Later that evening, the boys decided to race their cars outside of Peter and Sara's small country home. They hoped the racing would sound "cool" to Sara's cute sister who was babysitting that night.

Vesta was oblivious to the roaring cars on the street as she was getting Denise ready for bed.

"Let's read a book; it's almost time for bed." Vesta loved reading and cuddling with Denise. When Vesta had her attention, nothing else mattered. Just as they finished the book, the phone rang.

A young man's voice answered Vesta's "hello" with, "Are you alright? This is Jerry, Peter's brother."

Surprised, Vesta wondered why she wouldn't be alright. "I'm fine. Who is this again?" Vesta said, feeling a nervous excitement.

"This is Jerry. You know, Peter's brother. There were some guys from church who wanted to get your attention by racing down Sara and Peter's road. I was so angry when I found out that I told them to get out of here. Did they scare you or little Denise?"

"Well, no," Vesta confessed, "I didn't even hear them. There's lots of traffic in Lakewood, and cars are always roaring down the road close to our house."

"I'm so glad. Is it alright if I come by to check on you and Denise?" Jerry asked.

"Oh, okay, if you want to," Vesta replied trying to sound older than her fourteen years. She was excited that Peter's brother wanted to stop by. He was a senior at the Christian school in Chino that was founded by the dairy families who had moved there from Artesia.

Vesta hung up the phone and kissed Denise goodnight. As she walked to the living room, she heard a light tap on the door. She opened the door to find Peter's brother and a friend of his waiting with concerned looks on their faces.

"Hi, Vesta, I sure hope I didn't frighten you with my call," Jerry asked with concern in his voice.

"No, I'm fine, and so is Denise. I just put her to bed. Would you like to come in?" Vesta reassured him.

"No, no, we just wanted to make sure you were alright. I'll drive around a bit to make sure those guys are gone. Say hi to Peter and Sara for me, will you? Have a good night, and maybe I could call you sometime when you get home again. Would that be alright?" Jerry decided to be bold as he knew it wouldn't be long before some other guy snatched her up. When he saw the surprise on her face, he waited nervously for her reply.

"Um, well yes, that sounds okay," Vesta replied.

"Great, I'll see you later and hope to talk again soon. Have a good night and a safe trip home. You're going home tomorrow, right?" Jerry tried not to sound too excited, but the truth was he couldn't wait to have a date with Vesta, even though she was rather young. She didn't look too young for him, so he hoped his brother and sister-in-law would let him ask her out.

"Yes, that's the plan. It will be nice to hear from you. Thanks for being so protective of us tonight. See you later." Vesta was excited but stayed calm as they said goodbye. She couldn't wait to tell Peter and Sara about what had happened.

"Why you cagey guy!" Jerry's friend Andy shouted when they closed the car doors.

All Jerry could do was grin. He did what every guy wanted to do after church was over. They, however, only had the nerve to drive up and down the street looking ridiculous. Jerry already knew he wanted to ask Vesta out and was looking for an excuse to stop by his brother's house. He knew that Andy was both jealous and impressed by how he'd handled the situation. However, Jerry also knew that Vesta was still young and might not be ready to have just one guy in her life. Either way, it would be fun to see how things developed. After Jerry and Andy teased each other some more, they checked the road and headed home.

Comfortable on the couch, watching her favorite Sunday night TV program, Vesta anxiously waited for Peter and Sara to come home. She listened for any fast cars but didn't notice anything out of the ordinary. Her mind wandered to Jerry, and she wondered if he would call. He seemed nice enough but wasn't the cutest guy. He was a strawberry blond with fair skin and blue eyes, nice and tall, but he wouldn't be her first pick. He wasn't ugly at all, so Vesta felt guilty about being so picky. She also realized it had been an exciting evening and was anxious to share the story with Peter and Sara when they came home.

Jerry didn't wait long to ask Vesta out. He knew she was young but since his brother started dating Sara when they were young, why not try it? Vesta and Jerry dated for almost a year before Vesta realized that she wasn't ready to settle for one guy. She kept coming up with excuses to slow things down, saying, "My mom won't let me go steady" every time Jerry tried to ask her. Finally, Vesta let him go.

Vesta knew to let Jerry go was the right thing to do. Having a date every Friday night was the main goal of many teens in the early 1960s. She felt bad that dating Jerry was more of a status symbol for her than him being someone she cared about.

Vesta had become a single girl without a boyfriend and a regular Friday night date as she began her sophomore year. She was glad to have her freshman year behind her and ready to seek new adventures.

About this same time, Sara discovered she was pregnant again. This time, Johanna enjoyed her daughter's pregnancy more since she wasn't also dealing with a newborn. Another darling baby girl was born on January 30, 1962, just after Denise turned two and Rachel celebrated her third birthday. Vesta thought Annabelle was adorable with her big round eyes and cute face.

Another granddaughter was born soon after Annabelle. Matthew met the girl of his dreams during his last year at Calvin College. Her name was Cynthia Vanderhill. She was a freshman at the time, but that didn't stop Matthew once he made up his mind to marry her. They were both on college budgets, so a big wedding wasn't in the plans. It didn't matter to either of them. They hosted a nice family gathering and decided later they could have a reception. Before they knew it, they were expecting as well. Matthew had graduated with a teaching degree and found a job in Glendale, California.

Soon after, Cynthia and Matthew became parents to Candice Mae on April 23, 1962. Emotional new parents with colicky babies can be a trying thing to deal with for in-laws. Somehow, they all survived. Candice grew to be a full-of-life, happy little girl. Once again, Vesta was called on to babysit as needed. Vesta loved all her nieces, always enjoying spending time with them.

During her sophomore year of high school, Vesta had experienced some disappointments. For example, her grades often embarrassed her. Her parents, however, never made her feel bad about her grades because they knew how hard she studied. Johanna always wished she could be of more help, but with only an eighth-grade education herself, there was not much she could do. She was able to help Vesta with spelling as it came naturally to Johanna. Of course, this was long before computers and spellcheck existed.

Poor Vesta was a terrible speller, and her grammar wasn't much better. She loved her English and literature courses, but every time Vesta thought something was easy or believed she understood a lesson, her homework came back covered with red marks. Thankfully, her teachers liked her and worked with Vesta to help her improve.

One thing Vesta really enjoyed was cheerleading. She practiced hard for tryouts and was rather good, or so her friends told her. Unfortunately, the competition was tough, and she didn't make the squad. Another challenge that year was that her close friends—Caroline, Janie, and Diana—were going out on dates a lot more often than Vesta was. The truth was that since she broke up with Jerry, no one had asked her out.

Fortunately, toward the end of her sophomore year, things started looking up for Vesta. She tried out for cheerleading again and made it as a song leader for her junior year. A song leader was basically a cheerleader in song and music form. There were four cheerleaders and four song leaders at her school, and her best friend, Janie, was the head cheerleader. Vesta looked forward to an exciting summer full of learning the routines and getting fitted for her uniform.

Although Johanna worried about the extra expense for Vesta, she didn't want to worry her since she knew how excited Vesta was to be on the squad. Unknowingly, Sara came to Johanna's rescue by having Vesta stay with her girls for three weeks during the summer. Sara knew she could trust Vesta with the girls while she and Peter traveled to Michigan for the first time since their marriage. She even suggested Vesta have a friend join her so she wouldn't have to do everything herself. Sara also lined up babysitters to call if, by chance, both girls were asked out on a date on the same night. Sure enough, after their first day attending Sara and Peter's church, her friend Janie received a call for a date. Soon after Janie left on her date, Vesta read to the girls and put them to bed. She was getting settled on the couch to see if there was anything interesting to watch on TV when the phone rang.

"Hello," Vesta answered, wondering who would be calling and hoping Janie was safe. They didn't know her date well and being a member of their Christian community didn't guarantee his trustworthiness. Fortunately, the caller answered politely. "Hi, my name is Bobby. I saw you in church yesterday and was wondering if you would like to go out for a root beer float with me?"

"I'm sorry Bobby, but my friend is out with Jim, and I can't leave the girls alone. Can I take a rain check?" Vesta answered. She was pretty sure this was the Bobby who was one of the most sought-after guys in the area. Vesta was thrilled and couldn't wait to tell Janie.

"How about I just stop by and we can talk a bit? Our sisters are friends. You probably know her, Jennifer Tilstra." Bobby said, hoping to put Vesta at ease. He knew some of the other guys wanted to ask her out but needed more time to get up the nerve to call her. He had to think fast so they could meet while Vesta was in town. He could decide later whether she was worth driving to Lakewood for more dates.

Vesta was surprised by the call since she wasn't expecting anyone to call in the first place. Suddenly, she found herself talking to one of the cutest guys in the area, and he wasn't taking no for an answer. "Well, okay, I guess that would be fine. Do you know where Sara and Peter live?" she answered.

Since Bobby had questioned his sister thoroughly, he not only knew where Sara and Peter lived, he also knew when they were returning from their trip. "Yes, I do, and since I'm already in town, it won't take me long to get there. See you soon." Bobby replied, trying not to sound too eager.

Vesta was beside herself. She didn't know whether to be excited, nervous, or just plain scared. When the doorbell rang, she tried to play it cool. Bobby was very handsome though not extremely tall. Vesta could tell he was comfortable around children since he had several nieces and nephews of his own. They had a great time getting to know one another. Both Vesta and Bobby loved being open about themselves, which made their conversation even more fun. The time flew by, and they were startled to hear their friends returning from their date. Janie and Jim walked in, both with surprised looks on their faces.

When Bobby saw them, he laughed and said, "Well I couldn't be left out, could I?" Then he turned to Vesta and said, "Why don't Jim and I come by on Friday and take you girls out for dinner or something? Do you think you can get a sitter for Friday night?"

In the next couple of weeks, both Vesta and her friend Janie got to know Bobby and Jim better. The girls enjoyed their adventures with the Chino guys while taking care of Peter and Sara's girls and home. They both realized that being the new girls in town, they would have been asked out by others if Bobby and Jim had not jumped in so quickly.

Even though Denise and Annabel somehow caught the measles, the three weeks went by quickly. Since there was no measles vaccine yet, Janie and Vesta were relieved that they had both contracted measles as children. Vesta had much more experience in taking care of children and taking care of a home than her friend Janie, who had none. Vesta was glad for Janie's company, but since she had no homemaking experience, the responsibility for laundry, cooking, cleaning, and seeing to the girls' needs all fell on Vesta. By the time Peter and Sara arrived home, both their girls were recovering from the measles. Sara felt bad that Vesta had to take care of the sick girls, so she paid her extra. Vesta was happy to have the extra money to pay for her upcoming cheerleading expenses.

Bobby and Vesta dated for most of the summer. Eventually, Vesta realized that Bobby was too demanding to have a strong relationship with her. This realization came when Bobby laid out the rules that he wanted them to follow in their relationship. He was clear that if Vesta didn't agree, they would break up. Bobby also warned her that most guys would expect the same. Vesta decided to take her chances. Although the breakup caused some tears that night, Vesta was encouraged that Sara completely agreed with her to end the relationship with Bobby.

## CHAPTER 13
# Falling in Love

Vesta was excited to start her junior year. It was September 1962, and many things were happening in the world and nation. Neil Armstrong had been the first man on the moon while the US continued to try to keep communism out of power in Vietnam. Despite all these happenings, Vesta was more interested in the new dance step Chubby Checker had just made popular, the twist.

She was an upperclassman, on the cheer squad, and considered popular. She honestly didn't feel popular. She just did her best to treat people the way she wanted to be treated. Her primary focus was on her schoolwork and boys. She tried to be nice and was friends with a lot of different people. She dated different boys and made sure they stayed friends if, after one date, it felt like she was dating one of her brothers. However, there was one boy, Will, that Vesta was curious about and who had picked her out of a group of girls. They met the previous year at the Artesia Fair. Will noticed Vesta when she and her friends were flirting with a friend of Will's. Vesta's friends arranged for Will and Vesta to meet afterward, but nothing ever came of it.

Football season came and went. Vesta still hadn't found anyone special, but her life was full. One afternoon, the cheerleaders were at Vesta's house making new pompoms for the upcoming basketball season, and the phone rang. Johanna answered and knew immediately it was a boy. Johanna guessed the call was for Vesta, and she was excited for her daughter. Vesta deserved a nice young man, and maybe this was the one for her. The boy asked to speak with Vesta, so Johanna turned the phone over to her. Vesta's friends got quiet and excited when they realized a boy was calling her.

Will was nervous, but he'd already thought about Vesta for months and couldn't get her out of his head. He knew she talked a lot, but he loved hearing her voice and was sure she was the girl for him. If he was honest with himself, that night at the Artesia Fair, it was love at first sight. Now, Will just had to ask Vesta out on a date.

"Hello, this is Vesta," she said as her friends looked her way. They all had big smiles on their faces but were doing their best to be perfectly silent.

Will, trying to stay calm, croaked out, "Yes, hello! This is Will DeVee. Do you remember me?" Will said, hoping he didn't sound like a dork.

"Yes, I do!" said Vesta feeling both excited and surprised. She couldn't believe Will was calling. More than a year had gone by since they met. At the time, her friends maneuvered the two of them into a situation where Will was obligated to take Vesta home. They had a nice ride home, but he never called her after that night. Now here he was calling. She waited, wondering . . .

"Well," Will said cautiously, "I was wondering, are you busy this Friday night? If not, would you like to go out with me?"

"Well, we have our first basketball game of the season on Friday that I have to cheer for," Vesta explained, trying her hardest to stay calm as her friends hid their giggles behind their hands.

Thinking fast, Will asked, "Can I take you to the game and out for a coke or something afterward?"

"That sounds great, I'll plan on it. I need to be at the gym by 6 p.m. Is that too early for you?"

"No, that works. I'll come about 5:45 if that's okay with you."

"Perfect. See you then." Vesta hung up the phone as the room erupted with questions from her friends and mother, wanting to know who called and what he wanted.

"It was Will DeVee, and he wants to take me to our first basketball game!" Vesta answered, laughing at their surprise since they knew Vesta had all but given up on Will ever calling.

"Vesta, wait, what about Tim? I thought you were interested in him?" Her best friend Janie asked.

"Yes, I went out a few times with Tim, but he's out of town with his family for a couple of weeks and, besides, I'm not sure I like him that much." Vesta realized she sounded cold and uncaring, but she also knew it was wrong to lead someone on. Vesta was interested in Will because otherwise she would have been kind and told him that she couldn't go out with him because she already had a boyfriend. She knew deep down in her heart Tim wasn't the right guy for her. She didn't even know if he loved Jesus or attended church regularly. Vesta recognized that although she wasn't a perfect Christian, she wanted a husband and children who went to church and loved Jesus with her.

The girls had a fun time teasing Vesta for playing dangerously by dating two guys at the same time.

Vesta had no idea of the trouble she had gotten herself into. She almost lost Will when, after they had five dates in seven days over Christmas break, he learned about Tim. Vesta tried her best to be kind and say she was busy, but when Tim called, he was determined to talk to her face to face. Tim asked if he could pick her up from school the next day, and Vesta agreed. Vesta let Tim down as easily as she could, telling him that she decided to date someone else.

Since Will had already graduated, Vesta didn't expect anyone to tell Will about Tim. However, a friend of Will's saw Vesta get into Tim's car and told Will that Vesta was cheating on him. When he heard, Will was bowling with his friends and started throwing his ball too hard, resulting in mostly splits. He understood the irony of the splits and knew he had to break it off with Vesta. He didn't want to, but she had hurt him so much.

In later years, Vesta realized that neither she nor Will controlled what God had in mind for their relationship. They had responsibility, but it was God who softened the heart of Will. Eventually, Will decided to give Vesta one more chance when he heard from another friend that she agreed to meet Tim after school to break it off with him.

After several more dates, Will's best friend Carson warned Vesta at school one day, "Don't get too close to Will. He's known to love them and leave them."

After Carson said that, it was all Vesta could do to keep from bursting into tears. Instead, she acted tough as if what Carson said didn't matter to her one way or the other.

She didn't need to wait long before learning how Will truly felt about her. During their next date, Will timidly asked, "Um, would you like to meet my parents?"

"Well, that sounds nice," Vesta quickly replied. She had the impression that having a girl meet his parents was a big deal for Will.

Meeting Will's parents was quite an experience for Vesta. At first, she had difficulty understanding their strong Dutch accents. She had no idea that they were also nervous to meet her. They realized Vesta was the one their youngest son wanted to marry but wondered if Vesta knew this.

"What do you think, Daddy, is this going to work out for our Willie?" asked Annika, Will's mother, speaking in her broken English, "I can't help but worry. Vesta seems nice enough, but she's so young and a little talkative. Could you understand everything she said? I'm not sure she understood us."

Will's father, Dirk, tried to comfort his wife, "Willie is a smart young man. I think we can trust him to make a good choice. We need to trust God too. Let's pray right now that God keeps them in His hands and guides them to good and right choices."

Will's mother loved her husband Dirk so much, and his wise words gave her confidence. They immigrated to America when she was forty-five and Dirk was fifty years old. It was the hardest decision Annika ever made. They left their families in the Netherlands, including her precious father. Annika missed him so much that she cried every day during their first year away. Dirk and Annika worked hard to learn English because they knew their four children might marry spouses who didn't speak Dutch. They practiced speaking their English always, even to each other when alone, so they could be understood.

Dirk worked long days, and Annika took care of the family and their home while they wisely saved every extra penny to buy their own business. After years of hard work, they were finally able to buy their own dairy, and a few years later, a lovely home.

Before he retired, Dirk helped his sons build the DeVee Brothers Cattle Company. Many of their friends questioned whether Dirk's sons would manage the dairy as well as their father. One reason for the questioning was that the sons decided to raise beef cattle and sell some of the dairy heifers instead of concentrating on producing milk and dairy products. At the time, everyone believed that milk and dairy were safer businesses than beef. Unlike milk, the beef business wasn't protected by government price controls, so a cattleman needed to know how to protect their investment when demand was low.

Dirk had confidence in his sons and even more in his God. Never once was he concerned that his sons would fail. In actuality, Dirk was more concerned about who his sons chose to marry. His son Isaak married a woman from Minnesota who he met while attending Dordt College. They already had two young children. Dirk and Annika loved having their grandkids nearby, but he often prayed for them since they seemed to struggle in their marriage. Although their faith in God was strong and they were established in a solid church, Dirk wisely took his worries to his God, which brought him peace. He also prayed intently that his youngest son, Will, was making an intelligent choice with Vesta.

Will was extremely happy with his choice. He often dreamed of Vesta and how they would build their life together. He knew she was young but noticed the wisdom she had from taking on so many responsibilities at home. He also saw her caring heart and deep desire to make him happy. On their next date, Will planned to ask Vesta to go steady with him. It was 1963, and this was how you kept other guys away from your girl. If the girl said yes, they would exchange class rings. The guy would usually wear the girl's ring on his pinky finger or on a chain around his neck. The girl would wrap angora yarn around the band of the guy's ring to make the ring fit the girl's finger.

Friday night came, and Will was nervous. He was confident Vesta liked him enough to say yes, but for Will, going steady was close to being engaged. He had never asked a girl to go steady before, so this was a big step for him.

They went on their usual date—a drive-in movie and dinner in the car. They usually had a barbeque beef sandwich, fries, and a drink. Vesta loved watching movies, so Will was lucky to get a kiss or two in at the drive-in. Instead, he waited patiently until they could sit in her driveway and get a few more kisses in. They both enjoyed talking and cuddling in the car before it was time for her to go. If they took too long in the driveway, Vesta's mom would flash the porch lights. That night, Will kept his mind clear so he could pick the perfect moment to ask Vesta to go steady.

"Vesta, what did you think of my parents?" Will asked.

"They were very nice, but I was a little nervous about answering their questions since they were hard for me to understand."

"You were great! Also, I've been wondering what you think of people going steady. Do you think it's a good idea?" Will knew he sounded silly, but he couldn't come up with anything clever to say.

"I'm not sure. I guess it depends if they're ready to commit to each other. I don't like it when I hear couples who are going steady, and the next thing you hear is that they're sneaking out with others." Vesta was trying to stay calm as she guessed where Will was going with his questioning and she could hardly contain her excitement.

"I totally agree with you. You're right. Both people need to commit. So, is this too soon for you to commit to me?" Will asked with a slight tremble in his voice.

"Are you asking me to go steady?" Vesta asked, wanting to make sure she wasn't misunderstanding his intentions.

Will chuckled to himself. He loved how Vesta got right to the point and answered, "Yes, I am. I want you to be my steady girl if you'll have me."

"I will!" Vesta almost shouted, and they shared a few more kisses. Vesta was so excited because Will was the best kisser and so loving, gentle, and kind. She was thrilled to have this handsome guy as her boyfriend.

Now that she was going steady with Will, Vesta realized that she would need to decide if she was going to go to college. Since schoolwork wasn't her favorite thing, Vesta never really had college in mind other than perhaps going to beauty college. However, if she didn't go to college, she would have to face her mom, who had always wanted her to go and not marry young like her sister. It wasn't until Vesta's senior year when she was talking to some teachers that she considered college as an option.

"Vesta, you should give yourself some time to experience life before you rush into marriage," Mr. Smith said, trying to convince Vesta and her friend, Janie, that they would love college.

A fellow teacher, who was listening to them, enthusiastically agreed with his friend.

"Well, I don't think I have a chance to be accepted since I haven't taken any pre-college classes and my grades are just average." Despite this, Vesta couldn't help but feel flattered that these two teachers believed she could get into college.

Later, she shared the conversation with Will and was surprised at his response. He told her that if she decided to go to college, they would have to break up because other guys would want to steal her away. Vesta didn't realize at the time but that's what Will's brother Isaak did. Isaak went to college and found a girl who had a boyfriend back home. Isaak ended up winning the girl over, and they were married. In the end, Vesta didn't have any problem picking Will over college since she was never that interested in college anyway.

## CHAPTER 14

# Love and Marriage

I t was March 1964, and Vesta was enjoying the final semester of her senior year. She was surprised by the many things she had to do as the year came to an end. At the same time, she and Will faced some important decisions. Having dated for more than a year, they both wanted to get married, but the question was when to do it. Will was starting to worry about being drafted to fight in Vietnam. He tried, unsuccessfully, to get a deferment, so he was thrilled when Vesta came up with an idea to save him from the draft.

During their usual Friday night date, Will shared his problem with Vesta. She was concerned because she hadn't considered the possibility of Will being drafted. Of course, it made sense that it could happen, Vesta already knew of a friend whose fiancé was leaving soon to fight in Vietnam.

Vesta threw caution to the wind and said, "What if we marry sooner than we planned? Would that get you a deferment?" They discussed marriage often and knew that's what they both wanted. Even so, Vesta was afraid to look at him while she asked—what if he didn't want to marry so soon? She believed he wanted to marry her but wasn't sure if he appreciated her popping the question.

"Really? That would be great! I just hope we can convince your parents, especially your mom." Will could hardly contain his excitement. He loved Vesta deeply and was ready for marriage. He knew it would help him get a deferment from the Army and the Vietnam war. Throughout their life together, they always laughed that Vesta had proposed to Will. However, since Vesta was only seventeen, they still had to get her dad's permission (her mom was another story) before they could get married.

Will went home that night thrilled and ready to ask Vesta's dad for her hand. However, he decided to talk it over with his parents first. "Mom, Dad, can we talk for a bit?" Will asked when he sat down for breakfast the next morning.

Dirk and Annika were enjoying their morning coffee as Will sat down. They were surprised he hadn't left for work yet and knew something important was up. "Certainly," said Dirk. "What is on your mind, son?"

Will knew his parents loved Vesta, but he also knew she was quite young, so he wasn't sure how they would react. He decided not to beat around the bush and just spit it out. "Well," Will began, "Vesta and I decided last night we would try to get married shortly after she graduates. As you know, the Army is trying to draft me, and you know how hard it will be to keep the cattle business going if I must go. I wanted to let you know I plan to ask her dad for her hand this weekend. I would love your blessings as well. I know this is a lot to take in, but we have been dating for over a year already. Anyway, what do you think?" Will said with a nervous laugh.

Dirk and Annika looked at one another a little surprised. At the same time, they weren't entirely shocked. They knew Will was crazy about Vesta. Dirk spoke first, "Of course, we give you our blessing. We will pray for the Lord to guide you both in His ways as you begin life together in marriage."

"Yes, Daddy, I agree with you. We are so happy for you, Will. May God bless your words as you ask Vesta's father," Annika said as she hugged Will tightly.

Will smiled, "I would appreciate your prayers as I ask her parents. I know I will be so nervous! I love you both and your encouragement."

Will and Vesta were officially engaged on April Fools' Day because as soon as their parents gave their blessing, they immediately went shopping for the ring. Later, after realizing what day it was, they laughed and said at least they wouldn't forget the date of their engagement. They set the wedding date for July 3, 1964, three weeks after Vesta's graduation and two and a half months plus a few days before Vesta turned eighteen.

Vesta only had three months to plan the wedding and had no idea where to begin. Will helped when he could, but her main supporter was Sara. She helped Vesta pick both her wedding dress and the bridesmaid dresses. Sara also told Vesta that she would be the matron of honor. Vesta was grateful that Sara was not afraid to say how she felt. Vesta hadn't thought that her married sister would want to be part of the wedding party. Stephen also stood up at the wedding, and Isaak was Will's best man. Vesta included two of her closest friends, and Will had one of his friends stand up. Vesta also had Thomas along with one of Will's nephews as candle lighters. Vesta put her sewing skills to work to make Rachel's flower girl dress. Sara's little Denise and Isaak's little Dirk were the miniature bride and groom.

So many people helped make the day beautiful. Vesta knew she couldn't have done it without all of their help. Her father got in on the action and surprised her with some beautiful aisle candle decorations. She had admired them earlier but decided that the expense was too much.

Their wedding day arrived quickly and passed by in a whirl of activity. They spent the first night of their honeymoon in a lovely hotel bridal suite close to Disneyland. They were thrilled to be husband and wife but had so much to learn. Vesta remembered her doctor telling her that sex was like learning to play the piano. "Don't get discouraged if you can't play it perfectly right away; it takes time and practice to play it well."

Will, on the other hand, thought he'd never need sleep again. He just wanted to stare at Vesta, and was delighted that they would sleep together for the rest of their lives. By dawn, he was still so excited that he tried to wake Vesta. She could hardly get her eyes open but was able to ask in a sleepy voice if something was wrong.

"Nothing's wrong," Will answered with a hopeful grin on his face, "I just couldn't sleep and wondered if you'd like to wake up?"

Vesta, who had not slept much lately, just groaned and rolled over. "I'm sorry, honey, but I'm really tired and need more sleep. It's only 5:30 in the morning, and we're on vacation. Please, can you just try to sleep a little more?"

Vesta went back to sleep easily as Will just stared at his new wife. He tried his best to let her sleep, but by 7:30, he couldn't wait any longer. Vesta, on the other hand, could have easily slept until 10, but got up to enjoy the day with her new husband.

Their honeymoon was filled with discovery and learning how wonderful it was to say goodnight and go to sleep in one another's arms. Will and Vesta were an affectionate couple, so making love came easily to them. Despite this, it took many more years together before they realized you could always learn more about sex. Vesta never tired of Will's kisses and the tender ways he would reach out and touch her when he walked by.

As with most newlyweds, during their first year of marriage, Will and Vesta needed to overcome a few challenges. For example, Vesta was accustomed to her father being home on weekends and holidays. She was not familiar with the hours her husband had to work to build a successful cattle business. To help out, Isaak moved his family to Visalia in hopes that Will would not need to travel as much. Unfortunately, about six months later, the brothers realized there wasn't enough work for Isaak in Visalia to support his family. They made the difficult decision to part ways, and the DeVee Brothers Cattle Company became DeVee Cattle Company. This change left Will with a heavy workload running the business. Also, since Isaak originally took care of the books, Will needed to learn how to manage them himself. Will ended up spending every evening after dinner doing bookwork in an office bunkhouse next to their main house.

This was a tough way to start their marriage, but, thankfully, they were very much in love. At times, Vesta would break down, crying and begging Will to work less so that they could spend more time together. Will did his best to comfort her but knew he needed to keep working. He didn't tell Vesta, but he planned to become a millionaire by the time he turned thirty. Will was confident that Vesta was the right woman to help him accomplish his goal, even if she shed a few tears occasionally.

Will was right about Vesta. One day, when she was, once again bemoaning the fact that Will was not home with her, it struck her that she needed to build her own life. She began by deciding to paint the walls a new color. She checked in with Will since they shared a car and needed to make sure they had the money for the paint. In the early days, Vesta was easygoing about money and was glad to have Will make the financial decisions. She was content with the twenty dollars a week she had for buying groceries and any extra items they needed. Years later, Will and Vesta would joke about how they managed on such a small grocery budget. After a few months, Vesta and Will agreed that it was time to stop her birth control and try to get pregnant. Will was right about Vesta. Neither of them realized that decision would keep Will from being drafted.

In the meantime, Isaak and his family had moved to Visalia. It was a small, insignificant town in California. He took note of the fact that Southern California was becoming overcrowded, especially for the dairymen in Artesia and Norwalk. He suspected it was the perfect time to encourage the next generation of dairyman to migrate north to Tulare County. Isaak earned his real estate license and familiarized himself with the Tulare County area. He became acquainted with a real estate company selling ranches. His new career worked well for Isaak, who used his gifts of knowing the dairy industry and enjoying finding just the right property for someone. It took God's perfect timing and years of hard work, but eventually, Isaak established The Ranch Realty in Visalia. The two brothers never lost touch, even though many things happened that could have pulled them apart. Through the years, Will knew that if he had any questions about real estate, he could go to Isaak and get an informed, honest answer.

## CHAPTER 15

# Raising a Family and Life Changes

I t was September 8, of 1965, and after a relatively easy pregnancy and Will telling her that she made a great heifer, Vesta had no idea that the birth of her first child would be such an excruciating experience. As she held her precious daughter, Desirae Denise, in her arms, she felt so unprepared to care for her.

As much as Vesta had learned about giving birth, there were so many things happening to her that she didn't understand. She hadn't expected twelve hours of labor or passing out when the nurses insisted she try to use the bathroom. She was also surprised that when she carefully got out of bed on her own, she couldn't carry her bottom since it was full of stitches. So, she bent over and tried to hold onto herself for support. On top of everything, her breasts ached after just a few times of learning to nurse. Finally, she struggled to understand why she wanted to cry for no apparent reason. Vesta realized that having a baby was much more difficult than she anticipated. At the same time, she was totally in love with her new daughter.

The moment Vesta and little Desirae came home from the hospital, Will's parents wanted to stop by. Will and Vesta couldn't say no, although Vesta didn't want them to visit and couldn't explain why.

Vesta realized after a day at home that she needed more help and called Johanna to ask if she and Desirae could come to her parents' home a few days. Will thought this was a good idea since he was at a complete loss as to how to help his wife. Even with Johanna helping take care of Desirae, Vesta's melancholy continued.

Vesta felt good each morning, but at around 5 p.m., the blues would return, and the tears would flow. Little Rachel was confused by her big sister's sadness and would run to Johanna for comfort. From all her research, Vesta had not learned that women could suffer from baby blues after delivering their babies. Thankfully, Vesta was resilient and had a strong support system. She was becoming a confident mother and was soon ready to return to a normal life with her husband and new daughter.

Will and Vesta moved once in their short, married life to a rental house in Artesia after needing to sell the house they owned with Will's brother when the business was divided. Will made trips to Chino once a week for business, and Vesta, with Desirae, would accompany him and visit Sara and her girls, Annabelle and Denise. They loved being together, sisters and cousins. One day, it became apparent to Will it would be advantageous to move his little family to Chino. The business of growing cattle was leaving the Artesia area and moving quickly to Chino.

Vesta was excited and immediately called Sara. "Guess what! We're moving to Chino. We're even moving to a house near you. We'll see each other every day if we want to."

On a beautiful, warm August morning in 1966, Will and Vesta, along with the help of family, made their move to Chino, California. They were both excited to discover what was in store for them in this new place. In Chino, the sisters became closer than ever. Sara and Vesta did many things together, including babysitting for each other. Rachel, their younger sister, was growing up with their daughters and was almost more of a daughter to them than a sister. Since they were close in age, Rachel and Denise played together, which was difficult for Annabelle because they considered her far too young to play with them since she was only four and they were already six. Annabelle adored Desirae, so she was usually happy despite being teased or left out by the older girls. She was also a strong athlete, so no matter how hard Rachel and Denise tried to outdo her, Annabelle always managed to keep up with her sister and aunt.

Will and Vesta loved their Chino home. It was set on one acre, and there was room for Will to park his small cattle truck on their extra dirt driveway. Open fields bordered their home, and yet, the town was only a half-mile to the north. They had all of the advantages of country living without having to travel far for groceries or to attend church.

Will rented property for the cattle about four miles east of their home. One of their favorite features of the home was having Will's office in the great room. It was an enclosed porch that opened into the great room and had a wall separating it from the dining area. It also had a window they used as a shelf for knickknacks. The home was older than Vesta would have preferred, but since it was large and L-shaped, it made her feel rich. She loved walking from one end to the other just to enjoy the distance. It wasn't until much later that she realized what true riches were and how rich she really was.

In those early days, Will worked hard to make their business a success. Vesta wasn't familiar with any of the financial details of the business, but as time went on, Will shared some of the specifics with her so that she understood the life he was building for them. For Vesta, Desirae was her main focus, but she enjoyed learning about what Will was working on, and since his office was in the house, she picked up even more by overhearing his phone conversations. This was before cell phones were invented, so if Will made calls, he did it from their one home phone in the evening or at lunchtime.

Will and Vesta enjoyed married life; they were deeply in love, and their baby girl brought them immense joy. Vesta thought about having another baby, but for the time being, they were content to wait a while.

Vesta noticed that Will seemed more worried than usual. Vesta would answer calls from salespeople asking that Will call back as soon as he returned home, and the banker was calling as well. She let Will know about the calls as soon as he came in the door, only to have him say, "Okay" and leave again.

It occurred to Vesta that they might be having some financial difficulties when the bank kept calling. While they were on their way to deliver some cattle to the packing house in Los Angeles, Vesta decided to ask Will about the calls.

"Honey, I noticed something that I wanted to ask you about," Vesta said cautiously, wanting to make sure she wasn't jumping to any conclusions.

"What's that, honey?" Will asked, with the name they both used for each other.

"Well, I don't want to assume anything, but are we having any problems keeping up with our business bills?" Vesta asked carefully.

"Why do you ask?" Will had a sinking feeling in his stomach. He knew they needed to make up a cash shortfall since the cattle market had taken another considerable drop.

"It feels like you're avoiding some of the people that call, and I don't know what to say to them when you don't return their calls," Vesta said and decided to continue. "I'm wondering if we're having financial issues and there is a need to sell off some of the cattle or let some employees go. I will support you however you need me to. Please let me know if you need to work longer hours or if I should spend less money. Whatever you need, I will support you. I just don't want to watch as you run away when people call. Please tell me how we can face this challenge together."

Although Will knew he married the love of his life, until that moment, he didn't fully appreciate how wise a woman Vesta was. She was full of surprises. He realized he was trying to shoulder all the responsibility himself. He decided to make Vesta more aware of what he was going through. Together, they could encourage each other as needed. Her ideas would be difficult to implement, but with the help of his father and another loan from the bank, he was confident the business could survive this down market.

Soon, Will began working long hours, and as the business improved, he realized that he could use extra help caring for sick cattle and branding them when they arrived from the auction. Will talked with his sister Henrietta, who agreed to let her teenage son Dirk help with the cattle. He also trained a neighborhood boy, Guy, who lived near his small feedlot. Having Guy around was often more trouble than it was worth, but Will knew that hard work was good for the boy since his father was an alcoholic. At the time, Will didn't realize how important working with him was for the two boys and that it helped them build life skills they never forgot.

Dirk was a great help who loved working with cattle. He only had to deal with his mom (Will's sister), thinking Will worked too many hours with Dirk and didn't feed him properly. This was true enough as Will often forgot about the time when work needed to get finished.

Working with Guy was a different story for Will. Despite being a patient person, sometimes it would wear thin, and Will would end up firing Guy, which happened more than once. There was the time Guy decided to do a little target practice with his BB gun. When the BB whizzed close to Will's face, he couldn't contain his anger and broke the gun in half across his thigh. He followed that with shouting, "YOU'RE FIRED!" That incident was a bit much for both Guy and Will. It took some time for Guy to dare show his face to Will.

Vesta loved that Will was a wonderful father who doted on Desirae. When he arrived home from work, he would crawl around with her on the floor and give her rides on his back. Vesta was fully committed to Will building their business, but she also wished they could spend more time together. Since there was never enough time in his days, Vesta would often take Desirae out in her stroller and visit with the neighbors. Her routine included walking at least half a mile and seeing if her favorite neighbors were available to talk for thirty minutes or so. By then, it was usually time for Desirae's nap and to plan dinner. It was 1967, and even though there was a lot of trouble going on in the outside world, Vesta focused her energy on her family and close friends. She did this to avoid worrying too much, which had always been part of her nature.

During this time, Sara was her favorite person to call and visit. It was such a treat to have her close by. Every day, they either talked on the phone or visited each other's homes. They had so much in common. Their husbands both immigrated from Holland with their parents after World War II. They were both raising their families—Sara with two girls and Vesta with one. It was almost as if the girls were growing up with two mothers, and the little girls were more like sisters than cousins.

Will's sister, Henrietta, and her family also lived nearby. Vesta enjoyed Henrietta's company as well, but since she was eighteen years her senior, they weren't particularly close. One day, Henrietta stopped by for a visit and to talk to Vesta about her Bible study group. When she heard the knock at the door, Vesta hurried to answer it, always happy to have visitors.

"Hi, Henrietta, what a pleasant surprise. Come on in," Vesta said with a smile. "Can I get you a snack or something to drink? Desirae always wants snacks, so I have plenty," Vesta laughed.

"No thanks, anyway, I don't want to bother you. I just came by to invite you to a great Bible study group I've been attending. The group avoids the doctrinal subjects that might cause divisions. Instead, we study God's Word and what the Bible says to us personally. It is a two-hour class, which is so interesting that the time just flies by. I know you would like it, and they even have childcare." Henrietta could hardly hold back her excitement.

As she listened to Henrietta, all Vesta could think about were the hours she had spent sitting in Sunday School and Bible classes when she was growing up. At this point in Vesta's life, it sounded so boring. She was quite sure she didn't need any more in-depth Bible study. Her mind was spinning as she tried to come up with a good excuse to turn Henrietta down. Vesta didn't want to hurt her feelings, but there were so many other things that seemed more interesting than attending a Bible study with her old-fashioned sister-in-law. Later, Vesta learned she was not at all the Bible scholar she thought she was. She also learned that people make plans for their lives, but God is always in charge. Two verses in the Bible teach that plainly:

Proverbs 16:9: "In their hearts humans plan their course, but the Lord establishes their steps."

Proverbs 19:21: "Many are the plans in a person's heart, but it is the Lord's purpose that prevails."

"How sweet of you to think of me, Henrietta," Vesta lied. "But I'm very busy these days with Desirae. She's barely able to handle the church nursery on Sunday, let alone a two-hour Bible study class. Plus, I don't think I can find the time for another activity right now."

"Oh, I understand," Henrietta replied, trying not to sound disappointed. "You have your hands full, and Desirae is a shy baby. She reminds me so much of her daddy. Well, I better be on my way. I need to plan dinner for my boys. Have a good day." Henrietta left with a hug and a wave.

Vesta had all but forgotten the conversation, but Henrietta did not. When Henrietta arrived home, she headed straight to her favorite place to kneel before the Lord, and she prayed "I don't understand, God. I was so sure I was supposed to invite Vesta! I almost want to be angry with Vesta and You for the 'no' I received today." After shedding a few tears of anger, Henrietta decided to read God's Word. This calmed her down, and she felt a strong peace. It was almost as if God's voice said, "Don't worry, my child, she will come."

Henrietta believed that it was too presumptuous to think or know what God was saying. She did, however, have so much peace that she no longer worried about how Vesta had turned her down.

A few weeks later, Vesta's phone rang; it was her friend Cheryl. Cheryl and Vesta were so glad to reconnect after Vesta and Will made the move to Chino. They never forgot the day they first met on the bus one sun-drenched day in Southern California. They were both involved in the Speech and Music festival of several Christian schools in the state. They were on their way to Ripon, California. Valley Christian High and Ontario Christian High were sharing the same bus to take the competitors in. Vesta and her friend, Janie, sat in a seat in front of Cheryl. During the ride, Vesta and Janie turned around and introduced themselves to Cheryl and her friend Sandy. In no time, they were laughing and talking like they had known each other for years. Cheryl shared that they were worried about taking this trip as so many of the kids in their high school told them to beware of the stuck-up kids from Valley. Vesta and Janie got a good laugh out of this as did their new friends. Although they didn't realize it, it was the beginning of a lifelong friendship for Vesta and Cheryl.

After moving to Chino, Cheryl and Vesta became even closer friends. They talked on the phone for hours and had so much in common, everything from being the same age with baby girls to having husbands who worked with cattle, one in beef and the other in dairy.

One afternoon, Vesta had a free moment while Desirae was playing quietly; she was about to put her feet up when the phone rang. "Hi, Cheryl," said Vesta, excited to hear from her friend. "What are you up to today?"

Cheryl hesitated for a minute since she wasn't sure how Vesta would feel about what she was planning to ask her. "Actually, I've just come home from a class I've been attending."

"Oh," Vesta interrupted. "Are you going back to school or something?"

"Well, almost. This class does have quite a bit of homework," Cheryl answered cautiously.

"How do you make time for a class with caring for your baby and your husband?" Vesta wondered aloud.

"Well, my mom is babysitting for me while I go to the Bible study, and Joe supports me going since he thinks I'm calmer afterward, despite all of the homework," Cheryl added with enthusiasm. "I'm calling to invite you to go with me. I've learned so much, and it's so different from any classes I've ever attended. It's every Wednesday from 9 a.m. to 11 a.m. We start with a small group meeting and then attend a lecture together. The lectures are so interesting and funny. So, what do you say, will you come?"

"That sounds fun. Yes, I'll go with you. My sister can probably watch Desirae for me," Vesta replied, not realizing how easily she was persuaded by her friend to try a Bible study class in comparison to how quickly she had turned her sister-in-law down.

Vesta joined Bible Study Fellowship Class in spring 1967 to spend more time with Cheryl, but they ended up in different groups. Despite this, the class sparked a significant turning point in Vesta's life and her walk with her Lord and Savior. She realized later what a strong, almost impregnable force she was given in the class as she delved into God's Word. These teachings supported her in ways she couldn't imagine for the myriad of difficulties she would face in the future. Vesta often remembered this experience as the time when the light came on for her.

With taking care of Desirae, being a wife to Will, and her Bible Study Fellowship Class, Vesta was enjoying her life in Chino. If she needed someone to share her heart with, she could turn to Will, her sister Sara, or her friend Cheryl. With both Sara or Cheryl, Vesta could talk about anything since they fully trusted each other. She also noticed that as her life became more about what God wanted and less about what she wanted, she had a stronger relationship with others, especially Will's sister, Henrietta. She no longer seemed old-fashioned but a sweet sister of God. Vesta began to realize when her heart was in the right place, all her relationships improved. She made plenty of mistakes but knew she could bring those to God and begin again.

That same year, Vesta and Sara talked about how Sara's husband Peter was struggling with his new career. After Peter got an infection on his hands from handling milk products at the dairy, his doctor recommended that Peter find a new line of work. Since the real estate market in the Chino Valley was booming at the time, Peter decided to become a real estate broker, which he had been doing for a couple of years already. Since he was an outstanding salesperson, things started out well for Peter, but then, the market suddenly dropped. Neighborhoods of new homes sat vacant while interest rates rose to a point where hardly anyone could afford to buy a house.

Sara told Vesta that the day before, Peter came home from work and told her, "I just talked to my dad about our future and have done some research about starting a dairy in Washington state. I found an older farm for rent that has a home on the land as well. My dad would help us get started, and I would need to figure out a way to protect my hands when I'm working. What do you think?"

Sara didn't have to think very long, "I know this has been a rough time for you. Your parents have helped us financially, but this real estate market doesn't look like it will rebound anytime soon. I don't think we have a choice. The move could be hard on the girls, but they're young, and I'm sure they'll adjust."

Sara and Peter were surprised at how quickly everything came together for the move. There was a church near their new home and a Christian school for the girls to attend.

Vesta knew Peter and Sara were looking at making a change, but she had no idea they were considering an out-of-state move. As Sara shared their plans with her sister, Vesta almost burst into tears.

"What? Washington? That's so far away!" Vesta gasped.

Sara tried to comfort her, "I know it will be hard, but we can write letters and call from time to time. It's only a sixteen-hour drive, and since we have so much family in California, we'll come back often to visit. I know you know this, Vesta, but Peter can't make a living here anymore. We need to leave the area."

Sara recognized it was hard for her sister, just as it was hard for Sara to leave Vesta and start a new life somewhere else. Yet, Sara was looking forward to what the move would bring. "Keep us in your prayers, Vesta. I know God has a plan for us. I'll pray for you as well."

After they said goodbye, Vesta cried and cried. It felt good to grieve, and her tears helped relieve her feeling of loss.

Sara and Peter were able to move to Washington state rather quickly. They had sold their house earlier and were living in a rental home, located on the property near the dairy of Peter's parents at the time.

The sisters wrote daily after Sara and Peter settled in Tacoma. Vesta enjoyed receiving letters from Sara. The letters helped them to stay connected and healed the pain of loss. Phone calls were expensive so were reserved for special occasions. During one of their infrequent calls, they talked about their pregnancies and how excited they both were to be due around the same time.

Sara said, "I know a new baby will be especially good for Annabelle. She was so sad to leave Desirae when we moved away. She still tears up when she looks at your family pictures and sees Desirae."

Just as Vesta was adjusting to being pregnant again and her sister being gone, her friend Cheryl told her that she and her husband was considering going back to school to become missionaries.

"What?" exclaimed Vesta. "You're having another child; how will you manage financially?"

"Well, if God wants this, we believe He'll open doors so we can go," Cheryl replied. She knew Vesta was having a hard time but wished her friend would support their plan. Cheryl had always wanted to be a missionary, so she was thrilled. She and her husband would be giving up a lot to attend four years of college and then go through intensive Spanish language training.

Vesta didn't want her friend to leave but, over time, lost her completely when they became missionaries in Honduras.

Cheryl couldn't write often as life in Honduras was nothing like it was in the US. Later after Cheryl returned from Honduras for a visit, Vesta apologized to her friend for being demanding and expecting Cheryl to write as often as Vesta and Sara did.

Vesta knew God was always teaching and stretching her. She suspected God took her sister and best friend out of her life for some reason but had no idea what it was at the time.

It did seem that though God tested Vesta at times, He also surprised her in special ways. Soon after Sara and Peter moved to Washington, Stephen and his wife Joanie moved to Chino. Vesta loved Joanie, and it was wonderful to have some family close again.

## CHAPTER 16

# A Surprise from God

Before Vesta got pregnant, she suffered from uncomfortable vaginal infections. A specialist once told her that these infections were imaginary, so she never visited a doctor about them. When Vesta discussed wanting to have more children with Sara, she suggested Vesta go to a wonderful doctor in Chino who might help her understand why she wasn't getting pregnant.

During her first appointment, the doctor told Vesta that she had a horrible infection. The doctor was mortified when she told him about the specialist she had seen and immediately wrote a prescription for Vesta and gave her careful instructions on how to stay healthy. She also needed treatments for some cysts. The cysts may have made it difficult for her to get pregnant. Vesta was thrilled, and after a few months of seeing him, she was pregnant. It was early in 1968 when Vesta let the doctor know that she was pregnant.

Vesta had another easy pregnancy and even took swimming lessons that summer. She only gained twenty pounds but did notice that she was rather large. The doctor told her that women tended to be larger with their second pregnancy, so Vesta didn't worry about her size. Even though she was due in October, she began a new season of Bible Study Fellowship. In the end, she decided she would drop out when the baby came, even though she enjoyed the class and wanted to keep learning.

September 21 was Vesta's 22nd birthday. She joked with Will that she would have her baby on her birthday. Around 9:30 that evening, she started having pains. By ten o'clock, with Will sound asleep, the pains did not let up, so she decided to get ready for the hospital. After she was fully dressed, the pains stopped. Disappointed, she crawled back into bed, being careful not to disturb Will.

It was now the morning of September 26, 1968. Since Vesta hadn't experienced more false labor pains, Vesta and her friend Jean, who was also due in the middle of October, decided to attend a tea at the hospital together. Vesta was having some contractions but thought they would fade away because she wasn't due for three weeks. Once they were seated, Vesta decided to time her contractions. From the timing, Vesta realized she might be in labor. The pains didn't stop like they had before. She tried to calm her friend who wasn't sure if they should return home. After Vesta calmed her down, Jean immediately raced Vesta back home to alert Will and Henrietta to pick up Desirae and pack everything she needed for the delivery. Once she arrived home, Vesta called Will so they could quickly head right back to the hospital.

It was about 1:15 p.m. when Will and Vesta checked into the hospital. They were happily talking to Vesta's doctor when he confirmed that the baby was on its way.

A few minutes later, a nurse came to check the baby's heartbeat and Vesta's vital signs and said, "I hear you're having twins, congratulations!"

Will and Vesta just laughed, telling her, "We've been joking about having twins for the last few months since Vesta is rather large. But the doctor said Vesta was large because that sometimes happens with a second pregnancy."

The nurse chuckled and said, "In that case, I'm sure you won't mind if I take one of the babies home with me."

Vesta was so certain it was only one baby that she replied, "Of course, you can have one since I'm definitely not having two." Simultaneously, Vesta wondered how she would ever handle two babies at the same time.

The doctor came in and said, "We're ready to break your water and give you your spinal. Will, you can go to the waiting room until we come to get you." Vesta was surprised at this since her pain level was not bad and still ten minutes apart.

After her spinal, Vesta was wide awake and pushing, their baby girl arrived in no time at 3:00 pm. Vesta didn't feel any pain but was slightly tired from the pushing and thought to herself, *I knew I would have another girl. I'm so glad Will won't be disappointed. He said he loved having girls, and it was just fine to have another one. The most important blessing is the baby's health, boy or girl.*

Just then, the doctor said to the nurse, "Mary, I think there might be another baby. The one we just delivered is small given how big Vesta was."

Vesta reached for her stomach, "How can you tell my baby girl is too small?" The doctor wouldn't let Vesta touch anything, and before Vesta could think, the doctor put his hand and arm inside her. She was able to clearly see this in the mirror above the doctor's head. Fifteen minutes later, their son was born.

Their son was quickly taken away, as unbeknown to Vesta, his lungs were not working well. In the meantime, the doctor showed Vesta her interesting (according to the doctor) double placenta. It took a moment for her to realize she didn't like looking at the bloody placenta. While the doctor and his nurse were laughing about Vesta's reaction, Vesta asked where Will was waiting.

"Can I be the one to tell Will we have twins?" Vesta asked, knowing Will would be as shocked as she was.

When Will arrived, he was thankful to see that Vesta was okay as she smiled up at him. He felt something was amiss when the doctor asked him to follow him to the delivery room. That never happened. He saw a baby beside her and hoped all was okay with the child.

Vesta was nervous and excited at the same time. "Hi, honey, you are not going to believe what I'm about to tell you. This is your daughter beside me. But surprise, we have a son as well!"

"What! Are you serious?" was all Will could manage to say. His mind whirled. A son and a daughter! What a blessing!

They were both beside themselves with joy. As they wheeled Vesta to recovery and their daughter to the nursery, they worried about their son, surrounded by doctors. Later, they learned that their son was a little more premature than his sister and his lungs initially didn't work properly.

Will enjoyed telling friends and family that first evening about the surprise twins while Vesta was flat on her back, trying not to get the headaches the doctors warned her against. As she lay quietly, she had a lot to ponder, including what they would name them and how would she manage with two babies.

There were so many things to consider, and she was afraid she wasn't a good enough mother. After a while, one thought made its way slowly into her heart. If God gave her two babies, He must have planned to give her and Will the strength to handle this gift of two children at once. With that in mind, she relaxed and fell asleep for a few hours before the nurses came to take her vitals.

While this happened in the hospital, Will returned home and spread the good news of having twins. He enjoyed calling their parents first, knowing they were anxiously waiting to hear. Johanna was beside herself with joy and decided phone calling wasn't good enough. Instead, she went up and down her street knocking on the doors of her neighbors and friends. Many knew Vesta, so it was a thrill for all to hear the news. Will also didn't tire of thinking of who he could call next. It was great to hear everyone's shock as he told them he was a father of twins! A boy and a girl, no less!

The next day, the nurse from the labor room peeked in and politely asked, "Well Vesta, which baby do I get to take home?"

Vesta laughed quietly and thought about how much her life had changed in such a short amount of time. Will was working hard and called that morning to tell Vesta that he made arrangements with Sara, who knew someone with an extra cradle and crib. He also made quick work of ordering a diaper service and buying a clothes dryer for the house.

"Thank you, Will, those things will help so much, especially a clothes dryer! Having two babies to care for and hang clothes on the clothesline would add a lot of extra work. That is wonderful for you to think of that! I love what you do for me," Vesta said appreciatively.

The one thing Vesta was nervous about was leaving their babies at the hospital. She hadn't even touched them yet and hated the idea of leaving them there. Fortunately, as she was almost ready to leave, a nurse came in and asked if she had seen or held their babies yet.

"No," Vesta answered despondently. "The doctor said they have to remain in their incubators for several days because they are jaundice and premature. And even though they weigh five pounds six ounces and five pounds ten ounces, they were three weeks early, and both are a little behind in development, especially my son. His little lungs don't seem to be fully developed yet."

"Well, would you like to see them?" asked the nurse.

"Of course!" Vesta almost shouted.

One at a time, the dear nurse took the babies to Vesta. She held, hugged, and unwrapped them to count their fingers and toes. It was 1968, and people in the medical field didn't know how much newborns needed their mother's touch and to hear the sound of her voice. After meeting their mother, Steven Scott and Skylar Marie spent the next ten days in the sterile incubator under the care of the nurses who loved on them when they could.

In some ways, the ten days of separation were difficult for Vesta. She hardly felt like a mother of new babies; on the other hand, she could barely lift her head off the pillow as she had developed spinal headaches. Fortunately, Vesta's mother, Johanna, kept Desirae longer than originally planned since Desirae came down with a cold. Both Will and Vesta decided God had it all in His control. He was healing their children and Vesta at the same time. When Will and Vesta finally picked up the twins, Vesta was able to sit up for the first time in ten days without her neck and shoulders in terrible pain.

The nurses shared some thoughts before the trip home, "Vesta, your babies have stayed in a lit hospital room for twenty-four hours a day, so you may want to leave the lights on to help them sleep better at home. Also, be sure to feed them every three hours instead of the usual four hours since they're so small. They will do well on two to three ounces of formula per feeding; that was all we could get them to eat. Also, try to keep them on the same schedule so that you get enough rest."

"Thanks for the advice," Vesta gratefully replied. The nurses were sorry to see the babies go, but Vesta was excited to take Steven and Skylar home with her. She marveled at the fact that her headaches disappeared that very day.

Vesta was surprised to discover that the nurses were wrong about how much her babies would eat. During their first feeding, they opened their eyes wide and stared at her as she talked while they both finished their four-ounce bottles of formula. They continued to eat well until they were about a month old, and then both of them broke out into an awful rash. When the rash didn't clear up, Vesta made an appointment with her pediatrician.

"I think we should put your babies on soy formula since this rash is some type of allergic reaction," the pediatrician told Vesta.

Vesta was excited that the babies' rashes cleared up almost immediately and just before their baptism. She knew she was biased, but she thought they were so adorable, and as they grew, she dressed them up in the cute boy/girl outfits friends had given them.

Steven was a joy to Vesta because, in her family, he was the first grandson born after five granddaughters. Skylar was such a good baby, easier in many more ways than her brother. Steven had digestion problems until he was about six months, so he didn't smile much until then. He was also skinny compared to Skylar, and during the first month, he looked a bit like baby Frankenstein.

As with most babies, Steven's head was large for his body, but in his case, since he was premature, it had a square shape with veins protruding on each side. The doctor shared with Vesta that even though both twins were three weeks early, Steven was probably more premature based on his developmental signs. Soon after they came home, however, they both filled out and became much cuter.

CHAPTER 17

# A Sad Time

V esta often worried about the possibility of something unexpected happening to her or her family. She even woke up in the middle of the night sometimes thinking about all of the possibilities. As she read God's Word, she learned that worry wasn't the answer for contentment, so she tried to trust that God wouldn't give her more difficulties than she could manage. Since Vesta hadn't gone to Bible Study Fellowship during the year the twins were born, she realized she missed attending. At the time, she knew that staying home with three children under the age of four was a great reason for dropping out of the class.

When the twins were almost two months old, Vesta and Johanna anxiously waited for a call from Sara. Vesta and Sara had been pregnant together, and Vesta knew Sara had gone to the hospital an hour earlier. Since Sara delivered her babies quickly, Vesta expected a call soon. It also happened to be Johanna's birthday, November 22, 1968. Johanna shared that she was very excited to have a grandchild born on her birthday as she and Vesta waited for Sara's call.

The phone finally rang with Sara saying, "I have another girl." They decided to name her Bonnie Jo after Peter's mother,

Bonnie, and Sara's mother 'Jo,' which was short for Johanna. Sara also shared that Bonnie looked like Peter with her fair skin and blond hair.

The sisters kept talking until Vesta realized she needed to end the call before the phone bill became too large. She wouldn't want Will to have a stroke when he saw it. Sara and Vesta made plans to get their babies together and talked about how fun that would be. It didn't bother them that they lived hundreds of miles apart because they knew their new babies would love each other as much as Annabelle, Denise, and Desirae did.

A few weeks later, Sara called again and was concerned that Bonnie Jo was acting upset in an unusual way. She would scream like she had excruciating pain and then turn blue. Sara talked to the doctor about it, but he didn't seem concerned and told her Bonnie Jo probably had a severe case of colic. One evening, Bonnie Jo cried and fussed more than usual, but Sara was able to quiet her down and put her to bed. Bonnie Jo had turned three weeks that day.

Early the next morning, December 13, 1968, Sara woke with a start and thought, *Oh no, Bonnie Jo didn't wake up!* She ran to the baby's bedroom right away, fearing what she would find. She laid her hand on her cold baby and knew Bonnie Jo was with Jesus. Sara burst into tears but quickly calmed herself down since she knew she needed to take care of her daughters and break the news to her husband, Peter.

The strength of the Lord kept Sara and Peter going that morning. They called their pastor and family members to share their sad news. They held each other and cried long and hard, finding comfort in Jesus's promise that they would meet Bonnie Jo again one day.

When Vesta heard the news, her first question to God was, "How can I have two healthy babies and Sara had only one who was already taken home to You?"

Vesta couldn't fight off the need to offer one of her children to Sara. When Vesta told her dear sister how she was feeling, Sara replied, "Of course, you can't give me one of your babies. They're yours, and I can have more children. God will give us strength." Although Vesta didn't want to admit it, she was relieved that Sara said no, which took away Vesta's feelings of guilt.

Vesta attended the memorial service alone, leaving the twins with Will's sister, Henrietta, and Desirae with his mother. She was surprised at how much she cried every night for her sister and brother-in-law's loss. It felt to Vesta like she was going through Sara's grief with her.

The days ahead were not easy ones for Sara, but thankfully, her wonderful church family surrounded both Sara and Peter with love. She also had two busy, talented daughters who filled their lives with joy. Vesta and Sara sent each other letters every day and called as often as their budgets allowed. When time permitted, they also traveled to visit each other at least once a year.

Vesta understood that one's plans aren't always God's plans, and He gives one the desire to go where He wants one to go. In fall 1969, Vesta felt it was time to return to the Bible study. She decided she would leave Desirae with her mother-in-law (whom Desirae adored), and the one-year-old twins could stay in the Bible study class nursery. The twins both loved nursery at church, which made it possible for Vesta to attend without worry.

In early 1970, Sara called Vesta with the happy news that she was pregnant again. They praised the Lord together with their husbands. When Aaron Jon was born on September 4, 1970, he appeared to be a normal healthy baby boy, but a few hours after his birth, Vesta received another call from her sister. Vesta was thrilled to have another boy in the family and wondered why Sara would be calling back so soon. Sara began to cry, and Vesta's heart felt heavy as she asked, "What's the matter?"

Sara's voice cracked as she replied, "Our son has cerebral palsy, and they also think his insides are spastic. They don't know how severe his condition is or how long his life expectancy is. They don't have all the answers yet. Maybe God just wants us to trust Him. One doctor had the nerve to tell Peter and me that we should just put our son in an institution as he would get better care. That made us so angry! We made it perfectly clear that was not an option."

"Oh no. I'm so sorry, Sara. Do you need me to come stay with you?" Vesta was at a loss as her heart was breaking.

"Thanks, Vesta, but I have lots of support from Peter and my girls. Besides, you have a very busy family, so just stay home for now. I'll let you know if I need you. In the meantime, calling and writing letters is extremely helpful."

It was true that Vesta's life was very full. After returning to Bible Study Fellowship, she took on a leadership role. Vesta also encouraged Will to read an article about fostering needy teenage girls, and they decided to get involved with the cause. The first young woman they met through Vesta's Bible study class. A friend in the class knew of a girl who needed a home.

Lisa was their first attempt at helping someone having trouble. Will and Vesta met her through her aunt and uncle, whom Lisa had been living with. Lisa was a beautiful blond and easy to get along with. She had been raised as a Christian but seemed to rebel against everything she had been taught. She hung with the wrong crowds, experimented with drugs, and so on. Will and Vesta made it clear that to live with them, she must attend church and follow household rules. Lisa was okay with this. She was hoping to have a fresh start in her life.

Vesta enjoyed spending hours encouraging Lisa in her faith walk and discussing what made her abandon how she had been raised. A turning point for Lisa, after being with the DeVee family for about two months, was attending a Christian concert with Vesta. During the concert, Lisa went forward and gave her heart to God once again. At this point, her aunt and uncle took her back with high hopes. Although it took a few years for Lisa to truly let go of all her wrong turns, in the end, she solidly rediscovered her faith. Will and Vesta were glad they could be that small interlude to help. They kept in touch through their friendship with Lisa's aunt and uncle.

It was now fall 1970, and Will and Vesta began working with another young lady who had a son about a year younger than the twins. Skylar and Steven were two at the time. This young woman also came to the DeVee home through people Vesta knew at Bible study. Mary and Donnie, her one-year-old son, were rather independent and helpful. Mary needed a place to live until she could afford a place of her own. Vesta and Will shared their life of faith with her and prayed for Mary as she was not that interested in a life with God. She had a rough upbringing and just wanted what the world could offer her, not what God had to give. Her boyfriend was from a Christian home, but he had also wandered away from God. He just wanted to be with Mary without any true commitment. Will and Vista did their best to encourage this young couple with love and by example. They knew, in the end, it was in God's hands. No one can be forced to go God's way. After about six months, Mary found a home and moved out.

Vesta's children grew rapidly, and motherhood always provided new challenges. Fortunately, even at five years of age, Desirae was a huge help with the twins. When Vesta was busy preparing dinner, Desirae would often entertain her siblings while she played with her dolls. She would just chat away as her siblings did whatever she wanted. If Desirae decided to play store with them, she could persuade her siblings to come shopping, or if she wanted to pretend she was a performer, they would gladly sit and watch. They were thrilled if their big sister was willing to take time to play with them.

Although Vesta thought of herself as a loving mother, she knew she was a bit of a perfectionist when it came to her house and how her children behaved. If they weren't behaving the way she wanted, she could lose her temper. She would try hard to control herself but sometimes screamed at the top of her lungs. Whenever that happened, Vesta sat down with the children and apologized afterward, telling them that even though they did something wrong, it wasn't good for Mommy to yell at them.

Vesta often prayed that her children wouldn't remember her mistakes when they became adults. She loved them so much and appreciated how her children gave her insight into God's love and patience. Vesta understood how one is similar to disobedient children, and despite this, God continues to forgive and love. Though others may have thought her a good mother, Vesta knew how imperfect she was and needed God to forgive her inadequacies and lead her in better ways all the time.

Will and Vesta had a strong marriage, which helped them manage a business, children, and taking others into their home. They were confident as a couple and maybe that is why they didn't worry as much as others around them over what they took on. Their parents, friends, and relatives wondered if they were doing the right thing and prayed they weren't endangering their children by bringing others into their home the way they did. In the end, most people decided this was a special gift the DeVee family had.

In 1970/71, when Desirae was in kindergarten, Vesta had her hands full keeping up with her two-year-old twins and getting Desirae back and forth to school. Will worked long hours supporting his young family and still striving to become a millionaire by thirty. By this time, Will knew he loved the cattle business and was confident that if he was smart about it, he'd succeed and do well.

At the time, Will was alone in his confidence in the beef cattle market. The local Dutch dairy culture and many of his father's friends worried about what that DeVee boy was doing in those unstable beef markets. Will was a quiet man and didn't worry much about what other people thought; he simply did what he loved as his work and cared deeply for his family.

Vesta was Will's pillar of strength. She continued to give him the support and encouragement he needed, even though, at times, she complained to God about his long hours. She and the children took dinner to him when he needed to work late and couldn't afford full-time help. It helped her realize how hard Will worked for them, and her love continued to grow.

Will loved Vesta very much as well, and he appreciated her taking responsibility for the children and extra young women they took in while he worked long hours. When they could find the time, they would occasionally take a couple of days off and go to Palm Springs. The kids would stay with family, and the two of them would enjoy some romantic time together. Will would plan a cattle sale on their way to the desert so they could account for their expenses as a business trip.

Vesta learned more about Will's work since they discussed it during these trips. The more she learned, the deeper her love grew as did her appreciation of all he managed. Will was thankful for the easy life he had compared to many men he knew; they always seemed to want to get away from their wives. He felt lucky that he enjoyed being with her after a long day of work.

Vesta was a very loving woman, and Will was an easy-going loving man. Since neither of them enjoyed fighting, they rarely argued or bickered. Will loved the peacefulness he felt when he was with Vesta. Despite her responsibilities, Vesta made it work, and Will was glad he could support her, and they could occasionally have a fun break together.

Will also played a big part in raising his kids and loving on them. Skylar was always hugging her daddy while Steven would roll around on the floor with Will. To give Vesta a break, Will would take them to the ranch from time to time. Desirae loved going to "the place where their cattle were," as they called the ranch.

Will was also a strong male role model for the teen girls they took in. He was a wonderful example of faithfulness to God and family that was not always seen by these young women.

It was the beginning of 1971, and Mary and Donnie had moved out about three months earlier. They kept in touch and talked often on the phone in addition to visiting each other. Their children also enjoyed having a chance to play together. One afternoon, Mary called Vesta, complaining she had a terrible stomachache.

"I don't know what is wrong. I was up most of last night throwing up! I feel terrible and don't know what to do," Mary explained. "My problem is I don't have a doctor to call or much in the way of health insurance."

Vesta decided to go over to Mary's and see if she could help. When she arrived, she found Mary so sick that she could hardly sit up. They decided Mary should go to the emergency room, where the doctors gave her some strong medicine and sent her home.

The next morning, Vesta called to check on Mary. "How are you doing? Any better?"

"No, I think I'm worse. I think I have a high fever too now. I don't know what is going on. I have such bad stomach pain," Mary groaned.

That was it. Vesta decided to call her gynecologist, who always knew how to help. Sure enough, after Vesta explained what was happening, he told her to bring Mary back to the hospital and he would meet her there. This time, Mary's boyfriend took her to the hospital. He didn't want Vesta to have to go again since he knew she had a busy family to care for.

Vesta anxiously waited when a call came from Mary's boy-friend saying she was getting her appendix out. "Oh, my good-ness! No wonder she was in pain!" Vesta exclaimed. Will and Vesta were so grateful for the willingness of Vesta's doctor to help and see to it that Mary was taken care of. Vesta made sure she thanked him properly for all he had done. She knew Mary may not have survived without his quick actions.

They also realized God had saved this young woman's life through everything that had taken place. Will and Vesta were very beholden and took time with their children to thank Him during their devotions that evening.

As the days went by, Will was a constant, well-liked, and well-known buyer at the cattle sales. He continued his work with the beef industry association, even though it was difficult dealing with the unstable markets of grain, hay, or cattle prices. He was certain it was what he was gifted in and loved doing, so he was determined to make it work to support his family and enjoy life. He often came home for lunch to make phone calls since cell phones were a thing of the future.

Vesta kept busy as well, doing what she loved, taking care of her three small children and being part of Bible Study Fellowship. Desirae was now in kindergarten, and the twins had turned two. Vesta was now a leader in the class, so two mornings a week were required of her. Monday was for leaders' meetings, and Wednesday was the class meeting.

To help make ends meet, when Vesta needed the car, Will drove an old car with weak brakes. One day, Will came home for lunch to make some calls. As he drove down a narrow street in a nearby neighborhood, a small child ran out in front of his car. Will's heart stopped as he desperately pumped his brakes. The two-year-old didn't have a chance to survive.

The child's mother, who was talking with a friend, cried out, "NO, NO, NO!" as she ran to her son, who was lying in the street.

Almost immediately, neighbors came to help, and someone called the police. Will just sat on the curb and cried softly. The police questioned Will and other witnesses. In the end, they determined Will was innocent, even though Will felt guilty because of his old car. Will asked the police to tow his car away.

After they were done, the police dropped Will off at home, where he sat reliving the accident in the backyard.

As Vesta pulled into the driveway, she was surprised to see Will sitting on a lawn chair. He never sat in the backyard in the middle of a workday. Vesta realized that something didn't look quite right. She quickly got the children out of the car and ran over to him, "What is wrong?" she asked.

Will replied, "I just ran over a child."

Tears sprang to Vesta's eyes, "What? Oh no! Where, how, when? Is the child ok?"

"In the neighborhood near Desirae's school," said Will despondently. "He ran out in front of my car, and it just kept going; it was awful. He was only two years old, the same age as our twins. The mother was so shattered, she just cried and cried. The police tested my brakes, and everyone watching gasped when my car kept going as the officer tried to stop it. Thankfully, some witnesses saw the child run between the parked cars and said I couldn't have stopped in time even with good brakes, so the police didn't press charges."

Will and Vesta mourned for the child and prayed for the family. They knew they needed to find a way to let the family know how sorry they were for their loss. They talked with their pastor about what they could do. With his help, they contacted the family's priest, who interpreted for Will when he and their pastor visited the family.

Will was never the same again. Whenever he drove through neighborhoods, he drove slowly, looking underneath parked cars for children who might run out in front of his car. He also stopped caring if he was late for appointments when safety was involved. Needless to say, he never drove a car with old brakes again and hugged his children at every opportunity.

In the summer months of this same year, another opportunity came about to help a young teen girl. She was the adopted daughter of an older couple who struggled to handle her as she entered her teens. She had ended up in Juvenile Hall because she had run away often.

Will and Vesta met her and decided they would give her a chance to change. She seemed sweet and easy to talk with, so they took on the challenge. It turned out to be a significant challenge because young Patsy did not seem to understand boundaries. The children struggled to like her, and Vesta hoped she could keep her sanity. Then one day about six weeks after Patsy arrived, she ran away. Will and Vesta were shocked since they had no clue she would run. After she was found, she was sent back to Juvenile Hall. At first, Vesta was devastated. She felt she did not try hard enough and maybe they should offer her another chance.

Will was more practical, "Honey, I think we need to talk to the social worker. She will give us the best advice. We can't force Patsy to stay here if she doesn't want to. Running away tells me there is more going on with her. She may have mental or emotional problems that we aren't equipped to deal with. If we take her back, she may not get the help she needs and may just run again."

The social worker agreed with Will. "Yes, Will is right. I was hoping your home situation could change Patsy. I know now that she needs special counseling. We'll see to it that she gets it. Thanks so much for being willing to try."

A few weeks later, the social worker called again, asking if they would like to try with another girl. Vesta knew she wasn't ready and declined this time. In fact, she was seriously considering returning to school to become a nurse. She had been researching what it would take to go to a local college to get her AA degree. She wasn't thinking full-time but maybe some night classes. The idea had been in the back of her mind after her high school teacher told her she would make a good nurse. At the time, she didn't think it at all possible, but with age and experience, she thought she might even like it.

God, however, had other plans for Vesta. She discovered through the years that she might think she needed to go a certain way, but then God would put up a barrier she wasn't expecting.

This time, it happened one summer afternoon in late July 1971 when Vesta got a call from a psychologist in their church.

"Hi, Vesta. I'm sure you wonder why I'm calling. I know you and Will take in girls who are in need from time to time. I've been counseling a young woman I think would be perfect for your home. I don't do this often, but I have such a strong feeling that this young woman needs a stable place. Would there be any chance I could bring her by later to meet you and Will?"

Vesta couldn't believe a "yes" came out of her mouth. She hadn't thought she was ready so soon after their experience with Patsy. Will helped her recognize it was okay. Before they knew it, they were making room in their home and hearts for Terri.

## CHAPTER 18
# The Good Life Mixed with Trial

W ill, Vesta, and the children always enjoyed celebrating birthdays. It was already August 1971, and the twins were turning three and Desirae turning six on September 26 and 8, respectively. This year, Terri, who was now living with them, was also celebrating her birthday on September 4.

Terri came from an abusive home and had recently put her baby, born out of incest, up for adoption. She was a beautiful but troubled girl. At the time, Will and Vesta were still in their twenties, and Terri, at sixteen, was only nine years younger than Vesta. After meeting Terri, they wanted to help, and, thankfully, their children loved Terri. Although Vesta was considering going to college to become a nurse, she realized God called her in a different direction. A few years later, Vesta took counseling classes via mail and decided not to pursue a nursing degree. She realized after taking in teen girls that this was her passion.

Some of their friends at church believed Will and Vesta were foolish for taking in troubled girls. What if, for example, the girls abused their children? It never worried Vesta or Will. They had confidence in God to protect their family and guide them in handling whoever came to live with them. Terri was their fourth foster daughter; the others had moved on for various reasons. Will and Vesta felt this was a need they could handle, difficult as it was.

Far from being a professional counselor, Vesta gently talked to Terri every day to help her feel safe and protected. She also asked others, such as Terri's psychologist, for help. In addition, Will and Vesta attended sessions together with Terri and her psychologist. These sessions helped keep them informed about Terri's progress and gave them skills to handle tough situations.

While all this happened at home, beef prices were rising, and Will's business was doing well. Will leased a larger feedlot that included an option for purchase. He also found an honest, hardworking, and extremely knowledgeable employee to hire.

Will and Vesta upgraded their home with new carpet and drapes and an above-ground pool. After the pool was installed, Vesta immediately signed the children up for swimming lessons. Since she learned how to swim at about twenty-one, Vesta was determined that her children learn to swim much earlier. The summer was filled with swimming lessons for the children and hours of playing in the pool with Will after work. Will himself gained more confidence in the water since he could touch the pool's bottom.

As the business continued to grow, Will started looking for a larger ranch. He found a dairy with a lovely home for sale that had plenty of corrals and room for growth. When Will took Vesta to see the property, she was excited beyond belief.

"Can we afford to buy this? It's the kind of home I've always dreamed of owning!" Vesta squealed. The house they currently lived in had a small kitchen and no dishwasher, but Vesta always managed to keep it as clean as a whistle. This house looked newer on the outside and appeared to be much easier to maintain.

Vesta started making all kinds of plans for living in the house. Unfortunately, Will came home one day and said, "Sorry, honey. I know you had your heart set on that dairy and home, but the deal fell through. Another buyer came in with a better offer that the seller accepted."

Vesta tried to hide her disappointment from Will, "I understand. These things happen, and maybe God has something different in mind for us." Later when she was alone, she cried her eyes out. As she cried, Vesta had to be honest with herself. She realized her disappointment was due to the pride she felt that Will's business was going well, and they could afford such a beautiful home. She was hoping to look more uptown. When she confessed her sin before the Lord, she felt much better and more appreciative of the life she and Will had together.

The year 1972 was a time of hope for Sara and Peter and their little Aaron. He received therapy a few times a week, and Sara had learned how to work with him at home. Everyone loved on Aaron as his second birthday in September approached. It was the evening of August 22 when she tucked Aaron in his crib. He had trouble eating and often threw up with his spasms. Everyone prayed that he could be healed. The next morning, that prayer was answered. Aaron awoke in heaven. On August 23, 1972, he went home to Jesus. Sara again found a child of hers and Peter's dead in their bed. Once again, tears flowed.

Sara called Vesta with the news, and together they cried for Aaron. Vesta was preparing to attend the funeral when an emergency at home kept her from leaving. Sara said, "Don't worry, Vesta; we will get together at a happier time. My heart knew Aaron wasn't doing well, so it is not like the shock of losing Bonnie." More tears were shed, and then they said their goodbyes.

This experience helped Vesta realize that people and relationships are more important than material wealth. She knew it was time to rely fully on God's purpose and the places He wanted her family to be. She decided she needed to stop looking at what others had. It was time to be thankful for the abundance that she enjoyed daily.

Vesta spent time praying for her dear sister and Peter as they prepared to lay a second child in the grave and into Jesus's loving arms. She also confessed her weakness of wanting more than she needed or of any dissatisfaction she felt.

The school year went by quickly. It was a new season of life for Will and Vesta. Desirae was in first grade and Terri was a senior in high school. They both attended Ontario Christian School. It was a fun, full, trying, and very busy year for the whole family.

Terri was happy and yet confused. She was difficult for Vesta to fully understand. It wasn't until much later that Vesta realized it wasn't her doing that kept her life and Terri's together, it was God. She and Will's part in God's plan was to provide a safe and godly home for Terri's broken life.

In the middle of working with Terri and raising their children, Will needed to invest in property. He talked to his brother Isaak, who suggested Will look at Tulare County since land prices were relatively low. In Tulare County, Will could buy a larger property and use the remaining cash to build everything else they needed. Vesta and Will visited Isaak and Margot to understand their options. After much prayer and discussing the alternatives, Will and Vesta purchased a 360-acre ranch just north of Visalia.

It was summer 1973, and after spending seven years in Chino, Vesta realized that moving to another city would be a big change. Fortunately, their three children were young enough. The move for them was more of an adventure. Will and Vesta, however, were very involved in the community and with their church family. So, they would be leaving many friends behind. They also had to decide what to do about Terri since she wouldn't be leaving with them and was accepted at Azusa Pacific University in the fall. Fortunately, her psychologist and his family invited Terri to live with them for the six weeks before school started so Will and Vesta could get settled in Visalia.

They said their goodbyes in August and were excited about their new adventure. Vesta always loved trying new things but had no idea how hard this move would be. Her sister-in-law helped where she could but relocating to a place where Vesta didn't know anyone else was difficult. The phone seldom rang because people rarely made expensive long-distance calls, in 1973. Vesta was somewhat sad and lonely, so it helped that they moved into a neighborhood for the first time in their married life. Will planned to live in this home temporarily until they could build a new home on their ranch. The transition was also difficult for Vesta because Will needed to spend time every week at the cattle ranch in Chino. This required Will to leave home Wednesday at 3 a.m. and return as late as midnight the same day. During his trips, Will visited his parents for lunch, which they enjoyed. Vesta, however, missed Will on those days, which prompted her to get out and meet other young mothers in the neighborhood. Vesta met the woman next door who attended their church; unfortunately, she worked during the day.

After meeting several other neighbors, Vesta decided she would see if any of them wanted to have a Bible study together.

177

She knew some of the women had never studied the Bible before and thought it would be a joy and challenge to study with them if they were willing. Vesta hoped, with the skills she learned from the Bible Study Fellowship class, she could lead her own study group. Margot, Isaac's wife, gave her ideas for material to use. Vesta prayed about the idea and then started knocking on doors.

Regrettably, a couple of ladies said no. One answered with, "I don't believe there is a God, so no, I'd rather not come, but you certainly have beautiful eyes."

Vesta didn't know how to respond other than to say, "Um, thank you."

It made Vesta sad when someone shared that she didn't believe in God, and even though Vesta was quite knowledge-able about the Word of God, she wasn't good at sharing her faith in powerful ways.

Another woman Vesta met on the street appeared to be a per-fect candidate for the class. After a brief conversation, Vesta invited her to join, and much to her surprise, the woman replied that she was Jewish. Vesta could only stammer and say, "Oh well, it was so nice to meet you." She then scurried back home. She wasn't confident about how to reach out and just be friendly.

As the years passed, Vesta learned how to deal with this type of situation better. In the meantime, she prayed for each person she could not answer well. She knew she was inadequate, but her Lord Jesus was not.

Vesta started the Bible study in her home and became close to several women in the neighborhood. One neighbor accepted

Christ for the first time, and a few others started going to church again. Although Vesta didn't know if she made a long-term impact on the group, she did know that it didn't matter; it was God who made the impact. She was just the instrument in His hand.

In spring 1974, Will and Vesta were enjoying their new life when the cattle market crashed again. Vesta was glad she hadn't spent too much time on the house plans since they were on hold now. There was no extra money for a new home on the ranch, and they needed to work hard to keep the ranch.

Will had a great opportunity to raise heifers for the dairies, but he needed to convince his banker to loan him the money for it. He carefully laid out his plan and a step-by-step process to explain the opportunity to his banker. The banker knew that Will was trustworthy and hard-working, but he was also very conservative. Despite Will's careful planning, the banker refused to loan Will the money he needed. Years later, the banker apologized to him as he realized he should have loaned Will the money. Will decided God had other plans, but he did appreciate the apology .

Just before the crash, Vesta asked Will about taking a trip to Hawaii for their tenth wedding anniversary on July 3, 1974. They both thought it was the perfect time to go, but since it wasn't booked yet, she could easily cancel the trip.

Vesta approached Will that evening after she put the children to bed. Sitting close to him, she said sadly, "I'm sorry this deal didn't work out. I know it's a hard time financially again, so I'll just call the travel agency to cancel the trip to Hawaii."

"No, we're going," Will said firmly. "What did you say it would cost? Three thousand for the whole thing, flight, hotel, and food?"

"Yes, that's right," Vesta answered hesitantly. "But I don't know. Are you sure we can still afford it?"

"I've lost way more than three thousand dollars," Will stated. "Going to Hawaii won't make us any more broke than we are already. We need to just go. I haven't taken enough vacations with you."

Will was determined, so Vesta went back to the travel agent and finished planning their seven-day trip. Another critical piece of the planning was where to leave the children while they were gone. The twins stayed with Vesta's brother Stephen, who was still living in Chino. Vesta adored her sister-in-law and trusted her to take good care of the twins. Grandma and Grandpa DeVee, also living in Chino, was happy to help and took Desirae for the week.

After dropping the children off, Will and Vesta flew out of LAX. Although they enjoyed their time in Hawaii, Will and Vesta didn't take another trip without their children. During the trip, they couldn't stop thinking and talking about the children and how fun the trip would be if they came along. They both hoped, Lord willing, that one day they could take the entire family to Hawaii.

Early in 1974, knowing the twins were entering kindergarten in the fall, Vesta and Will decided to try to have another child. The twins would be turning six as they entered kindergarten since their birthday was at the end of September; it had been beneficial to hold them back a year. Desirae would be entering fourth grade. Before then, Vesta worried that it was possible, in her case, to have twins again. It would be far too difficult, she thought, to have two sets of twins at home full time.

When the twins started school, she was already in her first trimester. Vesta thought to herself, *If I do have twins again, I think I can manage since the others are older*. She had almost decided against it, only to find herself pregnant after her first month without birth control.

Vesta's pregnancy was going smoothly until one evening, she noticed a spot of blood. Since her mother had experienced two miscarriages, Vesta immediately called her. She knew Johanna would have wisdom to share with her.

"Hi Mom, it's Vesta."

"Oh hello, it's good to hear from you. I just arrived home from the grocery store. Glad you caught me since your Dad and I have plans for dinner and games with friends tonight. How are you doing?" Johanna asked happily as she loved hearing from her daughters.

"Well, Mom, I had some spotting today, and it has me worried," Vesta replied, getting a little teary. "I knew you would know what I should do."

"Are you still bleeding?" Johanna asked with concern in her voice.

"No, it stopped. What do you think I should do?"

"Call your doctor and see if he wants to see you. It will give you peace of mind. If there wasn't very much bleeding and it stopped, it will be okay," her mother answered calmly.

She immediately called her doctor, who sent Vesta and Will to the emergency room while their niece watched the children. After examining Vesta, the doctor said everything looked good and she didn't need to do anything special. If there was something wrong and Vesta couldn't hold the fetus, a miscarriage couldn't be prevented. Vesta and Will went home relieved and content that God knew what should happen.

Vesta's children were in the habit of regularly praying for their new baby. Steven only prayed for his new baby brother. No amount of discussion with Vesta would change his mind. He knew he wanted a brother, so that was that.

On February 5, 1975, three weeks before the baby was due, Vesta woke at 3 a.m. to her water breaking. Will had already left for his weekly trip to his feedlot in Chino. Vesta quickly called his car phone. Fortunately, Will had one of the early mobile phones in his car. It was such an early model that his car would honk if someone called when he was out of the car, and callers had to connect to the phone through an operator. Vesta reached the operator and explained what was happening, praying that Will hadn't reached the mountains and could still be reached.

After her conversation with Vesta, the operator was nervous, but she quickly dialed the number, relieved when a man answered.

"Your wife is on the phone, sir. Here she is."

Will couldn't imagine why Vesta was calling. He hoped all was well with the children; it never crossed his mind that she was in labor.

"Hi, honey, where are you? You need to turn around and come home. My water just broke, and the doctor said my labor will probably start soon. If it doesn't start, they'll need to induce labor. Right now, I feel good, but I'll call Margot to let her know what is happening," Vesta told him.

"Wow, that's a surprise! I'm turning around now and will be home in an hour and a half. The operator reached me just in time. I'm at the bottom of the grapevine. Another five minutes, and she wouldn't have reached me for another hour."

Will headed home more excited than he thought. His wife was about to give birth to their fourth child. He started wondering what God would give them—a boy or girl. He knew he was going to be in the delivery room and had to admit to himself that he was a little nervous about it. Will thought that experiencing his wife having his child wouldn't be anything like watching the birth of a calf.

Meanwhile, Vesta tried to dress without much success because she had to stay on the chair while also sitting on a towel. She managed to call Margot, Isaak's wife, to get the children off to school. Will would then pick them up from school unless the birth took too long.

Around 6 a.m., the labor pains started, and they were only five minutes apart. Margot arrived, and Will was already home. As they discussed what to do with the children, Vesta's contractions became more painful.

Margot noticed Vesta's voice slowing down and asked, "How are you feeling, Vesta?"

"Not too bad. I just must breathe and focus. I think I'll be okay for a bit longer at home."

Margot and Will disagreed. It was 6:45 a.m. when Will and Vesta headed to the hospital. Aaron Jon DeVee was born just over an hour later at 8:05 a.m. It all happened so quickly that Vesta didn't even need to think about having a natural birth experience.

Will watched the birth and became concerned when Aaron came out slightly blue because the umbilical cord was wrapped around his neck. Will turned white, sat on the floor, and a nurse got him some smelling salts. Aaron was a strong, healthy boy born into a family who loved him so much that Vesta never lacked time for herself again.

When they brought Aaron home, Vesta was excited to be nursing. It went well except Aaron seemed constantly sleepy. At his two-week check-up, the doctor noticed he was quite jaundice and had him tested. He told Vesta to take Aaron to the hospital and put him in the NICU since his jaundice levels were too high. They would put him under the lights for a few days, and he would probably be fine.

Vesta was not prepared to see her baby after the nurses called her back to feed him. He was all naked and screaming, with his little arms flailing in an incubator to heal his jaundice.

After Vesta had Aaron in her arms and wiped tears from her eyes, the attending nurse came in, "Well, I'm sorry that your baby is so jaundice. He should be better soon, but nursing can cause jaundice to be worse, you know."

"No. I didn't know that!" Vesta said, devastated and feeling guilty for her son's return to the hospital. When she got home, she lost her milk as she thought about the severe jaundice being her fault.

An on-call pediatrician put Aaron on formula when Vesta shared her predicament. He decided Aaron should be on a soy formula since the twins had needed soy. It turned out to be the worst thing they could have done and put all of them through six weeks of agony. Although Aaron healed quickly from his jaundice, he was allergic to everything except the Similac milk-based formula they were trying to avoid.

Once Aaron started to gain weight, he grew like crazy. Will and Vesta could do nothing but praise the Lord. They discovered anew how God walks through all the valleys with them. He taught them in a new way that life is never certain. They tried to love their children and be even more thankful for all the good times God gave them.

As Aaron grew, Desirae loved to hold and help care for him. At nine, she changed his diapers and knew how to feed him. She would often take over for babysitters who weren't quite as capable with a baby. Steven had not been at all surprised that God had given him a brother. After all, he asked, and at six, expected the answer to be "yes." On the other hand, he wasn't very impressed with Aaron's inability to do much. Soon, Steven was off playing ball on his own or with Will. Skylar could not hug Aaron enough and loved to call him her little "perciedy" (pronounced as precious with a *dy* on the end). It became Aaron's nickname.

Will loved all of his children very much and gave his time to them as often as he could. He knew Vesta was the main care-taker, but he loved giving her breaks. Desirae always wanted to tell him about her day. He decided to take her down to Southern California with him one Wednesday to have some time together. She talked all the way up and back, a four-hour drive one way. Skylar was his loving child who couldn't get enough hugs, while Steven was happy if they shot hoops together with his indoor closet hoop or the outdoor driveway hoop. Raising children was a joy and challenge for both Will and Vesta. They were amazed at what wonderful gifts God gave them. They tried to give the children all of the love and patience they were able to. During this year of 1975, they watched Aaron grow and had to tend to a few hard cases of chicken pox since there was no vaccine yet. Skylar and Desirae got it the worse while Steven and Aaron barely knew they were sick. Poor Skylar needed lotion every hour to keep her from itching. This, too, passed with everyone feeling like, "How did we endure that?"

## CHAPTER 19
## Country Living

L iving in a busy neighborhood was somewhat trying for the family. They were used to having more freedom and privacy as a family. When Steven and Will shot baskets in the driveway, neighbors would ask to join in. They didn't want to say no but also missed having some fun father-son time. Vesta didn't enjoy looking out her kitchen window with no view except the neighbor's house only two feet away. Their backyard was small, and when they played or talked, they knew close neighbors could hear. Although building a home on their ranch wasn't an option, Will thought his brother Isaak could help.

"We want to find a house in the country," Will told Isaak one day. "Can you be on the lookout for us?"

"Sure," Isaak replied, "There may be a few houses available right now that could work for you. I'll check and let you know."

It took a while, but Isaak found the perfect place for them— an older home on an acre of land that was four miles outside of town. It was on the northwest side of Visalia, close to their church, and the school bus stopped right at their door. They moved into their new (older) home on Ave 320 in January

1976 just after Desirae turned ten, the twins turned seven, and Aaron would be turning a year February 5.

Vesta delighted in her home life while Will kept DeVee Cattle Company running smoothly. Unfortunately, the cattle market continued to plummet that year, and Will had to decide what to do next.

"Vesta, I need to determine if I want to farm or raise beef cattle," Will said quietly so they didn't wake the kids. "If I raise cattle, we will have to sell the ranch and rent back part of it for a feedlot to keep the cattle. My employees could continue to work for me with the cattle, and whoever buys the land, they could hire them to farm."

Vesta knew it was a hard decision for Will. She was also saddened to sell their beautiful ranch. She was so proud of her husband and everything he had accomplished. They always had food on the table, and their children attended Christian schools. She enjoyed her life as a stay-at-home mom and knew she needed to fully support his decision, whatever it was. She realized she was blessed and had no reason to complain. Together, Will and Vesta prayed over this decision. With Isaak's help, Will found just the right man to buy his property. It went so smoothly that they both knew it was what God wanted for them.

The financial difficulty continued into the following year. With the sale of the ranch, Will underestimated the impact of capital gains on his taxes. One day, he came in the door looking miserable.

"What's wrong, honey?" Vesta asked uneasily, noticing that Will was extremely pale.

"I'm really confused. We just got a huge tax bill, and I have no idea how we're going to pay it," Will replied sadly. "This is worse for us than the losses we had in the cattle market."

Vesta and Will prayed long and hard. Vesta worried and tried to trust God, while Will worked determinedly to find a solution. Will knew he had to work as if it was up to him and pray like it was God's work only. He took out a loan and sold off some more cattle. He had learned his lesson and never let that happen again. Will made sure to pay their taxes every year to avoid having them balloon up again. He tried to pay more rather than less, not taking all of the extra deductions sometimes given to a business. This way, he had a cushion when he had a high-profit year.

After this experience, Vesta realized she worried about things that never happened and was surprised when the unexpected occurred. Prayer helped, especially when her worries woke her in the middle of the night.

Their church's Coffee Break program also helped Vesta fight her worries. It fed her soul and kept her absorbed in the Word of God. One of their pastors had heard about it and inspired the women of their church to start the program. It was a small group Bible study that was open to women who rarely, if ever, studied the Bible. Vesta became involved in leadership and invited women to join, including the women from her old neighborhood. Many of the women of the church were doing the same. One big attraction for young mothers attending was the childcare and children's preschool classes. Their class grew large and continued to be a blessing in her life for the next thirty years. Her involvement in leadership meant that she attended conferences, where she learned more than she realized.

While studying God's Word for the class, Vesta came across the verse from 2 Timothy 1:7, "God has not given us a spirit of fear but of power and love and a sound mind!" One night when Vesta was struggling to go back to sleep after waking up because of both real and imagined worries, she remembered that verse. After she repeated it several times, she drifted off to sleep, not waking again until morning. After that experience, Vesta began using scripture to get past her worries. She used the Word of God as her sword when any kind of trouble came, and it never failed.

When they were first married and now with their children, Will and Vesta did devotions together after their evening meal. They carried on this tradition from the families they both grew up in. After their children grew old enough to understand, Will and Vesta loved talking to their children and encouraged them to share their thoughts about God with the family. These interactions were a joy to both Will and Vesta. It helped all of them grow in their understanding as they questioned what they read in the Bible. They also made sure to use age-appropriate material to support their growing children's insight into God's Word.

The DeVee family did many other things together on their acre ranch home. The children raised calves to earn their own money. They also earned money from their weekly chores, such as helping with yard work and house cleaning. Will and Vesta wanted them to learn how to wisely manage the money they earned. They taught them how to save, spend for special things, and how to give. This was a particularly formative time for Will and his children as he was more involved in their lives than ever before.

During this time in his life, Will realized his children were growing up quickly. One spring day, he decided it was time to surprise his family. He came home, and at the dinner table that evening, he shared an idea with them.

"How does everyone feel about taking a trip to Hawaii? I think Christmas break would be a good time to go since farming slows down then and all the hill cattle are shipped to the pastures. Our employees can cover the rest of the feedlot work. So, what do you think?"

There was resounding agreement, along with some excited squealing, around the table. Vesta was on it, calling their travel agent first thing the next morning. Since Will wanted the trip to be somewhat educational for the children, they decided to travel to three different islands.

It was 1977, and Aaron was two, Steven and Skylar were eight, and Desirae was eleven. By Christmas, Steven and Skylar would be nine and Desirae twelve with Aaron almost three. It was a huge undertaking, but everyone helped. Well, everyone except Aaron, who was more like an extra suitcase for Will.

"This trip will be your Christmas gifts this year. Instead, you can have some spending money to pick out souvenirs for yourselves when we get there," Vesta happily told the kids.

"Another idea I had is that each of you can choose a place to eat and pay for the family meal out of your earnings," Will said, encouraging responsibility with their income.

Although it was tiring repacking and going to airports to visit the different islands, it was wonderful seeing the Hawaiian culture on the three islands they visited.

Later, they laughed about their experience in Maui. They landed on Christmas Eve and had reserved a rental car large enough for their family of six. When a compact car drove up for them, all Will could say is, "Are you serious?"

Two cars later, one driven by a car rental agent with their luggage and the other by Will carrying the family, they managed to make it to their hotel in their stick-shift vehicle. The kids laughed until their sides hurt as Will tried to remember how to drive as he slowly jerked his way out of the parking lot.

Christmas Eve dinner was ABC store snacks since everything else was closed! The DeVee family had a wonderful time but learned from their trip. After that if they went again, the trips would be spent on one island, in one hotel, and Christmas was celebrated at home before they left.

They all decided it was a blast to come home with tans in December, so their future trips (Lord willing) to Hawaii should always be in the winter. The DeVees hoped to make this their family tradition by taking these trips every two or three years.

Will and Vesta continued to work hard to teach their children strong values. The most important thing for the DeVee family was to follow the ways of God and His Word. Therefore, they went to church faithfully, and it never entered their minds to let their children decide if they wanted to come along. The children discovered, as they themselves had learned, that what one's family does, the children don't question. Nevertheless, Will and Vesta never stopped thanking God as they watched their children grow in their joy of attending church, Christian school, youth groups, and so on, never complaining that they didn't want to be there.

Through this village of church, school, and home, they would teach and give examples of being loving and patient with one another, often learning that just because a person was a

Christian did not mean he or she was perfect without mistakes in life. Will and Vesta also encouraged participation in household tasks and good work ethics with jobs well done, teaching the children that there were rewards, not only materially but emotionally and spiritually, when they did things right and honestly. Will and Vesta knew they didn't come by this naturally but by God's grace in giving them parents who had passed down most of these values.

While they taught their children by example, Will and Vesta learned as well, often realizing they were far from perfect and often praying for God's direction.

Skylar struggled with health issues since she was a young child. She was allergic to everything and was treated for asthma at two years old. She caught flus and colds twice as often as others and suffered more. She also grew rather quickly, and for a time, needed a lot of Vesta's attentiveness as her hormones changed. Vesta would be beside herself, not knowing how to encourage her sweet child to go to school. She knew some of Skylar's sicknesses were very real and others imagined. It was often difficult to discern the difference.

One morning, Skylar begged to stay home because her legs hurt. Vesta was certain she was having growing pains and sent her off to school with words of encouragement. By that evening, Skylar said she still had pain. When Vesta took the time to look at her, she noticed Skylar had red marks all over her legs. Vesta immediately called their pediatrician and took her in the next morning. It turned out that Skylar had allergenic purpura. She had broken blood vessels, which can be very dangerous and cause blood clots. Skylar had to rest for a week with her feet up. Skylar, of course, was in her glory being waited on by Mom. From that day forward, when her middle daughter said something hurt, Vesta believed her. She decided better be safe than sorry.

Although Steven started life as the weaker twin, as he grew, he was rarely ill. He was not allergic to the same things as Skylar and didn't get asthma like his sister. He was in constant motion and needed an outlet for his energy. His favorite outlet was sports. Will developed his interest in watching college sports as his son loved to share that with him. Will also enjoyed teaching his children to raise calves in the backyard of their one-acre country home. Steven learned quickly how to spot the sick ones and enjoyed going to the cattle sales with his dad.

Country living provided many opportunities for them to flourish as a family, but it also had a few drawbacks. Their home sat alone, surrounded by a field of grapes and other crops. The closest neighbor was about a half-mile away. They had a manual garage door with a manual gate that opened and closed to their fenced-in yard.

Will and Vesta became lax about shutting either the gate or door. One late morning, Vesta came home to find their home had been robbed. She immediately called Will. "Honey, we've been broken into!"

"Wow, that's terrible. Did they get a lot?"

"Well, it looks like all our electronics and my jewelry. It also appears they left in a hurry," Vesta replied with a shaky voice.

"Call the sheriff. They should be listed in the front of the phone book. Do you know where to look?" Will asked.

"I'm looking right now. Here it is. Okay, I'll call. Can you come home too?" Vesta asked.

"Yes, I'll finish a couple of things and be right there," Will assured Vesta.

The sheriff came and made his report. He also reminded them that if everything was closed, a person looking to break in would go to the next house. He advised them to be more careful when leaving. He finally said, "If I was you, I'd invest in a good dog. This is also a great way to deter robbers."

When the children heard what the sheriff said, they were all excited to get a dog. The DeVee family was between dogs at the time, so Will and Vesta were open to getting another one. The children promised to help take care of it as well. The Sheriff surprised them by mentioning that he might have just the dog for their family. He had a police dog who was too nice to do his job but would be very protective of a family.

The dog's name was Rebel, and he was just what Steven needed to overcome his nervousness about dogs. Rebel became Steven's dog, even though the whole family loved him. When Steven was around, Rebel was his shadow.

The DeVee family never grew tired of their country home. All their relatives enjoyed visiting. Stephen's family would often come from Chino to celebrate Thanksgiving in Visalia. Frank and Johanna made Thanksgiving at the DeVee's a yearly tradition too. It was close to Johanna's birthday, making it the perfect reason to celebrate with the Schuil family. Vesta learned to make turkey and pies from her mother, and Frank would help repair anything at their home or the ranch during their visit. The cousins loved playing together in the large yard and petting calves or the horse, Dollar (that had come with the house). Desirae was the only one who could ride Dollar. For some reason, he was unwilling to have any of the others ride him.

Busy lives make the years go by quickly. During these years of raising the children, Will and Vesta decided not to take in extra girls. Their children's ages were a factor, and a three-bedroom home with four children was another constraint. They always made room for Terri, who often came to stay during the summer months of her college years. She would share the room with the girls, and since they knew her well and loved her, it was never a problem. Terri even worked a few summers for Isaak, who owned a record shop at the time. The most exciting thing they helped Terri with was her wedding. They were all involved in one way or another. Soon thereafter, she was living in Southern California with her husband, Stan Bon, and expecting their first baby.

In 1980, Will was ready for another Christmas trip to Hawaii. The children were doing so well raising calves that Will felt they could afford to take the trip. They sold off the calves and sent the rest to their ranch while they traveled. Nothing beat going to Hawaii as a family, and they were all excited for their upcoming trip. At the beginning of December, however, a flu broke out, and the whole DeVee family was sick. It was only a few weeks away from their trip, so Vesta decided to take the children to the doctor.

"What should we do as we will be on a plane for five hours? All my kids have fevers, and Skylar is the sickest. The first day she sneezed non-stop, staying under the sheet of her bed, and now she is so congested. Should we cancel our trip?" Vesta asked her pediatrician.

"No, don't cancel. I believe you have time since fevers don't usually last more than five days, and getting your family in the sunshine will help everyone's recovery. Go have fun," the doctor told Vesta.

They made it on the plane with Skylar's fever finally ending that morning. When they came to their hotel, they all crashed on the beds for naps. The doctor was right, they were soon all healthy again after a few days playing on the beach in the sun. It was a special time to remember and joke about later.

## CHAPTER 20

# Running Businesses

The children always had needs, and Desirae was now ready for braces. While they were at the orthodontist, Vesta asked him, "I know my daughter's teeth need to be straightened, but I have to admit, I've wanted to get my own teeth straightened for years. Is it too late for me at thirty-four to be considering this?"

"No, you're not too old for them. In fact, I've straightened the teeth of people in their eighties," the doctor replied.

"Wow, let me talk to my husband about it, and thanks for looking at my teeth and giving me an estimate." Vesta was excited about the possibility but tried not to get her hopes up. Two thousand dollars was a lot of money.

After telling Will about the visit and finally getting the courage to share what she learned, he said, "Well, you could earn the money by raising calves in our backyard. What do you think?"

Vesta was excited by the idea of raising calves, and after about a year, she earned half of what was needed for her teeth straightening. All the children helped with raising the calves, but Will noticed that the girls, especially Desirae, who was in her junior year of high school, needed another outlet for her talents.

One night at dinner, the children were having fun talking about what they hoped to do when they grew up. Desirae mentioned that she would love to open a store. Will thought that sounded interesting and asked, "What kind of store would you want it to be?"

"I don't know," Desirae replied, "maybe a women's clothing store would be fun. But then again, I don't know, women can be picky, and that could be hard, but I think that would be super exciting."

They continued discussing various retail store options. Will, always the risk-taker, liked the idea of a store, and Vesta (also a risk-taker) agreed. Vesta thought having a store sounded like a thrilling adventure. She didn't worry about the work involved at this point in time. She proposed an idea, "A children's shop could work well since there isn't one on this side of Visalia. I feel the one on the other side of town doesn't offer a lot of choices. I'll talk to my friend who has the specialty children's shop in Chino where I used to shop. Will, remember the one I would sometimes get in trouble with you because I spent too much money there? She could help us with ideas and to understand if this is even achievable."

Will laughed and said, "Of course, I remember that store. Yes, it could be a troublemaker, and she would be a great one to get help from."

Before they knew it, their idea wasn't just an entertaining dinnertime discussion but a genuine business endeavor. That ended raising calves for both Desirae and Vesta and began their adventure of gathering information for a specialty children's store in Visalia.

The year 1981 began with plenty to keep the DeVee family busy. Vesta and Will continued with plans for the children's store that included talking to a banker about the feasibility of it all. They found out that they needed collateral other than the store itself, which they took care of by refinancing their home. It was somewhat frightening for Vesta to think she had encouraged this whole idea. Now it was really happening. They found the store space they wanted near to their grocery store. With the groundwork in place, they waited to see if all the other necessary doors would open for them.

Vesta enjoyed talking to her children when they came home from school each day to find out how their day went. When all four of them were in school, Vesta finished her work and dinner preparation before they came home. She also had their snacks ready, so she had time to talk and listen to them. It wasn't always easy since they were such different ages—kindergarten, seventh, and eleventh grades—and the boys were just as happy to answer with, "School was fine, Mom. Can I go play now or watch TV for an hour?" One hour of TV was the limit the kids had for watching their after-school shows. During this hour, Vesta had some quiet time to talk with Desirae alone. She had great stories about high school, and Vesta found it so refreshing to hear about her experiences at Immanuel Christian High.

Dinner was another important time for family conversation time. Will enjoyed hearing how his kids were doing in their school activities and how they reacted to their friends and teachers. The three youngest children were pioneers, so to speak, at Central Valley Christian (CVC). Will wanted to keep the school strong, and he knew his children's opinions mattered.

Desirae and Skylar had very different personalities. Skylar was as outgoing as Desirae was shy; fortunately, they rarely fought with one another. Maybe they didn't fight because they were so different, and both Skylar and Steven would do almost anything to please Desirae. Aaron was strong-willed and smart. He had to learn young how to make friends since there were only three boys in his kindergarten class. Establishing a new school created different issues for each of the children to deal with. Desirae was happy she was older and wasn't involved with CVC. She enjoyed her final years at Immanuel very much.

During early summer 1981, everyone was busy getting ready for the opening of their children's boutique. The entire family was excited to have a store with everyone involved in deciding many things about it, including where to locate it and what to name it. They found a small, 1,000-square-foot property near their grocery store that was not too far from their home. They called it Honey Bear Boutique after rejecting Honeybee since bees sting and bears are so cuddly.

From their friend in Southern California, they heard about a small store that was closing in the Fresno area. They purchased clothing racks, a cash register, and a nice check-out counter from that store. To tackle the challenge of how much merchandise to buy, they decided to hire an agency to teach Vesta and Desirae how to do this.

Desirae and Vesta learned quickly but continued to work with the agency for the first year. They were ready for their opening day in the middle of July. They were told that was the best time to have "back to school" ready for a children's shop. Just the week before, they heard about a huge children's specialty shop opening down the road at the same time. Vesta wondered if her mother, Johanna, was right when she questioned the idea of Vesta starting a business.

"Vesta, are you sure you should do this? You have four children who need you, and you are busy in ministry. How will you manage all of this?" Johanna asked with concern in her voice.

"Oh, Mom, I feel sure that God opened many doors so we could do this, the place and money we needed to get started, for example. It will be a great experience for Desirae, and it's perfect timing for me since Aaron starts first grade this year and Will is home a lot more these days. I don't plan to stop doing ministry or being there for my kids. It will be a family effort, and we feel it's a good time to try," Vesta replied to her mother, trying to sound confident. She didn't want her mother to worry needlessly.

In the middle of that night, Vesta woke up and went over her hopes and fears with her Bible in her lap and crying out to God.

"Lord, I know I can't turn back now, but if this is wrong, please help us decide what we should do." Tears flowed, and worry overtook her heart. She read as much scripture as she could, hoping that would give her strength and assurance. She repeated 2 Timothy 1:7, which was about God not giving the spirit of fear but of power, love, and a sound mind. Unfortunately, Vesta had no feelings of power in the moment, she only felt fear. Finally, Vesta became tired and crawled back in bed beside her sleeping husband.

In the morning, Vesta still felt fearful and could no longer keep it to herself.

"Sweetie, do you have a minute?"

Will was in the middle of his early morning devotions and preparing for his day. He looked up to see Vesta looking tired and worried.

"Of course, I have a minute. I thought you'd be rushing around getting ready for your big day. What is it?" Will grabbed his wife in a bear hug and waited for her to share why she looked so stressed.

"Well, you know the store down the street that Desirae and I visited a few days ago? It seems to me we don't have a chance to compete with it. Everyone will go to her store. She carries the same brands as we do plus a bazillion more," Vesta replied and started crying. "I'm afraid we'll lose all of our money and be a complete failure. Why did I think I could do this?"

"You'll be fine. I'm sure of it. Besides, even if you lose everything, we won't go broke. Please don't worry." Will held her close, and soon Vesta felt more confident. Will was an experienced businessman, and if he said she would be okay, she knew she would be. What a wonderful man God had given her.

In the years ahead, Vesta never knew how she managed to get everything done. It was difficult to run a business, and she learned to empathize with her husband's challenges in a way she never did in the past. She clearly understood why he agonized over high grain prices or low cattle prices. She appreciated what a heavy load he carried. She knew firsthand how exciting it was to have a great day of sales and, in contrast, how hard it was to have a very slow day.

Vesta felt lucky to have great women working for her and alongside her daughter. She was proud of Desirae, who was growing into a mature woman. Desirae took responsibility for running the store single-handedly in the early years. While their Honey Bear Boutique flourished, the woman who opened the extralarge store down the road failed. Her store turned out to be too large for the number of goods she could sell to cover the expenses. It was another good lesson for Vesta—wait and see how God directs. She didn't wish ill upon the other retailer but knew if she was meant to stay in business, God would make it clear one way or the other.

## CHAPTER 21

# Years of Plenty and Years of Learning

Will, Vesta, and their four children never lost touch with their parents and siblings and loved family gatherings. Vesta was closest to her sisters Rachel and Sara and also kept close contact with her brother Stephen. She found Matthew, Thomas, and their families harder to stay connected to. Vesta attributed this absence of connection to having less in common, not growing up together, or doing things together while they grew up.

She prayed for her parents and siblings often and assumed it wasn't always possible to be close to everyone since their family was large and spread out. Will's family was similar. Their two older siblings were not as close to Will as his brother Isaak. Despite this, if family members came to visit or if Will and Vesta went to see any of their siblings, they were welcomed. Their family ties were strong, and when the cousins got together, they always had a fun time together.

Both Will and Vesta's parents were healthy and able to travel with friends and family members. Will and Vesta loved seeing their parents enjoying life during their early years of living in Visalia. Vesta's dad, Frank, would often get a "daddy do" list when they visited. Frank was strong at sixty-three, even though, in his late fifties, he had a heart attack, which forced him to retire early. At the time of his heart attack, Frank was fifty-nine and traveling to construction sites to build water stations in remote areas of California. It was grueling work and stressful for his family. Johanna was left on her own to take care of Rachel and Thomas. Frank would leave first thing Monday morning and return home Friday evening. He quickly grew tired of living in motels, so he purchased a Fifth Wheel RV to pull behind his truck to the work sites. Since Frank didn't enjoy going to bars after work with his colleagues, evenings were particularly lonely. He dreamed of the day he could use his Fifth Wheel for fun trips to places like Alaska, where he heard the fishing was exceptional. One evening, Frank finished his day and was completely exhausted. He ate his dinner quickly, hardly remembering what he did next. The next morning, he woke on top of the bed covers, still fully clothed.

*How strange*, Frank thought to himself. *Well, I guess I was more tired than I thought.*

A few months later, a very worried Johanna called Vesta, "I'm sorry to tell you that your dad is in the hospital. He just had a heart attack."

"Oh no," Vesta exclaimed. "How can that be? He seems so strong and healthy."

"I know, I was shocked too. The doctor said he is doing good. He will keep him at the hospital for a few days for observation and more tests. He also told us that his heart had a scar, which means your dad already had a heart attack that he wasn't aware of at the time," Johanna explained.

Will and Vesta visited Frank and were glad to see he looked so good. He shared with them his thought, "I think when I was away at the out-of-town job site and woke one morning fully clothed and not remembering much, I probably had my other attack then. I told the doctor about it, and he agrees."

After his heart attacks, Frank unexpectedly got his wish to retire. His heart specialist said it wasn't safe any longer for Frank to handle that much pressure and responsibility. Finally, he and Johanna were able to travel around the US as he'd hoped.

Vesta was happy for her parents, and since her own life was quite busy, she was glad she didn't need to worry about them. Instead, she looked forward to their visits, especially when Johanna and Frank's siblings from Michigan or Idaho joined them. Johanna's sisters were the most fun to have visit. Each of them had a special giggle, and when they were together, they giggled constantly. Their giggling made everyone around them laugh since it was impossible not to laugh when hearing the three of them giggle.

Vesta loved Johanna, even though, at times, her mother made her a little crazy. Johanna loved talking about people from her church who she was positive Vesta must remember. Vesta found it difficult to listen to stories about people she hadn't seen in years, and she would get bored trying to pay attention. She confessed to God her frustrations when she grew impatient or bored with her dear mother.

Vesta and her father grew closer over the years. Vesta and Frank shared many interests, and she enjoyed talking with him. During this time, she realized her artistic talent probably came from her dad, and her love of people came from both of her parents. Frank would never have considered himself an artist, but anyone who could build and put things together as he could was truly a special kind of artist.

Will's parents were a joy as well. Will and Vesta made sure they joined family birthday celebrations in July and January at his parents' and would visit their home several more times a year. It helped that both sets of parents lived in Southern California so they could visit their parents whenever they were in the area. Vesta loved sharing in Will's father's knowledge of the Word of God. He had experienced so much in life—a war in his homeland, hiding people who were in danger, having a bomb land close to their home, moving to a new country at fifty where very few people spoke his native language, and starting over by working for others until he could earn enough to have his own business. He was wise and had so many interesting experiences to share. Through all of these experiences, good and bad, his faith never wavered, and Vesta loved hearing about it.

Will's mother also had wonderful memories and wisdom to share. Although they grew up in a different time, Will's parents were open to how Will and Vesta felt about things. Their attitude about life and openness to new ideas and experiences impressed Vesta the most. They came to America when they were fifty and forty-five and were determined to learn English since they were sure their children would find spouses who didn't speak Dutch and wanted to talk to them and their grandchildren directly. They never felt sorry for themselves, even though they left a country where they had worked hard and did well to come to a place with very little and needed to start over. For them, it was always about God and what He wanted for their lives. They were both humble people who never bragged about their accomplishments.

One day as Vesta cleaned out the cupboards, she found a diary of Will's father. Vesta loved reading it and gained more insight into her husband's family and how life was for them.

The diary shared details about their journey from Holland to America in 1948:

*El Cajon January 1949*

*When we said goodbye to the people in Holland, many asked us to write. But since it is not possible for us to write each one personally, the thought came to us to write a diary of our moving to America and send it to the Noorder Provinciale Groninger Courant for publication.*

*On December 10, 1948, at 11:30 a.m., we left Winsum by train. At the train station, Rev. Buitenbos was waiting for us and in the waiting room with many friends and townspeople who shook our hand for the last time. We left Winsum in brilliant sunshine—a sight we will never forget and the hands that waved us goodbye. The farewell from family, friends, and community of Winsum was not easy for us but full of energy, and with the strength of our God, we are going into our new future. Mrs. Witterholt accompanied us on the train to the head station in Groningen. It was a love deed from her to us, which we appreciated so much. And the sunshine made our spirits soar as we left the Province of Groningen. After a good train trip through Holland, we arrived in Leiden, where our good friend, J. P. Van Der Stoel picked us up with his large car. After stopping in Boskoop to say goodbye to friends there, we went to the hospitable home of the Van Der Stoel family and spent the evening having a good time in the midst of the large family that had gathered there. It was through the Van Der Stoel business connection that we were able to have the sponsorship we needed to enter America. His son was already living in America and was able to sponsor us by having work waiting for us when we arrived. We became acquainted several years earlier doing business as milk cow dealers who worked in export.*

*December 11. After a restful night, Van Der Stoel and his wife took us to Rotterdam, where we soon had to say goodbye. At the ship Nieuw Amsterdam, we met the Ridder family of Noorduvyk. Their daughter, Janny, will travel with us—she will visit an aunt and uncle in California. After much inspection of our papers, they were found to be in order, and we were allowed aboard the ocean liner. Going there, we were pleasantly surprised to see Harm Medema and his wife Dickie from Winsum behind the glass in the building almost next to the ship waving to us. We were thankful that we were able to greet people from Winsum, and it did our hearts good. Close to 4 p.m., the ocean liner left the dock pulled by tugboats, and then it went slowly ahead. Arms and handkerchiefs waved from the ship and the long arm of Harm Medema we were able to see for a long time. At 6 p.m., we passed Hoek van Holland, but it was dark, and we felt sad about that because it would have been the last of Holland that we could have seen. Soon the ship started to rock on the waves of the ocean. The dinner bell rang after that, and the food was so good. I don't remember how many courses we had, and at the end, ice cream and a foretaste of California—a delicious orange. In the evening, in the conversation room, we met many other immigrants, also the Kline family of Adorp, and we had fun traveling with them. The ship is large with a lot of luxurious things, and we are getting spoiled here. At 10 p.m., we went to our cabins, but the rocking of the ship and the drone of the engines prevented us from sleeping soon.*

*December 12 (Sunday). We woke up reasonably rested. We are in the harbor of Le Havre in France. It was a pretty sight. The city is built against and on top of the hills. The results of World War II are still visible. A sumptuous breakfast was ready for us, and we ate good again. In the morning, we were happy to have a sermon with us, which we read together. This way, it was Sunday for us because for the rest, there was no trace of it. Passengers and food boarded here. On this large ship, a lot is consumed by 1300 passengers and 600 crew. Close to 1 p.m., we left Le Havre to South Hampton, England, where we arrived close to 6 p.m. Going there, my wife, my daughter, and Janny Ridder felt their stomachs going around, but with the ship docked again; they got better fast. At 8:30 p.m., we left for the ocean again, and soon we were rocking on the ocean waves. After a good time in the conversation room, we crawled in bed again.*

*December 13. When we got up in the morning, many passengers didn't feel good in the stomach, and not many showed up for breakfast. Isaak, Will, and I were the only ones at breakfast from our family—the rest had no appetite. Many continued to be sick that day. We are now quite a way out on the great ocean. It is a beautiful sight. The waves are rolling endlessly. What a great example of God's creation! Not many people came to the table—from our family: only Isaak, Will, and I. We are sleeping better than the first night; a person can adjust to everything.*

*December 15 (Wednesday). The seasickness is not so bad anymore. Today, my wife was also on deck, and the others were at the table. It is really something when you cannot enjoy the abundance at the table. In the afternoon, the waves of the ocean are bigger, and toward evening, the chairs in the conversation room are tied down, and that means something, and sure enough: When we are lying in bed, the large ocean liner starts to move from side to side—it is lifted high in the air in front by the waves and then tossed into the deep, and in bed, we are tossed to and fro. Before daylight, it is much calmer.*

*December 16 (Thursday). Not much going on. The waves are high, and as a result, again, many people are sick. It is no fun on deck. Toward the evening, the ship is tossed so bad that a few people in the conversation room tip over—chair and all—and it made many people laugh. At night, the sea calmed down, and we had a restful sleep.*

*December 17 (Friday). Beautiful weather, the sea is calm. A big relief from the storm yesterday. Everybody is on deck, and my wife is getting better fast. We are meeting more and more people and talking with them, and the time is now going fast. Every night, the clock is set back one hour—we notice that the world is round.*

*December 18 (Saturday). The sky is dark, and a few snowflakes are starting to fall, and it is getting colder. The suitcases have to be packed. They have to be set ready tonight because Sunday morning, we will arrive in New York. We go to bed early because Sunday morning, we have to get up early.*

*December 19 (Sunday). We woke up at 5:30 a.m., and many people were up already because the city was in sight. It was fantastic—all the lights—and in the background, the skyscrapers of this great city. We had to eat already at 6:30 a.m., and for the last time we ate good aboard the ship. When we went on deck again, the sky was gray with snow so that we could not see anything anymore. The Americans were the first to go on shore. We had to wait, and the checking of papers took so long, it was after 12 o'clock when we were able to set foot on the ground of our new country. The checking of our suitcases went pretty fast, and after that, we went to the Christian Seaman's Home, which was close by. The immigrants were welcomed by Mr. Dahm. Coffee and bread were served. There they gave us also a helping hand with any of our needs. We had thought to stay here until Monday, but the weather was so bad that Mr. Dahm advised us to leave that same night. With taxis, we were taken to the train station, where a black man took us and our suitcases into the waiting room. This same man took us to the 7:30 p.m. train. We were so happy to have learned a little English; otherwise, we would have been really stuck. We got into a large, well-furnished train but got a rocky ride. The train was well-lit, thanks to the marvelous lights in the city.*

*December 20 (Monday). In the morning when we woke up, we saw a pretty countryside and high hills with houses on the side and on top. Everything had snow on it. This was the state of Pennsylvania, and the hills were later not as tall. Part of it was still barren ground, but there was also farmland and farms everywhere but not in the style of the Hooge land (where we came from)—you don't see that here—the houses stand separate from the barns. We also passed through the states of Ohio and Indiana. When we arrived in Chicago, there had been snow all the way. Someone is waiting for us there. Kudos to the stranger Traffic Bureau who sent the information from station to station. Here we had to wait four hours, so now we had time to take care of our insides by ordering and eating a hot meal. After that, we went into the city to buy bread for the rest of the trip because in the train it was very expensive. We looked and looked for a bakery but found none until we walked into a large warehouse, where we could buy what we needed for little money, and no rationing coupons, of course (World War II). Back at the train station, I went to the barber to get a shave. It wasn't cheap, and with many movements by the barber, I still didn't get a good shave for seventy-five cents. Very efficiently, at 9 o'clock, we were taken to the train, which looked gorgeous. When we went to sleep, we pushed a button, and the seat went backward. With a small pillow under the head, we slept well. There were also sleeping quarters, but they were too expensive for us because we are now poor.*

*December 21 (Tuesday). When we woke up, I remembered that the cow sale mart in Groningen had already ended because we were now seven hours behind Holland time. The sun was shining brightly, and we rode through the state of Missouri. There was beautiful scenery here, and good, but more bad pastures with skinny cattle outside in the winter. Later, through the state of Kansas, we saw soil that looked better, more productive, and big herds of good cattle. When we went to sleep, we were tired from taking it all in.*

*December 22 (Wednesday). In the train, we met many people, mostly Americans, who gave our youngest boys candy. They were friendly and helpful, and we noticed that there is not much in the way of social classes here. Many people found it nice to talk with us. We rode through the state of New Mexico, a big, barren landscape, which we crossed. On the horizon, we saw the mountains loom up—a majestic sight when you see it for the first time. The train later slowly zig-zagged through the mountains with deep ravines, sometimes on both sides of the train. It is really an untouched country. New Mexico is a poor state, and out in the country, it is thinly populated and very poor. We saw Indians in their colorful dress. We saw a few women at a train station making colorful towels and trying to sell them to the people on the train. These people live in shacks—the chicken coops in Holland are so much better in contrast. Then we rode through the state of Arizona, also partly desert. At 10 o'clock, we went to sleep but would wake up through the shock waves of the train when it made stops. The train stopped at every little station and then moved on with great speed.*

*December 23 (Thursday). Wide-eyed, we look outside. The train is riding through the orange groves of California! The trees are green here, and vegetables are growing in the field. We are riding through nice cities and towns—how prosperous—hundreds of cars are riding through the streets. And the mountains rise up like dangerous icebergs on the horizon (Holland is flat like a pancake)—insert by Bram. We are getting closer to Los Angeles and see sights we had never seen before. We are riding over mountains, and we look in the valleys and see white houses hiding in the green and sometimes built unto the hillside. In Los Angeles, we have to change trains. The uncle and aunt of Janny Ridder, J. Koining of Willington, are standing at the train station waiting for us. In the waiting room, we drink a cup of coffee and have a good time. We have to wait here a couple of hours for the train to San Diego. This is a colossal train station, and everything looks neat. At 12:45 p.m., we board the train that will bring us to the last station. After riding through orange groves, we see on our right the sea, the Pacific Ocean, and on our left, the hills with different sights. It was a wonderful trip from coast to coast through America, but we are now glad that we are nearing the end. At the station in San Diego, we are warmly welcomed by a son of Van Der Stoel and his wife, who have already lived here for fourteen years. They take us with their car to our temporary home in El Cajon, California. We have a rented furnished home that we can now rest in from the long trip.*

*Now I will stop. Maybe at a later date I will write about the land and life in California.*

*With many greetings to family, friends, and acquaintances.*

*D. DeVee*

Vesta was disappointed that her father-in-law didn't continue writing in the diary. She knew that soon after they arrived in El Cajon, they moved and rented a dairy in Artesia. It only took about six months in El Cajon for Will's father to make enough money to start his own business with a partner in Artesia. Her father-in-law loved to sell dairy cows, a business he learned in Holland, and was soon able to buy out his partner in Artesia and own the business himself. Dirk rented the land, barns, and the home that was on it. It always impressed Vesta how much he had accomplished in such a short time. He was already fifty when they moved to America, and neither of them knew much English. They were both very determined to learn the language because they wanted to speak and understand when their children married Americans and had children.

Vesta also found a short story of the DeVee family life in Holland during the war. It was written by Will's oldest brother Bram. When Germany invaded Holland, he was only eleven and was sixteen when they retreated.

The story read:

> *When the Germans overran Holland in 1940, my dad was on his way to Leeuwarden in the province of Friesland to the weekly Friday milk cow market. When he got word that war broke out, he went home in his car as fast as he could while bridges were blowing up behind him. We were so glad to see him back home!*
>
> *When boys were fifteen, they had to register with the Germans. I had to do that at fifteen. The Germans made them work in the German war efforts when they turned eighteen. I never had to go, yet I did have to hide a few times as they thought I was older. Thankfully, the war ended by the time I was sixteen.*

*I remember our churches filled up when the Germans were in our country. People turn to God when there is trouble, that is for sure.*

*We lived in the country and had cows and could get food more easily than people living in the city. The people would share their food, but, often, the Germans would confiscate the food! Hunger was a big problem during the war.*

*On a Sunday, two men came to our church to thank the Lord for their deliverance from the concentration camp in Germany. For me, at sixteen years, it was a sight that I've never forgotten—man's inhumanity to man!*

*There is one more item about the war time that pertained to electricity. Since we milked cows and shipped milk to the factory, the Germans let us have electricity only in the barn and in the cow departments. In the house, we only had candlelight. We got plenty of sleep that way. Dad hid a radio in the loose haystack in the barn and plugged it into the electricity at the barn. He would listen to BBC in England and keep track of the war and the liberating forces.*

*When we heard the Germans had surrendered and were leaving town, they left with only horses and wagons, a few cars, and trucks. We were glad to see them go. We noticed that while they occupied our country, there were some good men who would look the other way when we didn't obey German rules. We were thankful to see that too.*

*I was so happy to hear they were leaving that I climbed to the roof to hang our Dutch flag up and, mind you, I am afraid of heights! Then word spread that they were coming back, so I scrambled right back up and took it down. A couple of hours later, we heard it was a false alarm, so I went right back up to put up the flag!*

*Written by Bram*

Vesta had heard bits and pieces of Bram's story from Will and his brother, Isaak, but neither of them was old enough to be directly involved in the war. It was a dangerous time for parents to care for young children. They were thankful that nothing terrible happened to them where they lived in Holland during the war. Vesta loved having these stories to share with her children and future generations.

Will and Vesta felt blessed to have parents who shared the same faith and had common worldviews. When Vesta talked to friends who had strained relationships with their in-laws, she felt particularly fortunate to have a good relationship with hers, as they surrounded her family with love and support.

Throughout the years, Will and Vesta's parents and other family members visited them many times. One visit stood out to Vesta.

"Vesta, did you say your parents and aunts and uncles were stopping by tomorrow?" Will asked one June day.

"Yes, they should be here later today. I'm planning to cook a roast in the crockpot and make a good salad and some sides to go with it. They plan to leave first thing tomorrow morning for

Alaska. They're taking three motor homes on the trip, so will you make sure our car and pickup are out of the way?"

"Sounds good. I'll be back after the cattle auction, which shouldn't last past 5. I'll come right home when it's done and look forward to a great dinner," Will replied as he raced out the door after giving Vesta a big hug and kiss.

Everyone arrived that afternoon and had a great time around the dinner table laughing and talking about their trip. They decided to park their motor homes at a nearby trailer park to make it easier for Will and Vesta. The men talked most about their fishing plans.

"All the sportsmen magazines say that this time of year, the best fishing in Alaska is at night. It will be amazing to be out on the lake at 1 a.m. while it is as bright out as 1 p.m." Frank never thought he'd be able to afford the trip and could hardly contain his excitement.

"You're so right, Frank. It will be an experience we'll never forget. Just seeing the landscape during our drive will remind us of God's great handiwork," Vesta's Uncle George replied.

The ladies played Scrabble and talked about what they would do during this adventure. They knew they would enjoy the sights but weren't particularly interested in going fishing in the middle of the night. They looked forward to being together and creating memories.

On their way back, Vesta's parents stopped by again while the others took a different route back to Michigan. Everyone enjoyed seeing the polaroid pictures Frank took in Alaska and hearing all about the trip. However, they weren't quite pre-pared for one of the stories Frank shared.

"We went on a fishing trip in the middle of the night, but it was rather short," Frank began. "Since it was cold, we wore heavy jackets, but when we got to the middle of the lake, it was warm. I stood up to take my jacket off, but before I got my arms out, the boat started to sway back and forth from my weight. Suddenly, all three of us were in the water, and it was freezing cold!"

Vesta was shocked and started peppering Frank with questions. "Were there other people around? Did you have on life jackets?" She knew her father couldn't swim and that the three men were fully dressed and wearing heavy shoes.

"No, that was a problem. We were alone on the lake. When I fell into the water, I remember looking up, seeing the overturned boat, and wondering how drowning would feel," Frank calmly replied.

By this time, Vesta was beside herself—three men who couldn't swim, on a lake all alone with no life vests.

"As I was sinking, I remembered something your brother Tommy told me. He said 'Dad, if you ever fall out of a fishing boat in deep water without a life vest, just start kicking.' So, I kicked hard, and the next thing I knew, I was out of the water, staring at your uncles who were holding onto the upside-down boat." Frank continued his dramatic story as everyone sat, spellbound.

"What happened next, Grandpa?" Will and Vesta's children asked in unison.

"Well, for a minute, we just stared at each other. Then I realized we were going to freeze quickly if we didn't yell for help. I started shouting, and the guys joined me. We could not believe our eyes. A few minutes later, a man in a speed boat came roaring over. We had no idea where he came from. He dropped us back on the shore, and we rushed straight back to our motor homes." Frank ended his part of the story as Johanna took over.

"Frank banged on the door, scaring me since I was still sound asleep. I ran to the door to find him standing there dripping wet and shivering. I had no idea what happened but helped him get out of his clothes and put on dry ones. We jumped into bed until he warmed up and stopped shivering. Finally, when Frank was able to talk, I heard the whole story." Johanna finished with relief and gratitude to God in her voice.

That afternoon, they tried to find the man who rescued them but couldn't and decided it was a guardian angel God had sent. With so many miracles surrounding the story, Vesta was convinced a guardian angel had rescued them. Her father and uncles never should have survived and lived to talk about it. Vesta thanked God for His special care and remembered this day often.

## CHAPTER 22

# Business Ventures and High School/College

O ne evening, Will and Vesta enjoyed their Saturday family night out to dinner with their children. They reminisced about how God had made amazing things happen in 1979. While growing up in Visalia, the children attended Christian schools in both Hanford and Reedley. Both schools were more than twenty-five miles away from their home and not easy to get to when fog would set in during the winter months. Will often wondered about the feasibility of starting a school in Visalia and discussed this idea with his brother Isaak. Isaak heard about a small, local Christian school that was closing due to a lack of support, and the two brothers thought this might be an opportune time to start a new Christian School in Visalia. For the initial discussions about the feasibility of this, Will brought five men from Visalia and Hanford Christian Reformed churches together at their home.

Their children, Steven, Skylar, and Aaron were part of the first group of students who, for the first three years, met at their church. It was tough on their children to be this type of trail-blazer. In the beginning, many tears were shed, but they appreciated what resulted over time. This school came to be named Central Valley Christian School (CVC). The school grew rapidly, and Will and Vesta knew God was behind its success and that they were only His instruments.

As their children took part in the first classes and started many of the school programs, Will and Vesta were members of its first boards and Mother's Club. Isaak helped the board find land to build the school along with leading them through the approval process with the city. They struggled in the early years; it was as if an invisible force didn't want them to succeed. Ultimately, the success of the school was due to the hard work of so many people in the Christian community and the mighty hand of God. As the years passed, CVC became well known, and parents wanted to send their children there. Will recognized that one man, Dr. Joshua VeBrea, was instrumental in helping the school prosper when he became superintendent in 1992. Although the twins had already graduated from CVC, their youngest son, Aaron, attended high school during this time.

By this time, the Honey Bear Boutique, which had opened in 1981 as Aaron entered first grade at CVC, had become a local favorite. As it grew to a 3,000 square foot store, Desirae and Vesta decided to change the name to Honey Bear Kids. They renamed it to let new customers know they offered merchandise at a variety of prices and carried children's sizes 0 to 14 in both boys and girls.

Most stores in town didn't carry the wide assortment of children's clothing, shoes, socks, and infant gift choices that Honey Bear Kids offered. They also carried a large assortment of crib bedding and could order baby furniture. The DeVee girls did their best to stay on the cutting edge of all that was popular and in-demand at the time.

While Vesta and Desirae worked hard at the store, the boys found their place in the cattle business with their father. Skylar discovered her passion for cleaning and yard work. When Skylar was a toddler, she wanted to make her bed, even though Vesta would say it was too hard and Mommy would do it. However, if someone believed Skylar couldn't do something, it made her more determined to do it. She loved being at home, and both she and Desirae loved to cook and bake. Skylar also raised calves with Desirae and Steven, but Steven kept with it after the girls gave it up. Their Avenue 320 one-acre lot was difficult to keep clean since a yard full of baby calves came with flies and dust. The boys were responsible for mowing the lawn every Saturday while Skylar kept the weeds out of flower beds.

One weekend, a cousin (Matthew's daughter, Candice) came to visit Will and Vesta. She marveled at how hard their children worked without complaining. Her comment reminded Vesta to thank God more often for His provisions.

The children worked hard, but like most siblings, they also knew how to fight. They just didn't fight much because they were so busy.

Will believed in teaching his children how to manage money. They were paid for raising calves, doing extra work in the yard or house, and working at the store. Will and Vesta tried hard to model frugality and always gave a good portion of their earnings to the Lord and helped the children set up savings accounts. They watched their children respond to having money in very different ways. For a couple of the children, money never lasted long while another child would save almost every penny earned.

As he grew, Steven, became more involved in the cattle business with Will. Will took him to the auction yard and taught

Steven about the cattle he bought and how he chose them by size and shape. By working closely with Will, Steven became quite skilled at purchasing cattle, and Will often allowed him to buy some of his own. Will also strongly encouraged his children to consider going to college to learn more about life and try other options before making their career decisions.

In 1982, as Desirae entered her last year of high school, her passion for retail grew. Vesta and Desirae scheduled their buying trips during school holidays and summer vacations. They treasured their trips when they could talk with no interruptions and rehash their hilarious encounters in the fashion world at the California Mart in downtown LA. They often ran into movie stars on the elevators, and one day, Vesta even noticed a new underground train entrance.

When they both looked more closely at the entrance, Desirae exclaimed, "This could pass for New York City. See all the extra stuff on the street. It looks like they're getting ready to make some kind of movie."

After a few trips, they stopped being surprised by their adventures. They learned that taking the escalator at the Mart was a feat unto itself. It traveled incredibly fast, and once they were on, most people kept racing up the moving stairs since everyone in LA seemed to be in a hurry. After some practice, Desirae and Vesta were able to keep up without tripping.

Breaking for lunch also required speed. At the lunch line of any deli, there was no extra time for deciding what you wanted to order. When you got to the front of the line, you needed to order immediately, or the next person in line would be served.

That year, Desirae's fashion merchandising class teacher asked if Desirae would plan a field trip for the class to the Mart. Vesta and Desirae were delighted to plan the trip and share their experience with the class. Until then, they hadn't realized how much they'd learned about buying and the workings of the Mart. Their salespeople knew them well and happily shared great tips from the world of fashion with the class. The visit was a wonderful success, and Desirae and Vesta laughed years later about the teacher's comment that the escalators moved so fast it made their hair blow.

Desirae did great in her senior year, and to her surprise, was nominated to be on the homecoming court. At her school, the candidates had to perform in a talent show. Desirae had a blast performing the song "Adelaide's Lament" from the Broadway musical, *Guys and Dolls*. She surprised many classmates with her song since it was very crazy and funny, and she was normally quiet and shy. Vesta was so proud of her and knew her daughter was a performer at heart. Even though she wasn't selected homecoming queen, it was a wonderful time for the family.

That year's graduation was exciting as Desirae was a salutatorian along with several others in her class. Their school let all of them give a speech. Steven and Skylar also graduated from eighth grade that year. It was a busy time with lots of excitement and parties to celebrate their children. Will and Vesta never tired of celebrating the accomplishments of their children.

The year 1983 brought some big changes for the DeVee family. The twins entered high school, and Desirae moved to Fresno to attend college. Even though Vesta knew Desirae wasn't that far away and she would see her often, packing up her first child to leave home was a huge adjustment.

Tears flowed as she told Will, "I don't know why I'm so sad. It's just hard, I guess. Desirae and I are so close, and letting her go is not easy."

As Will hugged his wife, his own eyes grew misty. "Yes, this is a new road for all of us to travel. Now we know what it feels like to let go of our kids and let God lead when we can't. I admit, I'm not ready to let them go either."

It turned out to be a good time for Will and Vesta with their twins. Since it was such a small school, CVC needed every child to participate in sports, so Will and Vesta attended every game. Steven loved every sport, so he was thrilled. Even when winning was almost impossible, especially for the freshman/sophomore boys who had to play against juniors and seniors, but the CVC fans cheered the loudest. Skylar also played every sport and was a natural to help lead the cheer squad.

With Desirae at college or working at their store, Vesta enjoyed very special times after school with her twins and Aaron. Will and Vesta grew in their abilities to manage their businesses while being actively involved with their children. They also continued their involvement in their church and Christian school. They both felt blessed to have such full lives, even though it was challenging at times.

Some of Vesta and Desirae's favorite times together were their trips to LA. They often stayed with Vesta's parents so they could visit with Frank and Johanna. There were times, however, when Vesta and Desirae stayed in a hotel close to the Mart. For one trip, they booked a nice-looking hotel online, but when they arrived, the neighborhood wasn't very welcoming.

"Yikes!" Vesta said to Desirae. "I don't think I want to stay here. In fact, we shouldn't even get out of the car." Even though they were in the parking garage, everything seemed too scary for them to get out. Vesta and Desirae drove down the road to a much better-looking hotel. They were able to get a room and quickly canceled at the other hotel. Another lesson was learned; be careful when booking hotel rooms online.

In fall 1983, Aaron entered fourth grade, and, thankfully for Vesta, he was a good student. He worked independently on his homework and yet needed time to talk, so Vesta went out of her way to give him attention.

When Aaron was younger, Will and Vesta thought he would grow up and be a cattleman more quickly than Steven, so they were surprised it didn't happen that way. Although he raised calves with Steven, Aaron really liked helping at the store. He was naturally disciplined, quick to learn how to work the cash register and take inventory as needed. When he was a freshman, Aaron became an official employee at the store. He had a commanding presence and worked Saturdays so Vesta could take some Saturdays off from time to time.

This same fall of 1983, Desirae started her first year at Fresno State. She wanted to stay close to home so she could work Saturdays and holidays at the store. Her goal at college was to expand her fashion merchandising skills but soon realized she knew more than most of her professors. Despite this, college was a good learning experience for Desirae, and it is where she met her husband, Brock Estrada. She liked meeting guys but felt that dating was more trouble than it was worth. She found it nerve-racking, and the guys she was interested in didn't seem interested in her or, as Vesta told her, didn't have the confidence to ask her out on dates.

Desirae didn't even notice Brock when he first came along, but he couldn't stop noticing her. He arranged to eat his lunch near the place she usually sat and walked to class using a path where he would conveniently run into her. Through patient planning, Brock finally approached this beautiful blond woman and asked her to coffee. After a few dates, Desirae talked to her parents about Brock. They were quite surprised that she wanted to seriously date a Mexican guy who was Catholic. It wasn't like their daughter to be interested in someone so different in life experience and especially so different in faith.

"You know we have concerns about you dating Brock," Will stated, "but at the same time, we know that you are mature for your age. We want you to pray and contemplate to be certain that Brock is the right man for you. Let's pray together right now. We firmly believe that God will lead you to the right choice."

The three of them prayed together, and in the coming days, continued to pray separately. Desirae and Brock dated another year, and it soon became apparent they were on a path to marriage. Vesta had well-meaning friends, including their pastor at the time, who shared their concerns about the relationship with her. Although they understood their concerns, Will and Vesta strongly believed in allowing their children to make their own choices. They knew that the Bible teaches to raise children in the way they should go, and when they are old, they will not depart from God's way. They trusted that Desirae's Christian upbringing gave her the necessary foundation to make the right choices.

Brock and Desirae were engaged. Together, they decided Brock would continue his education. Desirae finished her year of college and started planning the wedding while working full-time at the store with Vesta. In the meantime, Will decided to take a family trip before things changed drastically with a child getting married. They found roundtrip plane tickets to Detroit for

$150 each. Off they flew on their whirlwind tour of Niagara Falls, New York City, Washington DC, and the Pennsylvania Amish country. In every big city, they made sure to look for wedding dresses. High necks with lots of lace and satin, large puffy sleeves, and flowing trains were the style for wedding dresses at that time. Desirae found a lovely cream-colored dress in a small Michigan town, ordered it, and had it shipped to Visalia. She had tried on white dresses but loved how the cream looked next to her rather pale skin.

They arrived in Washington DC on the Fourth of July. They were not at all prepared for the city and all the holiday commotion, "Oh my goodness," Vesta gasped. "What are we going to do? All of the streets to our hotel are closed."

"Let's drive around a bit," Will replied calmly. He was certain they could find a way in.

A few minutes later, they stopped a police officer for advice. He told Will, "Sorry, sir, every street is blocked off for the celebrations. All you can do is find a place to park and walk from there."

"Can you tell us where we might be able to park?" Will asked politely.

"Sorry, sir, I can't help you. The streets won't reopen until about midnight after the fireworks. You need to move along now; I need to keep the cars moving."

"Maybe we shouldn't have stopped to hear the Liberty Bell ring in Philadelphia," Vesta said sadly. "What are we going to do? People are parking all over the place, and we can barely get through the streets. This city seems to go in circles, and I'm quite sure our hotel is down one of those closed roads." Vesta looked up from the paper map they used for navigating.

Will wasn't sure how to get there either but noticed that cars were parking on freeway off-ramps in the grass area. He decided to take a space on the 110 Freeway right across the water from the Lincoln Memorial. They were perfectly positioned to watch one of the country's best firework shows.

As soon as they stopped, they saw a sign threatening to tow cars. Aaron, at nine years old and with a strong need to obey rules, saw the sign and shouted, "Mom, Dad we can't park here; we'll get towed."

Will tried to calm his son, "Look around us. There is no way they can tow all of these cars tonight. I'm sure if anyone tried to stay here after the fireworks are over, they would have a problem. Let's go join everyone who is sitting on the grass over there. We don't have much of a choice since there is nowhere else to go."

It was starting to get dark, and more people were parking near the DeVee's rental car. They couldn't move, even if they wanted to. They had never experienced anything like this before. Aaron was convinced they would come back to find their car gone, so Vesta kept him distracted with other sights, so he didn't worry too much. With the Lincoln Memorial shining in the background, the fireworks were breathtaking.

It was close to 11 p.m. as they made their way back to their hotel. With the streets open, they easily found it. They parked under the building and noticed that the gate was locked after they entered the garage. Once they were in the hotel, they asked if the restaurant was open.

"No, sorry, it just closed. You could try the one down the street. It's about two blocks away," the man at the reception told them.

Vesta couldn't help herself and blurted out, "Really? Would you send your family down that street at this time of night?" The street they had just driven down they noticed was where drug dealers and hookers hung out.

He thought for a minute and then replied, "Well, maybe not. There is a store across the street where you should be able to get some snacks."

Will and the boys headed across the street while Vesta and the girls settled in their room. Vesta noticed that their window overlooked the street and watched as Will and the boys came out of the store and passed several seedy-looking gentlemen. When they were safely back in the room, they all talked at once about how the people in the store were almost scarier looking than the ones they saw on the street.

A few minutes later, they heard a blood-curdling scream and peeked out the window to see a man running away with a woman's purse. Vesta wasn't sure she liked this city until, suddenly, they heard a clap of thunder and watched an amazing lightning storm, the likes of which they had never seen in California. They all agreed that God's fireworks far outweighed man's puny efforts. Shortly after the lightning storm, it started to rain, and everything grew quiet. It was almost as if God took over the streets and sent everyone home.

After a good night's sleep, everyone was ready for sightseeing. After their neighborhood experience the night before, they were a little nervous about venturing out. Much to their surprise, the street was filled with people in suits and business attire; the thieves, drug dealers, and prostitutes had disappeared.

One thing that troubled the DeVee family was the number of homeless on the streets of our nation's capital. It made everyone's heart ache. Vesta worried about Aaron keeping up with all the walking, but he turned out to have more energy than the rest of them. By the end of the day, everyone was looking to sit on a bench, any bench, while Aaron was jumping around enjoying the sights. Will appreciated that all the museums and other sites were free and enjoyed benefiting from some of the taxes he paid. Despite all of the ups and downs, everyone was glad that they visited Washington DC for two days.

Their last stop was a one-day, whirlwind tour of New York City. It began with a bus tour until noon, then an afternoon walking the streets, and ended the day with a Broadway play. After the play, they discovered they needed two taxis to get everyone back to their hotel. This caused a bit of a panic until the children convinced a limousine driver to take them back across the river to New Jersey. Since Will and Vesta were unprepared for this situation, they felt, once again, that God protected them from harm in this big city environment that was so foreign to them. For years after their trip, Will would say that visiting New York City was like having a vacuum in your wallet sucking out all your cash. It was a harsh contrast to Washington DC, where everything was free.

Although the trip flew by, they had such a great time together that no one forgot this happy (though somewhat crazy) experience. After returning home, they started a new chapter in the DeVee family life. Desirae and Brock married, and as Vesta moved their oldest daughter's belongings out of the house, she was heartbroken and shed many tears.

The wedding was beautiful and took place in their church with a wonderful reception at the nearby Holiday Inn. Will and Vesta were thankful that the Estrada family was willing to have the wedding in a Protestant church. They worried after hearing stories about marriages that didn't work out because the families didn't accept their child's spouse from a different background. Fortunately, the Estradas loved Desirae and accepted her fully into their family just as the DeVees accepted Brock into theirs.

Despite having their families' blessing, however, Brock and Desirae realized that their upbringings were very different. They knew they had a lot of learning and growing to do. Vesta prayed and encouraged Desirae when she shared some of their marriage difficulties. From this experience, Vesta learned to listen closely and encourage her children to love their spouses. She knew from watching other families that, in some cases, the parents would split up marriages by taking sides. They would push couples apart when all they needed was some encouragement to communicate in the right way.

At home, Skylar and Steven enjoyed high school. With Desirae married, Skylar had Vesta's undivided attention and liked talking about the day's activities after school. Since Skylar and Steven were part of the second class to enter the new Central Valley Christian High, in many ways, it was great fun, but in other ways, it was a challenge. They were both positive and upbeat and tried to encourage their classmates as much as possible.

Skylar was a people person and never tired of making others happy. As a result, she was surrounded by young men wanting to befriend and date her. Steven was her protector, which at times she appreciated and other times she detested. For example, when they went to parties, Steven would always ride with her since they shared a car. Skylar didn't think this was fair since Desirae had her own car. However, Skylar discounted the fact that Desirae drove thirty miles each way to her high school while the twins only drove four miles and went to most places together.

It was now fall 1984, and Steven and Skylar entered their sophomore year and Aaron started sixth grade, and Desirae lived in Fresno about forty-five minutes away. She drove to Visalia five days a week to work at Honey Bear Kids with Vesta. It was her first year of marriage, and she enjoyed sharing life with both her mom and Brock as he finished up at Fresno State.

Vesta also enjoyed her children at home. She found communicating with them came naturally, particularly in comparison with other mothers who complained about constantly arguing with their teens or preteens. Of course, Vesta and Will had disagreements with their children during their teen years, but the arguments were always manageable.

Skylar and Steven would come home from school and share the good and the bad of what was happening in their lives. They often asked for Vesta and Will's opinions and encouragement about whatever was occurring. Vesta liked hearing about their love interests and who was dating who. Dating had changed since Vesta and Will were young; one was no longer considered a loser if there was no date on Friday night. Instead, if one had a boyfriend or girlfriend, one would hang out with friends or family over the weekend, so Vesta loved having her children around. They enjoyed inviting friends over and stayed involved in school and church activities.

While Steven and Skylar shared interesting tales of school events and happenings, Aaron entered puberty. These years came with lots of worries and questions from Aaron.

One evening as Vesta and Aaron sat in their backyard jacuzzi, he asked with worry in his voice, "Do you think I'll ever get married, Mom?"

"Of course, you will, Aaron, if God wishes and you desire it. The Bible says God gives us the desires of our hearts. It is not something you need to worry about," Vesta answered in the best way she could without trying to predict the future.

Aaron responded and was close to tears, "I knew I would never marry! God won't want me to. I just know there won't be a girl who will like me anyway."

More tears flowed as Vesta wondered what to say next. She didn't realize that he was dealing with raging hormones. Vesta tried to encourage and comfort him, assuring Aaron that he would have a great future, wherever God led him. Then, to distract him, she changed the subject away from girls, a tactic that usually worked well.

During his early teens, Aaron excelled academically, even though his body grew more quickly than his mind could manage. Aaron enjoyed finding the best prices for items they needed to buy. As he honed his skills, Aaron helped Will by calling car dealers and getting prices for pickups and cars. Even when he was younger, Aaron was blessed with a deep voice, which was a real asset when he talked to the dealers. He also used his voice for another favorite pastime, which was to practice being a DJ with his home entertainment mic and recorder set.

From the time she was a toddler, Skylar was her mother's most challenging child. Vesta knew it was because they were so alike. She loved her strong-willed, second daughter, and hated being at odds with her.

"Mom, can I have ten dollars for school tomorrow?" Skylar asked.

"What's it for?" Vesta wanted to know.

"There's a fundraiser for the cheerleading squad, and I need to do my share," Skylar responded, trying not to sound annoyed.

"Didn't I bake cookies and give you money for the same thing last week?" Vesta reasoned.

"Yes, but I'm the head cheerleader, so I need to do extra. I'm also a class officer, so we'll need to do some more baking for Grandparents' Day and the harvest festival." Skylar's mood lifted as she thought about the fun class activities they were fundraising for. She also knew her mom would eventually give in; she always did.

Vesta sighed, knowing there was no use arguing with this active young lady. Skylar was so different from her sister. Sometimes Vesta had to beg Desirae to take part in some of the fun activities at school. Vesta knew she needed to love and encourage Skylar as she used the gift of leadership God gave her.

Steven was busy as well but a much easier child to raise. He was calm, like his father, and often helped his sister understand the consequences of her actions.

"Hey, Steven, are we going to the party tonight after church?" Skylar asked.

"Sure, it sounds like some fun kids are going to be there. Let's ask Mom to make sure it's okay with her," Steven stated.

"I'm sure she won't mind, but yes, I'll check."

After getting the okay, they went to the party. Much to their surprise, some older guys showed up with twelve-packs of beer. Steven wasn't pleased. He knew his coach would not be happy if he found out that they were attending such a party.

"Come on, Skylar, we need to go," Steven said urgently under his breath.

"Oh, Steven, we just got here." Skylar felt uncomfortable, but at the same time, thought that some of the guys were pretty cute. She really wanted to stay and flirt with them.

Steven wouldn't have it. "We're leaving right now. Say your goodbyes, and remember, I have the keys."

Skylar delayed leaving as long as possible, but soon they were walking out the door.

"Thanks, Skylar," Steven said. "I know you wanted to stay, but I don't think this party is going to end well. Those guys were drinking when they came in, and they're acting like they want to be back in high school." It irritated Steven that these older guys were trying to swoop in on high school girls.

When they arrived home, the twins told Will and Vesta about the party.

"I know Steven was right, Mom, but I'll be honest, I wanted to stay. Those older guys are so good-looking, and I wouldn't mind dating a few of them," Skylar confided.

Vesta understood completely; she felt the same way at that age. However, she never liked guys who drank too much and was grateful her son was wise beyond his years. Vesta and Skylar talked until it was bedtime. Vesta would often stay up talking with the kids. Will would have too, but he needed to wake up to the alarm at 5 a.m.

Her children's friends all knew that Skylar and Steven shared everything with their parents. When something significant happened, their friends would always say, "I suppose you're going to tell your mom about this."

Skylar would quickly answer, "Yup." She didn't care if her friends approved. Sharing everything with her parents, especially her mom, was something she loved the most about her life.

## CHAPTER 23

# More Life Changes

F un runs were a popular event in Visalia, so Will looked into using one to raise money for Central Valley Christian School. As a member of the school board, Will was also in the perfect position to bring the idea to them. Before he knew it, he was in charge of organizing the entire fundraiser.

As a person who enjoyed taking on new ventures, Will quickly had everything in place. The plan included soliciting prizes for each group of runners and a way for each kid to get sponsors based on how far they ran.

The race was scheduled for spring, and each group was assigned to run during a specific hour. Will's group ran last, later in the afternoon. It was a beautiful day, but by the time Will's group ran, the wind had picked up and dust was blowing everywhere. Will needed to run the entire hour to collect on the generous pledges from his sponsors. By finishing all of it, he would raise a nice sum of money for the school.

Will finished the race and was pleased with running a full seven miles in an hour. He thought this was quite good for a forty-two-year-old. He coughed quite a bit after he finished but didn't think too much about it.

Will caught bronchitis easily and often needed antibiotics. He had also suffered from pneumonia a few times. He called himself a "lunger," which was a name given to cattle with lung problems. Will would often comment, "If I hadn't quit smoking in my late twenties, I'd be dead now."

About a month later, Will felt sick and had a low-grade fever. At first, he thought it was the flu and just took it easy. The fever persisted and numerous visits to the walk-in clinic didn't help; the doctors didn't know how to treat him. As summer gave way to fall, Will only grew weaker. Since Steven worked closely with Will during the summer, he understood the feedlot well. As he and Skylar started their junior year, Will was so weak from the fever that Steven got permission to come late to school to help his dad with the morning chores. Vesta also hired additional help for the store so she could drive Will to his cattle sales. Will and Vesta began thinking the worst was happening and started discussing their will and what Vesta should do if Will passed away. It was one of the most difficult times of their marriage thus far.

Finally, during one of their clinic visits, the doctor said, "We need to do an X-ray of your lungs, Will." After reviewing the results of the X-ray, the doctor returned looking gloomy and told them that Will had three or four spots on his lungs. Then he added, "Before we talk about options, there are some other doctors here who I'd like to get an opinion from."

Will and Vesta remembered very little about that visit except that Vesta knew she felt hopeless. As they drove home, between her tears, she said, "This sounds like it could be lung cancer. What else do spots on the lungs mean?"

"I agree. I never heard of spots on the lungs meaning anything other than cancer," Will replied with a sad voice. "Lung cancer is also a bad thing to have. We need to make sure our will is in good shape, and I want to review my life insurance policy. Don't worry, Vesta. I know that God will take care of us."

Almost a full year after Will developed his fever, he had lost thirty pounds and his skin had an ashen tone. Somehow between Vesta and Steven, the business continued to run smoothly. God took special care that year by providing decent cattle prices and perfect weather for feeding their hill cattle.

Each morning, Vesta took time for her devotions, which she followed with a three to five-mile run. Out in the fields, she was able to cry her heart out to God and tell Him exactly how she was feeling. She thought she was doing pretty well but realized how much of a burden she carried when, one morning, Will woke up and said, "I don't think I have a fever."

"That's wonderful!" Vesta shouted. "Should we go to the doctor one more time to check the spots on your lungs?"

"Yes, that's probably a good idea." Will was glad Vesta thought of doing that.

At the doctor's office, Will and Vesta shared that Will had been two days without a fever. After he heard their news, he immediately checked Will's lungs. He came back after the X-ray and told them that the spots were gone, and this confirmed that Will had suffered from Valley Fever. Even though it was a rare illness, it was more common in areas with farming and cattle where certain dust spores infected people, like Will, who were more susceptible to it. Eventually, Will fully recovered, but the doctor still recommended he avoid running in the open fields.

The next day during her run, Vesta realized a huge weight had been lifted from her shoulders. She praised God for healing

Will and felt grateful for being given another season of joy to share with her husband. Never again did Vesta take this wonderful man for granted.

Life continued for Vesta, Will, and their children with all of them learning to manage everything they did in a fast-changing world.

During the 1980s, computers became more pervasive and a regular part of everyday life. Steven and Skylar needed a home computer to keep pace with their schoolwork. Before home computers, Will always did his business books by hand using a desk calculator. He remembered when the first handheld calculators were introduced and cost between 300 to 500 dollars. He loved using his handheld calculator at the sales yard while bidding on cattle. At the same time, Will and Steven recognized that the California cattle business was changing, and they decided to visit some feedlot owners in Kansas, Texas, and Oklahoma. After they finished some of their trips, they both started calling them, "cold turkey visiting and meeting feedlot owners."

Will and Steven were in the business of purchasing 200 to 400-pound Holstein bull calves from dealers and at sales yards. The huge dairy industry in the valley meant that Holstein cattle were abundant. They raised their cattle to sell to feedlots when they were 500 to 550 pounds in size. They worked hard to sell the Holsteins in the Midwest since most of the feedlot owners were not familiar with the breed. In the Midwest, they traditionally raised colored cattle and were skeptical that Holsteins would not grow fat enough to sell for beef. However, Will and Steven persisted, and, after some ups and downs, they developed a good Midwestern market for their Holsteins as a result of their hard work.

Vesta understood the traveling was necessary, but she still didn't like sleeping alone. She worried that something would happen to Will and Steven and wondered how she would manage life without her dear husband. She reminded herself, "Life is uncertain, and worry is easy to fall prey to. I must not let worry take hold of me. I must trust that God will give me the strength to walk where He wants me to." She often comforted herself with the knowledge that what she worried about rarely happened. It also helped that Skylar and Aaron were home with her while Will and Steven traveled to expand their business to the Midwest.

During this time, Will saw that Steven was a natural when it came to understanding the cattle business. Despite this, he encouraged Steven to go to college and make sure the cattle industry was where he wanted to spend his life. Will knew better than most how hard it was to make a living with cattle, so he wanted Steven to be confident in his decision.

Neither Will nor Vesta was sure where Skylar was headed. She attracted young men easily and seemed more interested in becoming a housewife than attending college. But, starting in her junior year, she decided to apply herself to her studies. To her surprise, her grades jumped from being average to making the honor roll. Skylar was excited that she seemed to have as much scholastic ability as Desirae, who had been one of the top students in her class.

During her senior year, Skylar also became acquainted with Tommy Ridder at church. Even his family noticed when she greeted him each Sunday. Tommy wanted a good woman as a life partner, but after having his heart broken a few times, he began to wonder if he would ever find her. He had all but given up looking when he noticed this cute DeVee girl.

"Is she actually interested in me?" Tommy asked himself. She kept turning up wherever he stood and would talk to him. She wasn't afraid of anything, which he liked a lot. "I wonder how old she is, maybe too young." Tommy did some asking and found out she had just started her senior year of school. *Well okay, so I'm five years older, not too bad*, Tommy thought.

Finally, Tommy got up the nerve to ask Skylar on a date, and his family was thrilled. Will and Vesta were also excited for her. Even though they knew people who believed Skylar was too young for marriage, Will and Vesta were unconcerned since they had started dating at around the same age. As with Desirae and Brock, they continued to feel strongly about letting their children make their own life choices. However, they still prayed for and talked openly about their children's choices with them, sharing thoughts from God's Word and praying together with them.

As Tommy and Skylar got to know each other, they discovered that they had a lot in common. In the spring, Tommy searched for the opportune time to ask Will for his daughter's hand in marriage. Will gave Tommy his permission to propose. The DeVees had known Tommy's family since they moved to Visalia twenty years earlier. The Ridders were a bit rowdier than their own family, but Will and Vesta appreciated their strong faith in God. The wedding date was set for September 19, 1987, at their church with the reception taking place in the Ridder's backyard.

Will and Vesta were thankful they had the means to make their daughters' weddings special. They thanked God together for bringing two good men into their daughters' lives. Will and Vesta also appreciated that both daughters lived nearby so they could still enjoy family time together. Desirae and Skylar were happy too since, once they were married and suddenly had more responsibilities, they realized how wonderful it was to have their parents nearby for support.

Skylar and Desirae both loved their home life before they married. However, Skylar had a harder time adjusting to the fact that living with her parents and siblings was over. The realization of how much her life was changing hit her hard just a few days into their honeymoon.

"I don't know exactly why, Tommy. I'm sorry, we're having a great time, but would you mind if I call my mom just to hear her voice?" Skylar choked out between loud sniffles. She just couldn't help herself and didn't understand why. Skylar was thankful that Tommy thought it was cute and didn't get annoyed at all.

"Of course, you should call your mom," Tommy said, hugging her. "I know she'll be glad to hear from you and give you the advice you need."

Tommy's words made Skylar cry more. Calling Vesta made her feel better and reassured Skylar that her family would be there whenever she needed them.

## CHAPTER 24

# Grandchildren

Desirae and Skylar were now married while Steven took a gap year to determine if he wanted to attend college or go into the cattle business with his father. In parallel, Will decided that if his sons joined the business, he would keep it running, but if not, he would sell it and retire. By retiring, Will knew he could enjoy more freedom and find work buying cattle for other people if needed.

After his gap year, Steven decided to attend college in Michigan. Vesta watched as he packed his bags. She could see he was nervous and concerned that Michigan was a long way from home. Shortly after he arrived, Steven decided to finish the semester, even though he knew that college wasn't for him. He made lots of friends and had fun teaching his friends how to check out the girls using the same methods he used to separate cattle, "in and by, in and by." His friends had a good laugh, but Steven was often disappointed to discover that the girls he considered dating already had boyfriends.

With Thanksgiving just around the corner, Steven prepared for a serious conversation with his dad. The biggest issue was that Steven had already paid for his entire first year of college. When Steven arrived home, he shared with Will what was in his heart. "Dad, I just don't like school. I thought about it a lot and know I can't do it for four more years. I talked it over with Todd, you know, my teacher from high school, and he agreed with me. He feels it is better to do something I love. So, what do you think?"

Will listened with excitement and joy in his heart, hoping that it was God's will for his son to give up on college so soon. Both Will and Steven talked and prayed about this decision long and hard. They agreed to donate the money to the college scholarship fund. Although Steven had more learning to do, Will was confident he already had a solid understanding of the cattle business.

Desirae continued working with Vesta at Honey Bear Kids. They loved working together, and it came so easily to them. After their year of living in Fresno, Desirae and Brock decided to move closer to her work. They found a nice apartment down the street from the store. Desirae could walk to work so they could share a car and save quite a bit of money. When Brock graduated, he started selling insurance. Two years later, he had done so well that they bought a new home in Visalia.

After their honeymoon, Skylar and Tommy settled in a home on the Ridder Farm. Skylar asked Vesta for a job cleaning her house. Vesta loved the idea since Skylar knew exactly what she expected when it came to cleaning.

With all the changes, Vesta was surprised by how much time and attention her family continued to need. With Steven back in Visalia, his friends kept trying to set him up on dates. Unfortunately, each time he went out on a date, he came home and said, "No, I don't think so."

Almost every day after work, while Vesta cooked dinner, Steven jumped on the kitchen counter to talk things over with her.

"What do you think of Laura? Should I go out with her? Some of my friends want to set me up with her, but I don't even know what she looks like, and they don't know my type. To tell you the truth, I'm getting a little sick of blind dates," Steven complained one evening.

"Well, Steven, sometimes it takes time to find the right girl. It's up to you if you want to go. Who knows? Maybe she's just what you're hoping for." Vesta wished she could make it easier for him but knew not to rush him through this critical life decision.

The boys liked having Vesta's full attention with the girls married. They especially loved it when their mom joined them in the jacuzzi so they could talk with her. If Vesta encouraged Will and the boys to use the hot tub without her, they would complain. They claimed that they couldn't get a conversation going without her. This always flattered Vesta and, invariably, she would laugh and join them in the hot tub.

It was now 1988, and Ronald Reagan was president. Will and Vesta hoped that another good Republican would be voted in when his term ended. They felt he had done such an amazing job. Vesta didn't enjoy politics as they made her anxious. It was difficult for her to listen to discussions about what was wrong with both parties. She knew she needed to pay attention to a point but left the rest up to Will since she agreed 100 percent with his views on life and politics.

Vesta's family life was busy and full, at times too full. She continued sharing her faith with others and was very involved in their church's women's Bible study class that focused on outreach. Being a class leader required continual preparation and study. It also required personal contact with the women in her class and extra meetings with the leaders. Vesta had the time to be involved with all these activities, but as she entered menopause, she started getting migraine headaches.

"I'm getting headaches lately, and I don't know why. I never had this problem before. It scares me a little. Could I have a tumor or something? I doubt it, but I can't figure out where the headaches are coming from," Vesta mentioned to her friend Lois, who also worked for her at Honey Bear.

"Do they seem to come at the same time every month?" Lois asked.

"Now that you mention it, yes they do." Vesta was surprised that she had not noticed that before.

Sure enough, the headaches came about once a month. Vesta also noticed she had some abnormal bleeding between her cycles. Her doctor recommended to Vesta that she consider having a hysterectomy. One day while Vesta was reading her Good Housekeeping magazine, she read about an easier way to take care of her bleeding problem. She talked to her doctor about getting an ablation of the uterus. He was willing to try the procedure, and it cured Vesta's bleeding problem.

Her bleeding stopped, but the headaches continued. Vesta had a new appreciation for the woman who bled for twelve years and approached Jesus to be cured. With medical care scarce or unavailable, women in biblical times endured difficult problems. Vesta realized that this is the case today as well, for people in third-world countries.

It was well into January, and Will and Vesta were enjoying the winter months with their children. Vesta was a runner and ran five miles in forty minutes; she loved fun runs and won her share of trophies. However, one Saturday, she came home from her run feeling like she was coming down with the flu. Throughout the night, she had a stomachache, but in the morning, decided she felt good enough to go to church. Vesta never liked missing church with her family as it filled her life with God's truth. After the service, her stomach still felt strange, but Vesta still thought it was the flu. At that same time, Will and Steven were getting ready for a trip to check out some of their cattle in El Centro. It was a six-hour drive, so they planned to leave immediately after lunch.

As he watched Vesta lying on the couch, Will felt uneasy about leaving. It wasn't like her to slow down so much, although when she had the flu once or twice before, it had hit her pretty hard.

"I'll be fine, I'm sure it's just a flu bug. Aaron is here, so I'm not alone. You and Steven should go; you'll be back on Tuesday, and I'm sure I'll be better by then."

Will and Steven left for El Centro right after they finished lunch. After saying their goodbyes, Vesta felt sicker and her temperature rose.

"Does it hurt in any particular place, Mom?" Aaron asked.

"I didn't think to check that." Vesta felt her stomach and told Aaron that the pain was coming from an area on her right side.

"I'm going to check the encyclopedia and see what it says about the symptoms of appendicitis."

"Good idea, Aaron." Back before the internet existed, an excellent source of information was the encyclopedia. Fortunately, Will and Vesta had invested in a set for their children's schoolwork.

"Sure enough, Mom, you have all the symptoms," Aaron reported.

"I'm calling my doctor," Vesta said as she looked up his number in the telephone book.

Luckily, her doctor was on call, and even though he was a gynecologist, he knew Vesta well. He knew that she rarely complained and wasn't often sick. When he heard her symptoms, he agreed that Vesta may have appendicitis. He contacted the emergency department at Visalia's Kaweah Delta Hospital so that they would be ready to see her immediately after she arrived.

As Aaron drove them to the hospital, Vesta said, "Please don't tell your dad anything until we know if I need surgery."

"Well, Dad would want to know that you went to the hospital. I don't think we should wait too long to tell him," Aaron replied, wishing his dad was with them.

"Yes, you're right, Aaron. We'll call him soon. Hopefully, he'll be in an area with good phone reception." Vesta didn't feel at all well and was glad to have Aaron with her.

When they arrived at the hospital, they were immediately ushered into an examination room. When a nurse popped her head in, they were delighted to see Cindy, a friend from church, was on duty. She let them know that a surgeon was being called in to take out Vesta's appendix. Vesta's blood tests and other symptoms indicated that she had an infection. It seemed strange to Vesta that, at age forty-two, she had appendicitis. She had always thought it was a childhood disease.

Now Vesta had to reach Will. Cindy got her a phone. When she couldn't reach Will, she called Skylar and Tommy. Vesta told them, "Be sure to tell your dad I'll be all right. I don't want him to drive home tonight since I'll be recovering anyway. He should do his work with Steven and just come home tomorrow."

"Oh Mom, I feel awful. Isn't there anything we can do?" Skylar asked, feeling helpless and worried about her mom. Later, Skylar and Tommy joined Aaron in the hospital waiting room. Tommy also went to Will and Vesta's house to pick up some family photos. He hoped seeing them would help Vesta feel less lonely when she woke up.

After her surgery, Vesta wondered, in her fuzzy state of mind, if she was dreaming there were family photos on the shelf of her hospital room. After her mind cleared, she realized she wasn't imagining the photos. When she was told what Tommy had done, she couldn't get over what a thoughtful thing it was for him to do for her.

Will was quite upset when he heard that Vesta was going to have surgery.

"What? We need to go home now!" Will cried to Skylar.

"No, Dad. Mom said you need to stay and get your work done. She'll be fine, and we'll keep you posted. We're staying with Aaron at the hospital until everything's done. If you come home now, she'll just be asleep anyway." Skylar tried to comfort her dad as best she could under the circumstances.

As far as Vesta could tell, the surgery went well. She felt a lot better with the infected appendix gone. After the surgery, Vesta spent three days in the hospital, and her recovery went well, even if it was a bit slow. The food wasn't very good, so one of the days there, she was surprised by her daughters bringing in Kentucky Fried Chicken. It was a wonderful treat and tasted amazing compared to the hospital food.

After Vesta's appendicitis, Will and Vesta had a new appreciation for the unexpected. They understood how precious life was and how things could change in a heartbeat. Vesta had feared having surgery and discovered it wasn't scary at all. She reflected on how often she worried about things that never happened and how things she never thought would happen did, yet God always provided the strength needed. She resolved to face each day as a spiritual adventure and see what God would do with their lives.

Once again, Christmas seemed to arrive faster for Vesta. They decorated at home and the store. Christmas parties, programs, and busy days at the store filled the season. Holiday sales were important at the store and came with extra work. Free gift wrapping for customers was also offered, so to save time and stretch dollars, Vesta would take her family gifts and wrap them at the store. When the season was over, Will and Vesta would escape for a few days to someplace warm. One of their favorite places to go, after the last party with their foster family in Southern California, was a nice hotel on Huntington Beach. From there, they would head to El Centro and sometimes Arizona to check on Will's cattle. It was great to have some time for just the two of them. As they grew older, they were always thankful for how much fun they had together.

For several years, they skipped shopping for gifts and took trips to Hawaii with their family, a tradition they tried to do every other year with their children. After the first year of visiting several islands, they would go to their favorite place on Waikiki Beach on Oahu and stay at the Outrigger Hotel for their entire stay. They would get two adjoining rooms, and since each room held three people comfortably, it worked well. Will would carry the single bed for Aaron through the adjoining doorway while the maids giggled and looked the other way. Will always put it back when the trip was over, but it was wonderful for Will and Vesta to have some privacy. When needed, the kids shared Will and Vesta's bathroom, but no one ever complained. This particular year, Aaron was the only one to come since Steven needed to care for the ranch and the girls were married. Aaron had not remembered as many trips as his siblings because of his young age. Will and Vesta decided Aaron needed an extra trip. This time, they were given a suite with two bedrooms and a living room. It also had a large patio overlooking the beach.

During their trips, they took early morning swims, went snorkeling, visited the Polynesian Market Place, went to the North Shore, and watched the huge waves. They also went to the Polynesian Culture Center for the best Hawaiian evening show on the islands. They never tired of enjoying this special place. Maybe it was because it drew them closer as a family or they felt so privileged to go. Their trips to Hawaii were a time in their lives that would always be remembered fondly.

Earlier that same year in 1988, Desirae and Brock came up on their fourth year of marriage while Tommy and Skylar were finishing their first. Desirae and Brock had just discovered they were expecting their first child, and Skylar and Tommy were trying to get pregnant as well. She and Tommy decided they would have children right away so they would be young enough to enjoy them. Late in September, soon after Desirae discovered she was pregnant, Skylar came to the store with yet another pregnancy test. She had been teary-eyed lately because she wasn't getting pregnant. Although she was only a few days late, she decided to test once again.

As she came out of the restroom, Vesta looked at her daughter and guessed what the test results were. Skylar, crying and laughing at the same time, announced, "It's positive!"

Everyone was overjoyed. A few months later, they discovered Skylar was expecting a boy and Desirae a girl, both due in May 1989. Vesta was thrilled to watch the ultrasounds of her first grandchildren. They ordered all the furniture, bedding, and baby items needed from the store. Luckily, Vesta was on the frugal side, which helped her avoid going too far overboard in her purchasing.

May arrived quickly, and everything was ready for the babies. Their rooms were beautiful with lovely bedding. Desirae struggled for weeks with Braxton-Hick's contractions, so when her due date arrived, the doctors induced her labor. After long hours and a difficult birth, little Sienna was born on May 12. Desirae had barely left the hospital when Skylar arrived and birthed Joshua two days later. Her birth also wasn't easy. When the new mothers arrived home, Vesta had two needy daughters on her hands. She jumped right in and spent the morning with one daughter and the afternoon with the other. Somehow, they all made it through that busy time of baby blues and neediness.

Desirae and Skylar never forgot the week Will decided his girls could use some fun during the summer of 1989. They both had tiny babies at home, and Will thought his mother would love to see her new great-grand babies.

One afternoon, the girls stopped by Will and Vesta's, and Will said, "Hey girls, I think we ought to surprise Grandma DeVee with a visit. Also, I think we ought to take in Disneyland! Aaron can come too and help with the babies. We could all take turns going to the park. I might even have a chance to do some book-work in a nice Disney hotel room. What do you think?"

Vesta, who was always up for an adventure said, "That sounds like a great idea! What do you girls think?"

Desirae almost shouted, "Yes, I love Disneyland! Let's do it! I know Grandma DeVee would love to meet our babies."

Skylar agreed. "This sounds like so much fun! I think I could handle it, especially with Aaron along and us taking turns in the park. We'd have to take a lot of supplies along, but I'm up for the challenge!"

It turned out to be a little over the top with newborns and all that was needed for a few days' trip. At the same time, Grandma DeVee was thrilled to see the children with the new great grandbabies, making them glad they came. Some special pictures taken saved the expression of joy on her face. Disneyland was still the happiest place for Aaron and the girls as they took turns enjoying some rides. Will added to their joy by taking them to great places to eat.

For Will and Vesta, learning to be grandparents while their daughters and sons-in-law learned to be parents was challenging at times. When Sienna discovered she could scream at the least little thing and scare the adults, she used this for extra attention. After a few years and a few more grandkids, everyone realized they needed to be more relaxed and not fret so much when the children were fussing in the playroom. Soon enough, Grandma and Grandpa's house was calm and fun when the family gathered there.

It was a busy time, but Will and Vesta both knew it was a special time in their lives. They often discussed how blessed and challenged they felt. In addition to their growing family, they ran two businesses. A banker once told them that beef cattle and retail were two of the hardest businesses to make a consistent profit in, and they were doing just that. There were a lot of ups and downs, but Will and Vesta were risk-takers, and so, with their children, they stuck with it.

The year before their first grandchildren were born, Will decided to build a new home for Vesta. They both loved their fifty-year-old home, but it needed significant repair. Vesta's dad Frank went through the house to see if it was worth remodeling and suggested that they tear it down and start over. There were very large trees planted too close to the house that were uprooting the foundation. Frank advised that it would be more cost-effective to build something new. Will and Vesta agreed and drew up the plans.

The new house was finished as their first grandchildren turned six months. At the time, Will reminded Vesta to never put her beautiful home before her grandchildren. So, when her girls helped her clean and get ready for their first Thanksgiving in their new home, Vesta remained calm when one of the babies spit up on her new carpet. She kept reminding herself that things can always be cleaned or repaired while children took love and patience.

Vesta enjoyed entertaining and taking care of her grandchildren. As their family grew, Will and Vesta were surprised at how full their lives became. They loved babysitting but were also happy that they could send the kids home with their parents.

## CHAPTER 25

# Handling Life Changes

Vesta meditated on God's Word and prepared for her Coffee Break Bible study class. She was so grateful for the women who worked at Honey Bear Kids on Tuesday and Wednesday mornings so she could take part in the class and its leadership team. Although things constantly changed in her life, Vesta knew that God never changes and was always there for her to lean on. Looking back over her life, she pondered how the loss of Will's dad had affected her spiritually. She and Will, along with his family, mourned the loss of his father three years back in July 1986. His death was Vesta's first experience of losing someone close to her, besides her sister's two babies. Thinking of a dear one buried in the ground shook her faith, but after much prayer and reading of God's Word, Vesta was grateful for the peace she received. Vesta knew that her faith was one of the most important things in her life, and every time she experienced another difficulty, she felt it was even more essential. She loved talking to Will about all these feelings and gaining from his wisdom.

After her father-in-law's death, her mother-in-law had a particularly tough time adjusting. Dirk and Annika had shared a long and happy life together, especially in their later years. Their love was deep and strong. They were very dependent on each other. Annika could hardly move out of her grief, but she had a wonderful friend who helped her through this time by visiting often. Her daughter, Henrietta, lived in Escondido and would pick Annika up and bring her to her home for visits. Even though they lived four hours away, Will and Vesta also stopped by as often as they could, as did Isaak and Margot.

Seven years later, Annika celebrated her ninetieth birthday on July 27, 1993. They celebrated her birthday with a party at the Inland Home in Ontario, where Annika lived. Will and Vesta's family, along with Isaak, Margot, and their children, and Case (Henrietta's husband) and Henrietta, with their sons and grandchildren, all came for the party. Vesta was impressed that her mother-in-law made it to ninety. Although Annika seemed frail and had even broken her hip a few years earlier, God had other plans for her. The day was filled with food, laughter, reminiscing, and great all-around family time.

A few months later, Annika showed the first signs of Alzheimer's. It was the start of a rough three years, especially for her daughter Henrietta, who made most of the care decisions. She would call her brothers, Will and Isaak, often, and they would do their best to encourage her. The brothers and their wives would also visit as often as they could. At one point, Annika lost her ability to speak English, which made communicating with her daughters-in-law and grandchildren difficult. Throughout her battle with Alzheimer's, she never forgot her favorite granddaughter, Desirae. They were both kind, gentle spirits, and Desirae adored her grandmother as much as her grandma adored her.

During these same years, Aaron attended Calvin College in Michigan. When he was home on break, he still worked at the children's shop. Vesta enjoyed Aaron so much; in many ways he was still her baby. The funny thing was that he didn't seem to mind when Vesta referred to him as her baby. Each year, when Aaron returned to college, she cried as she waved goodbye to her youngest son. Vesta was certain Aaron would find a Midwestern woman to marry and feared he would settle down there. Despite her fear, Vesta knew she would support Aaron in whatever decision he made since she wanted what was best for her children. She prayed daily for a strong Christian home and spouse for all her children. Will encouraged Vesta in letting go of their children to make their own choices. He was certain they would make good ones.

Will and Vesta's family grew with Skylar and Tommy having another son, Jacob. With two rambunctious boys at home, Skylar had her hands full. Vesta knew it was time to find another house cleaner. When Vesta discussed this with her daughter, all Skylar could do was cry. Skylar wanted to continue doing the cleaning, not only for the money but also to have more social time with her parents. Since she and Tommy planned to have four children close in age, Skylar knew she would eventually need to give up driving to her mom's to clean, but she was sad about it. It ended up working out since, soon after she left, Skylar became the main bookkeeper for Tommy's family's farm.

While all this happened, Steven found a wonderful woman to marry. He went to a young adult bowling night with a friend. They both noticed an extremely attractive young woman who neither of them recognized. They agreed to go together and see if she might be interested in one of them. Steven and his friend shook hands, saying, "May the best man win!" They introduced themselves to Brooke and talked for a bit. After meeting her, Steven was smitten. He came home and told Will and Vesta that he had met the girl he was going to marry.

"Mom, I just met the greatest girl. I think she's perfect for me!" Steven told Vesta as he sat on the counter in the kitchen while she cooked dinner.

"So, what makes her perfect?" Vesta inquired. She loved it when her children shared their deepest feelings with her.

"Well," Steven said thinking out loud, "She's cute and great to talk to. She seems like an awesome Christian woman. You would love her, Mom! Actually, she reminds me a little of you and Skylar."

"I would love to meet her. That is if you go out on a date with her." Vesta couldn't help teasing her son. She was sure Brooke would accept her sweet, handsome son if he asked her out. Not that she was biased, Vesta thought, laughing to herself.

After Brooke went on a date with him, Steven complained to his mom and dad, "Can you believe it? She said she only wants to be friends. I'm not looking for a friend, I'm looking for a wife to be my best friend."

"Give her time. I'm sure it will turn out in the end. Make it a matter of prayer as well, Steven. This is an important decision in your life. You don't want to take it too lightly." Vesta trusted her son, but she trusted God more and knew He would open or close the door for Steven and Brooke.

Will agreed, "It will work out, Steven, if she's the right one for you."

While these things happened, Desirae gave birth to her second child. Sienna turned four a few weeks after her darling brother, Brody, was born on April 30, 1993. As with all her grandchildren, Vesta helped out for the first week after Brody's birth.

Once Desirae took her six weeks off, she, Sienna, and Brody were with Vesta every day at the store. Vesta was able to help with all her grandchildren from time to time, but since she worked with Desirae, she did end up seeing her children quite frequently. Brody would end up at his grandma's house when Sienna was in school and Desirae was working. Vesta would do her bookwork while she cared for little Brody. As a toddler, Brody would ask Vesta to walk him to the river (the water canal in the field about a quarter mile away) so he could throw a rock in the "riber." Brody also loved having stories read to him, but if it was naptime, he would cry, "No," because he knew he would fall fast asleep and miss the end of the story.

Soon after Brody was born, Skylar became pregnant with her third child. Beautiful, strong-willed Elizabeth was born almost a year after Brody on March 29, 1994. Brody used to beg Elizabeth to play with him when they were both toddlers, but she was rarely interested. She had a mind of her own. Elizabeth loved horses and started vaulting with her cousins at a very young age.

On August 6, 1994, Steven and Brooke were married. Vesta, Desirae, and Skylar had a great time helping Brooke with all the arrangements. Steven asked Aaron to be his best man while Desirae, Skylar, and their husbands were also in the wedding party. Joshua and Jacob were charming ringbearers, and Sienna, an adorable flower girl. It was a beautiful day for the church ceremony and reception in Will and Vesta's backyard.

Vesta was thrilled when Will offered the yard for the reception since it provided the excuse to finish their landscaping. Initially, there was a big expense putting in a beautiful rod-iron fence with brick posts around both their lot and pool area. Now, almost four years later, they were going to put in the grass with a sprinkler system along with trees and flower beds.

Vesta was beyond excited to design and plan how it would look. Since it was a very large project, it took until a week before the wedding to finish. They all breathed a sigh of relief when the final flowers and plants went in.

After their wedding, Will and Vesta were glad Brooke and Steven came over often to learn and grow in their relationship. They both valued spending this time with the newlyweds.

Will and Vesta never tired of enjoying the grandchildren and seeing them change as they grew. They were also happy to shower love on the grandbabies and be available to babysit as needed. It always made them laugh with how exhausted they'd feel when they had the grandchildren stay overnight. "How did we ever manage to raise our own kids? Why does this feel so much more tiring?" Will chuckled as he waved goodbye to the kids one evening.

During these years, their children with their families came over about once a month. Vesta loved cooking yummy meals for them while Will spent time playing outdoor games with his sons, sons-in-law, and grandkids. He had put in a basketball court with one end that had a short hoop that could be raised as the children grew and the other end with an adult height hoop. Between the court, pool, and large backyard, everyone played for hours. Another outdoor game they often played was Wiffleball. The rules were like baseball, except that Wiffleball used a lightweight, plastic ball instead of a baseball or softball. This way, no one had to worry about breaking any windows.

In June 1995, just before her ninety-third birthday, Annika DeVee went home to meet her Lord after a bout with pneumonia. Vesta remembers Annika's death being easier to handle than Dirk's. Maybe it was because Annika had declined so much with Alzheimer's and was now reunited with Dirk in heaven. Or, maybe it was because, at the gravesite looking up at the sky, Vesta profoundly felt the presence of God. God's presence gave her absolute reassurance that her family lived on, even if they were no longer visible on earth.

Steven and Brooke started their family a few years later. At the same time, Skylar was pregnant with her fourth child and Desirae with her third. It was a busy time for Vesta, who cherished babysitting as often as she could. Things were so busy that she realized something needed to change. When Desirae became pregnant again, Vesta recognized it was time to sell the store. It was a heartbreaking decision for both Vesta and Desirae.

"Mom, are you really sure you want to give up the store?" Desirae tried to reason with her mom. "We've had such a great time buying merchandise, traveling together, and getting to know our customers. Our customers will be so upset if we sell. Maybe I can get a babysitter more often."

"It's been fifteen good years, and Dad even told me I built our new home from the store's profit." Vesta appreciated the encouragement from Will that those fifteen years weren't wasted. Will was always a great help to Vesta with her emotional highs and lows. He was continually strong and calm, especially compared to Vesta's excitable nature. "I'm just getting tired of all the work it takes to run the store. I know we have great help, which I am thankful for, but I still have to come in every Saturday. Sherry mentioned that she might be interested in buying the store. If that happens, you could be an awesome support for her," Vesta replied, trying to help Desirae understand. Sherry was a friend and customer who loved shopping in their store. Vesta knew that she and her husband were financially able to purchase the store if they were interested.

In the end, Sherry didn't buy the store. After talking to a friend who recently sold her children's shop in Southern California, Will and Vesta prepared to sell out. They began advertising in October and November and were able to close the store by year-end.

During the last few years of owning the store, Vesta was also busy helping her parents. Her mom was diagnosed with Alzheimer's disease and her dad with prostate cancer. Vesta spoke to Frank often now that Johanna was easily confused and tended to repeat herself. Vesta felt guilty that Johanna frustrated her when they talked, so she would gently ask, "Mom is Dad at home? Could I talk to him a minute?"

"Why do you want to talk to Dad?" Johanna would reply. "I want to talk to you right now!"

"Okay, what do you want to tell me?" Vesta asked patiently.

"Well, I don't know. Oh, alright, here's your dad. He keeps standing over me," Johanna responded angrily. "I bet you two just want to talk about me."

It was a similar conversation whenever Vesta tried to talk with her dad. She sympathized with him as he tried to keep Johanna out of trouble and dealt with his cancer. She called frequently and tried to visit as often as possible. She and Will discussed the possibility of moving them to Visalia. Will was even open to building a small home for them in the corner of their one-acre lot. In the end, it turned out that their health insurance was only available in Southern California. It also didn't seem fair to take them away from their doctors and other caregivers or their church, which was full of close friends who had supported them throughout their lives.

The doctors told Vesta's father that his prostate cancer would be easy to cure. Radiation and some chemo usually eliminated it. They advised Frank not to have surgery and just do radiation therapy. The radiation made Frank so ill he asked to stop the treatment.

A friend of Frank's thought that he needed a second opinion, so he took Frank to a doctor at UCLA. The doctor told Frank he looked great and should enjoy life. Vesta thought this was good advice and asked her parents, "How would you like to visit Peter and Sara in Washington and stop at your sister Jackie's in Idaho? You and I could share the driving, Dad. What do you think?"

Frank was up for the challenge, "That sounds wonderful, Vesta. Let's go! I'll get in touch with my sister and make sure she is home then."

Will thought it would be great for Vesta to take this trip with her parents. They left in June to enjoy the lovely weather. Johanna's mind was not working well; she kept thinking they were traveling through Michigan. By this time, Vesta had learned it was better to be patient and agree with her mother than to try to explain and make her upset.

Their first night in Bend Oregon did not go well since Frank started feeling uncomfortable. Vesta carried all of the suitcases up two flights of stairs while she persuaded Johanna not to follow her. The next day, they arrived safely at Sara and Peter's house in Sunnyside, Washington. They went to bed early to get a good night's sleep with the hope of attending church with Peter and Sara the next day.

Early the next morning, Frank thought he was having a heart attack and needed to go to the emergency room. After they finished all of their tests and didn't find anything, they sent him home again. By Monday, Frank wasn't feeling much better and wanted to head home. Vesta was sorry they couldn't stay longer but knew her dad did not complain needlessly.

After they arrived in Visalia, Will offered to drive her parents' home but Frank was sure he could manage the drive. After hitting a major traffic jam, Frank and Johanna finally arrived home five hours late with Vesta beside herself with worry. They had no cell phones to check on them. That same night, Frank could no longer handle the pain and called an ambulance. They called Vesta the next morning. Fortunately, Terri was able to take care of Johanna until Vesta arrived.

This was when the doctors discovered the tumor on his spine. Although they tried to remove the tumor, they were only able to relieve Frank's pain. After the surgery, he was never able to walk again and spent his last year in a wheelchair. Vesta was beside herself, trying to keep things running smoothly at home and the store while running back and forth to her parents.

She came home one evening and made dinner for her and Will. As they sat and enjoyed their food, she poured out her heart, "Honey, this is so hard. I don't know if I should be closer to my parents or what."

"It's alright, honey, we will get through this. God will lead us day by day. Right now, Terri is willing to help, which is wonderful. You can go anytime you feel you should. If I can go, I will too," Will encouraged.

She was so grateful to have Terri, her foster daughter, living close to her parents and being willing to spend time with Johanna. Terri took her to visit Frank in the hospital when Vesta wasn't available. Sara and Rachel also came to help and were able to encourage Frank during this difficult time. Since Frank had seen so many friends endure chemotherapy and die anyway, Frank chose to go on hospice. Fortunately, Vesta found a Christian-skilled nursing home for Frank and Johanna to live together in one large room. She never forgot sitting outside the home and crying out to God for help. When she went in to talk with the director, she learned that a large room had just opened that would work great for both her parents. She knew that God was watching over them. Vesta loved that her parents could be together, and their church friends visited often.

During this time, Johanna couldn't understand why the nurses constantly looked in on Frank. She was convinced they were trying to steal her Frank from her. Thankfully, as time went by, Johanna fell into the routine.

As Vesta supported her parents' transition to their new life, Skylar and Tommy were expecting their fourth child. One morning in spring, April 17, 1996, Sharyl Desirae came into the world. Sharyl weighed six pounds three ounces. She was the smallest of Skylar and Tommy's children. Being tiny and short, and a little shy by nature, she had inherited traits from both families. She turned into a darling bundle of energy as she grew and often ran circles around her cousins and friends.

Along with joy comes sorrow; there is life, and there is death. Frank went home to be with his Lord on May 7, 1996, which happened to be Will's birthday. It would be an easy date to remember, Vesta thought. Vesta missed him so much but was glad Johanna was settled in a good place to live. Her poor mother hardly knew what happened at the memorial service. She asked Vesta when Vesta was bringing her back to the home, "See all the beautiful flowers on the trees. Is it Easter?"

Vesta replied gently, "No, but those are such beautiful flowers."

In retrospect, Vesta wasn't certain how she managed during that emotional time. She did know that God walked beside her and gave her strength she didn't know she had. Will and Vesta, with their children, along with all her siblings and their families, enjoyed a time of shared memories after the service in a reserved room at the hotel they all were staying at. The service itself took place in Frank and Johanna's church in Bellflower, California.

The summer seemed to pass swiftly, and it was again time for Aaron to pack up for his last year at Calvin College. Vesta couldn't believe how rapidly the time had passed and secretly hoped he would come back home to live after graduation.

The week before Aaron left for college, they worked late every night at the store, getting ready for the sellout. Vesta would often be the last to leave, and on weekends, Will would take her to dinner. On this particular Friday, Vesta was behind on bookwork, so she let the others know she was staying at the store for another hour to finish up before Saturday.

Soon after everyone left, Vesta's phone rang. "Hi, honey, what's up? I asked Aaron to tell you I'd be late. Did he let you know?"

Will choose his words carefully. "Yes, he did. Actually, why don't you come on home? We'll get a bite to eat and then we can stop back at the store, and I'll help you with that bookwork."

"Oh, that sounds so wonderful!" Vesta quickly replied. She loved having a cozy evening with Will, so she hurried to pack up her things, locked up the store, and headed home.

On her drive home, she sang praise songs, enjoying the sight of the open fields on a hot summer night. As she turned down her road, Vesta noticed cars parked close to her home. *That's odd, probably just some people working in the field*, she thought to herself.

As she drove closer, she saw people running in the road with big "Happy 50th Birthday" signs. It turned out that her children decided to throw Vesta an early surprise party before Aaron left for college. Since it was an entire month before her big day, they knew Vesta wouldn't expect it, and they were right; she was totally surprised! The evening celebration with family and friends was wonderful. Will enjoyed watching his shocked wife, although he worried he hadn't sounded very convincing when he had called her to come home. Later that evening, as they crawled into bed together, Vesta assured him that she was extremely surprised by the party. They felt life couldn't get much better for them.

Soon it was time to wave goodbye to Aaron. Later that night, as Vesta wiped her tears away, she prayed for his safety on the long drive to Michigan. Although Aaron was gone, life never slowed down much for Will and Vesta. Another granddaughter, Amanda Joy, was born on September 8, 1996, and Joseph Caleb arrived just three weeks later, on September 27. Once again, Vesta was delighted to help with her new grandchildren. Vesta wasn't quite sure if her daughter-in-law wanted her assistance with Amanda or if she preferred to just have her own mother helping. When Vesta talked to Brooke about it, she enthusiastically accepted Vesta's offer saying, "Oh, Mom please come! My mom works during the day and doesn't know as much about this as you do. This is also her first grandchild, so I'm definitely going to need your help!"

Will and Vesta were thrilled to welcome more grandchildren into their lives. They were also very thankful for their rather large home and yard. It was a delightful place to create memories of family dinners and parties with their children and their growing families.

Vesta enjoyed helping Brooke with Amanda, who was the most darling curly-haired blonde and blue-eyed baby. Brooke was eager to care for her baby properly, but as with most new moms, it involved a steep, learning curve. Since Brooke had a difficult childhood, she decided to go to professional counseling to help her become the mother she wanted to be. Steven also went to counseling with Brooke so they could understand some of the negative experiences she had as a child and how they could approach and overcome them together.

By the time Joseph Caleb was born, Brooke was ready to go it on her own so Vesta could have time for Desirae and little darling Joseph. It was over a weekend, so Vesta had fun making a nice Sunday brunch for the family. Desirae and Brock had a new learning curve with the life changes of three children. Thankfully, little Joseph was an easy baby, and a big sister was a wonderful help.

The year ended with the closing of Honey Bear Kids. Vesta couldn't help but feel relieved. The store had become a burden in many ways. So many changes in her life hadn't helped. Losing her dad and feeling the pressure to visit her mom enough was always at the back of her mind, not to mention having enough time to enjoy her now eight grandchildren. She was happy to lose the extra responsibility of running a business. It ended up working out well. Since Will didn't like using computers, Vesta learned to pay the business bills and do the payroll for DeVee Cattle Co. on the computer.

It began a new era in the DeVee family. They no longer owned a children's shop, but as their family and the cattle business grew, new surprises lay ahead.

## CHAPTER 26

# More Babies

With eight grandchildren, Vesta never stopped marveling at how different they were from each other. She was also surprised at how exciting each new birth was. They had a nice mix of boys and girls—Desirae and Brock with Sienna and Brody, and now little Joseph, while Skylar and Tommy were enjoying Joshua, Jacob, and their girls, Elizabeth and Sharyl. Brooke and Steven had a sweet little cutie in Amanda. And although Sienna prayed for a little sister, she decided her baby brother Joseph was special to help with.

During these years, Vesta and Will praised God for the wonderful blessings of healthy grandchildren, their married children living nearby, and the cattle business doing well. Even though life always had trials, they knew they had much to be grateful for.

Desirae wisely shared with her mother, "You know, Mom, I'm starting to realize that we get trials, and then we get a rest or good times for a while, but we need to stay alert for the next trial. This is why you always told us to stay close to God. I see now, we can't do life alone."

Vesta agreed completely with her daughter. They had both experienced many ups and downs in life. They knew God was good, held them up in difficult times, and gave them plenty to rejoice over.

The next few months were busy ones for Will and Vesta with Palm Sunday and Easter. Will was busy with spring cattle sales and shipping his hill cattle. Together, they were involved in various programs at their church and school. Vesta also led the church drama program at the Visalia Christian Reformed Church. She found a good play for Easter and gently persuaded people to play the different roles. When Vesta first started, the plays were held on Easter Sunday evening, later they moved to one of the Sunday morning services.

With Vesta so busy on Easter Sundays, Will and Vesta started a new tradition of having their children and grandchildren over on Palm Sunday to celebrate Easter. After Easter service, the two of them would take a hike and have a picnic lunch together. They loved both celebrating with family on Palm Sunday and enjoying each other while their children spent Easter with their in-laws.

Will and Vesta enjoyed hiking and biking together. Vesta also liked to run. As they hiked more often together, Will and Vesta became familiar with the beautiful mountains and Redwood and Sequoia forests, which were only two hours away. They also explored biking trails during their trips to Idaho each September. On their way to Idaho, they spent a day or two at Lake Tahoe and rented bikes. It was always challenging for Vesta to ride her bike up the hills. Most of the time she made it, but now and then, she ended up walking the bike. Will was tough and rode up the hills, where he patiently waited for Vesta. What Vesta couldn't understand was how sore her legs were after their rides while, since neither of them rode at home, Will's didn't seem to hurt at all. She decided her husband was a natural strong athlete as she remembered when she taught Will to play tennis. In the beginning, Vesta won a few games, but soon, he was winning almost every game. It was a good way to stay humble, Vesta decided.

A short fifteen months later after Amanda Joy was born, January 17, 1997, Steven and Brooke welcomed their second daughter. Janelle Skylar was a demanding child as dark as her sister was blonde, with big brown eyes and cute as a button. When she was young, Janelle stomped her feet and screamed when she didn't get her way. Brooke quickly became the family disciplinarian, and before going to counseling, she had a hard time understanding how to properly show love to her girls. Thankfully, the girls were still young, Amanda was two, and Janelle was almost a year when Brooke worked with her counselor and became a remarkable mother.

As the years went by, Brooke and Steven began to open their home to children from disadvantaged backgrounds. Will and Vesta were continually impressed by how much room they had in their hearts for whoever needed their love. God had clearly given the gift of loving to them both.

As their family grew, Will and Vesta prayed for them daily. Although there wasn't anything she could control, Vesta wished she could and occasionally tried. Will was very helpful when Vesta would unburden her worries on him. Will knew how to direct her to let go and allow her children to make their own choices or mistakes. She realized that prayer was the best method of sheltering her family with God's direction and love. His perfect love was more valuable than her flawed love. Vesta also had a habit of opening her mouth and inserting her foot. She often found herself apologizing and wishing she wouldn't make the same mistakes over and over again.

After Janelle's birth in January, they learned that Desirae and Brock were pregnant with their fourth child. Having grown up in a family of four and both girls having four children, Will and Vesta laughed that their children must really like the number four. Colt Steven was born on July 24, 1998. As Will and Vesta visited in the hospital room, holding him, Vesta thought that Colt was one of the most beautiful newborns she had ever seen. Poor Sienna wanted a little sister in the worse way but quickly became the passionate leader of her three younger brothers. They all adored her and enjoyed being led by her. She became a great helper for Desirae as the boys grew, and their family life was full and busy.

During these years, Desirae worked a variety of jobs to help supplement the family income. With four small children at home, having a job was difficult, but thanks to Will and Vesta helping where they could, especially with childcare, she was able to try various things. At one point, Desirae hosted parties and particularly enjoyed selling Pampered Chef products. She loved cooking and baking, so it was straightforward for her to encourage women to buy products for something she enjoyed.

Finally, as DeVee Cattle Company grew, Desirae started working in the office. Desirae liked working with her father and brother while they, in turn, appreciated her business skills and ability to be economical. She oversaw ordering supplies and always managed to find what they needed at the best price. While Desirae worked for the family business, Brock pursued a master's degree in education. After receiving his degree, he worked for many years as a teacher and then a principal at various schools.

At the same time, Skylar and Tommy were doing well working with his family at Ridder Farm. Skylar was skilled with the computer, and with her strong leadership skills, she soon became the head bookkeeper there. She and Tommy often used their gifts at their church as well. Vesta was impressed at Skylar's ability to lead large groups of children at Vacation Bible School. One year, in only a week's time, she had 200 children singing together and putting on a wonderful program for their parents.

Will and Vesta were so proud and thankful for their children. They often wondered how they were so blessed. Not that there weren't problems, but they seemed to get through things together, even though tears came. As their family grew, they hoped they could afford a trip to Hawaii with the entire family; they also wanted to take this trip before the grandchildren were too old and no longer wanted to go.

CHAPTER 27

# Wedding Celebration

It was the year 2000, and leading up to the new millennium, people feared that the power would go out on January 1, 2000. Vesta didn't understand why this was a worldwide concern, so she asked Will about it.

"What does this all mean, sweetie?"

Will calmly answered, "From what I understand, the power grids around the world are run by computers that don't recognize dates after 1999. Truth is, I think it's all being blown out of proportion. I'm sure everyone's working hard to make the necessary changes to the computer systems in time."

Since Will was always levelheaded, Vesta thought he was probably right. The end-of-the-world pastors and other Armageddon worriers were having a field day with all the negative possibilities. Vesta prayed during this time to calm herself and knew that if the power grid went down, God was still in control.

The big day came while everyone watched the first country, Australia, enter the year 2000. Everyone was relieved when Australia's power grid didn't miss a beat.

*Well, so much for the end of the world,* Vesta thought and then said aloud, "Lord, You have shown me once again not to worry about something before it happens. We must always wait upon You and watch what You will do." She cherished talking to God as if He was in the room with her.

Around the same time, Aaron worked for a local Christian radio station and moved to his own place. He valued his DJ job and had a great voice for the work. His childhood dream had come true. He really appreciated that he could do what he loved since he knew people didn't always get that privilege.

The winter and spring months were again filled with busy times for the DeVee family. Before they knew it, summer and the valley heat came with its triple digits. Every summer, Aaron's radio station took part in "Spirit West Coast." It was a fun event on the central California coast when radio stations brought together Christian singing groups, known and unknown. It also offered a time to escape the heat of the valley. Lots of volunteers were needed to help with the extra work. One of Aaron's friends from the station invited her friend, Christine Hawkins, to come along.

After the weekend, Aaron told Will and Vesta, "I think I met the girl I'm going to marry! Her name is Christine Hawkins. You might be surprised, Mom and Dad. Maybe it seems quick to make that statement, but I'm so attracted to her personality and looks. She is such a fantastic Christian woman."

"That's all that's needed. We'll see how your relationship develops from here. Your dad and I will pray for the right things to happen," Vesta replied. She could hardly contain her excitement for Aaron.

The year 2000 also brought Will and Vesta another darling granddaughter, Casandra Danielle. Casandra was Steven and Brooke's third daughter and was born on December 1, 2000, another beauty with large round brown eyes and a calm demeanor. It was a joy for Vesta to help Brooke take care of her newborn and older daughters as needed.

Christmas season arrived, and with it, a lot of time to enjoy their children and grandchildren. Vesta loved finding everyone's special gifts and decorating the house. Her favorite thing to do was dress the grandkids in costumes and have them perform a short Christmas play. Will would read the story while the children, under Vesta's direction, acted out their parts. It was a special way to help the children learn about Christ's birth. They would sing praise songs and have a prayer time led by Will. Then it was time for food and gifts.

"Oh my, that was wonderful," Vesta said to Will after the children left. "It is so much work, but I love watching everyone have a fun time together."

"I agree," Will said. "I've been thinking about taking all of them to Hawaii next Christmas before the grandkids get too old and too busy with their own lives. What do you think, honey?"

"That would be so wonderful! Do you think we can afford it?" Vesta was excited but tried to think practically.

"I think we could do it. God has been good to us this year. There are always things to save for or improve and spend on business things, but I think we should just take the time to do this," Will said with determination. "Life can change so quickly, and then the window of opportunity is gone."

The year 2001 dawned brightly, and Vesta began to research, taking the entire family to Hawaii. She knew Aaron was getting serious with Christine, and she was looking forward to their wedding as well.

The months flew by, and Christine and Aaron fell deeply in love. They set their wedding date for July 6, 2001. Christine was a grade school teacher, so she finished her school year with just enough time for any last-minute planning. The wedding ceremony took place at their Visalia CRC church with the reception at Vesta and Will's home, but this time, Vesta was able to plant lots of flowers in the yard. She appreciated the extra quiet time down on her knees and planted them with joy in her heart and thankfulness to the Lord. Will and Vesta had learned many things after having Steven and Brooke's wedding reception in their yard.

Everything was ready with the wedding day fast approaching. The month of July started with a heat wave. Fortunately, they found umbrellas to set up for the guests, but then, on the morning of the wedding, it began to rain and pour.

Vesta couldn't believe it. "How can this be happening?" she cried to Will. "It never rains here in July. We need to pray right now!" Vesta and Will got down on their knees, begging God to make this a beautiful day for the wedding.

It stopped raining, and though the sun didn't come out, it cooled down quite a bit, and the cloud cover in the evening allowed for beautiful pictures and mild temperatures for everyone to enjoy. The umbrellas weren't needed after all since the Lord provided His own umbrella of clouds.

The next day, both Will and Vesta spent substantial time thanking God for answering their prayers. They knew that not every prayer gets answered exactly the way one thinks it should.

When Will and Vesta reflected on their lives, they realized how much they had to thank God for. Their youngest son, just married, planned to settle down nearby. The rest of their children with their eleven grandchildren all lived close as well. They remembered the joy in their hearts when each of their children came to know that Jesus was their Savior and professed their belief at church. They all married spouses who believed, and they found good churches to attend.

Steven and Skylar, with their families, attended the same church as Will and Vesta, which they considered a special blessing, while Desirae and Brock attended another strong Christian church in Visalia, and Aaron and Christine decided to go to the church of her family background in Visalia; also, a solid Christian church.

With all four of their children living on their own, Vesta and Will's home was busier than ever. The kids came over for every occasion and joined for dinner whenever Vesta called to say there was extra food available. Since her mother worked outside the home and she grew up eating fast food, Brooke, in particular, appreciated the opportunity to learn how to cook and entertain from Vesta. The grandchildren also enjoyed coming to Grandma's house to play with their cousins whenever possible.

Will and Vesta had more time to travel and were glad that they could leave Steven in charge of the ranch. When they traveled, they often combined business and pleasure. Every fall, for example, Will went to the cattle sales in Orland and Cottonwood, California. Will and Vesta would usually stay in Redding for two nights during the trip.

Vesta loved traveling with Will and would take projects along to keep herself busy while she waited in the car at the cattle sales. Since she led a Bible study, she would use the time to prepare her lessons for the Tuesday class. During cattle sales in mid-November, Vesta completed addressing her Christmas cards and even went Christmas shopping in Redding.

When they traveled together to ship cattle out of New Meadows, Idaho, they started hiking there. They always stayed in McCall at a lovely hotel right on the lake. On their first hike in the area, they noticed a sign recommending a one-mile trail nearby. They both thought, "No problem. We run five miles all the time."

What they didn't realize was that this trail was one mile downhill over rough terrain, and then they had to hike back up again. Vesta wore boat sneakers with no socks, and Will wore his good tennis shoes. At the bottom, they arrived at some beautiful falls. Unfortunately for Vesta, large blisters had developed on her heels, and they still had to climb back up. Will gave her his socks, which helped and, thankfully, his feet were in good shape after the climb up. Vesta, on the other hand, could hardly walk for three days. Despite this difficult lesson, they both realized they enjoyed hiking.

On their way back home, Will and Vesta found a sporting goods store and purchased proper hiking equipment. They discovered wonderful hiking areas nearby Sequoia National Park and soon overcame their fear of heights and learned to maneuver rocky terrain. When they hiked the Marble Falls trail in Sequoia, a 2,000-foot climb and almost four miles long one way, they were thrilled. Regardless of where they hiked, they always made sure to carry plenty of water and snacks or lunch so they could take their time and enjoy God's wonderful creation.

Once, a few years prior, during a trip to Idaho in September, it was unusually hot, still in the 90s. They decided to go white water rafting and looked in the telephone book for places to call about a possible trip. They soon found a place in Riggins, about an hour away, where they could take a half-day rafting trip.

"Oh look, Will," Vesta said. "You can ship cattle in the morning, and then we can drive over for the rafting trip. I really want to try this, but I'm nervous about it. I'm afraid of falling overboard and getting caught in a rapid. Maybe, since it's September already, the rapids won't be as wild."

When they arrived for the rafting trip, Vesta's heart beat rapidly as she asked the girl, "Are the rapids calmer since it's the end of the summer?"

"Well," the girl answered, "the Salmon River water is actually rougher this time of year since there is less of it."

*Yikes!* Vesta thought to herself, but she really wanted to try rafting at least once. She also noticed that Will seemed calm, which helped settle her nerves.

As they boarded the raft, Vesta was still shaking. She thought they sat on the floor of the raft, where the big puffy sides would protect and keep them in the raft. However, after they got in the raft, they were told to sit on the sides while balancing with their paddle to help steer the raft over rapids. Then, just before they took off and started down the river, a few people in kayaks floated by. Suddenly, one of the kayaks flipped upside down. Vesta never saw the woman flip back up, so with that scary sight at the top of her mind, they headed down the river.

It seemed that only a minute went by when their guide started yelling, "We're coming to our first rapid; get your oars ready."

Vesta felt her heart pounding and braced herself. One leg was against the rafting side and the other on the side of the ice chest that contained snacks and drinks for later in the journey. Will and Vesta were both nervous but looked at each other with excitement as well.

That first rapid was so much fun. Vesta had the perfect spot to sit and stay balanced. As the water splashed into the boat, she found herself completely soaked, which was perfect for a ninety-degree day. When the guide said "smile" for their picture going through another rapid, Vesta was ready. She even used that picture on their next Christmas card. After they returned to the hotel, Vesta realized how tense she was on the trip when a large bruise appeared on her leg where it was anchored against the ice chest. She and Will agreed the bruise was worth it as they both loved the trip.

## CHAPTER 28
# The Year of Armageddon

T he year 2001 was passing quickly with Aaron and Christine's wedding in July and the grandchildren growing up. Will had told Vesta he wanted to take all his children and grandchildren to Hawaii that year. Vesta worked diligently with their travel agent to schedule their trip to Hawaii in December. Everyone was thrilled and put plans in place for their days away from work.

Suddenly, it was September again, and Will and Vesta were excited to take a break together to ship their cattle grazing on grass from a lush mountain valley in New Meadows, Idaho. On their way out of California, they stayed at their favorite spot in Lake Tahoe. They loved bike riding along one side of the lake and doing some hiking or rafting. After their usual two-night stay, they started their drive to Idaho to the Bear Creek Lodge. They found this lodge when their favorite one on the lake closed for remodeling. The Bear Creek Lodge offered wonderful meals, including a free, full-course breakfast. The only drawback was no television or outside communication in the rooms.

Will left early to ship cattle the following morning. Vesta woke around seven, taking her time with devotions and getting ready for the day. As she ate her breakfast, the waiter mentioned that the Pentagon had just been bombed and how the world was at a standstill. Vesta only half-listened and thought he must be joking. She finished her meal and left, not having the faintest idea what the waiter was talking about.

When Will returned to the room, he shared with Vesta the full story of what was happening.

"Vesta, have you heard about all that is going on?"

"Well, no, the waiter was telling me some things, but I didn't quite understand."

"Honey, the World Trade Center had two planes fly into them. They both collapsed, and there was another plane that flew into the Pentagon. Our government is in an uproar, and all airplanes worldwide are grounded," Will shared quickly.

"WHAT! Then what the waiter said was true! Without a way to watch the news, I had no idea," Vesta answered with uncertainty rising in her voice. Finally, she said, "Do you think we should see if we can get to another hotel, so we have a TV and the ability to keep up with what is going on?"

"Yes, absolutely. I must know for the shipping of our cattle as well. They may be closing roads, so it would be good to have more information available to us," Will stated as he went to talk to the person in charge.

Vesta followed and said, "I'm worried about the kids. Let's call them later and see how they are all doing." Will agreed, and soon they were moving their belongings to another hotel.

It was a crazy and scary time. They were a long way from home and were anxious to talk to their family back in Visalia. Vesta and Will decided to move to another hotel in New Meadows. It was also closer to the area where Will was shipping his cattle if the roads stayed open. When they arrived at the new hotel, they stayed in their room and watched the news for the rest of the day.

The day was September 11, 2001. Vesta and everyone she knew remembered where they were and what they were doing. The world stood still, and it was the closest thing to an Armageddon that Vesta ever experienced. It was the beginning of the war on terror. She watched as people turned to God and filled churches across the nation. Fear was everywhere, Vesta would wake up in the middle of the night over the next few months, thinking she heard a loud warning siren of some sort. Once again, Vesta tried hard to turn her fears over to God.

This day was not soon forgotten. It resulted in so many changes to a country that had considered itself free. Slowly, freedoms were taken away to keep terrorists out of the US and other countries. There was constant news from the Middle East of terrorist plots against the US. Some succeeded, and others failed. Somehow, over time, life returned to normal for Will and Vesta.

The events of 9/11 brought the DeVee family closer to God and helped them live life to the fullest. They focused on doing the best they could and to let go and let God.

No one wants to reminisce over the story of Job and how God tested him by taking his family and business away from him in one day. However, Job is a good reminder that, sometimes, when God tests us, He has a purpose and plan. As with Job, God doesn't always explain why. Will and Vesta realized that people wouldn't understand God if He did explain Himself. Then, they decided, He wouldn't be God.

During the years after 9/11, Vesta and Will read many moving stories about the tragedy. It was sad to hear how many lives were lost as the two large skyscrapers came crashing down in New York City. Vesta couldn't imagine what it was like for those who had to return to their jobs in the city. They later learned of the heroic efforts made by men on another plane taken over by terrorists who had planned to crash into the White House. The heroes forced the plane to crash in an open field instead, killing everyone on the plane.

Over time, hearts began to heal, especially when the trouble seemed more contained and controlled. The churches went back to their regular attendees, and people went on living their lives.

That year ended with the entire DeVee family going to Hawaii right after Christmas. Will asked Vesta to plan one main outing for the whole family. He wanted them to be free to also do their own thing. When they arrived and were settled in their rooms, they heard about a breakfast that would help them plan some tours. Their daughters, along with Will and Vesta, attended the breakfast.

Skyler was excited. "Let's go snorkeling at this bay. It sounds like a blast! And look, we need to go to the Polynesian Culture Center. Look, we could also do this Luau."

"I'm in," said Desirae, knowing her family loved the beach and water along with going to exciting places.

Will added, "Those ideas are great. We also need to get tickets to see the Arizona Memorial. It is such a moving experience; one I know the children could learn from."

"Yes, good idea," both girls agreed.

Steven and Brooke had their hands full with a one-year-old, but everyone took turns playing with little Casandra. The children especially enjoyed the beach, digging big holes to sit in, or making a sandcastle. Swimming at Waikiki Beach, which was right outside their hotel, the Outrigger, was the best. The water was warm and shallow in areas, making it great for the little ones to swim.

Will and Vesta also treated their kids with a date night while they did kid duty. They had their hands full and were thankful for the older grandchildren who helped them.

Aaron and Christine felt like it was their second honeymoon since they were married only six months before. Watching his siblings with their children, Aaron enjoyed his time with his new bride. After having paid for the honeymoon himself, it was a treat to enjoy his dad's generosity on this trip.

Will was surprised that the kids and grandkids wanted to do almost everything together. They also took time to meet during their ten days together in one of their rooms to have devotions. A different family was in charge each time they gathered. They sang, prayed, and shared a special scripture and devotion. The devotions helped powerfully at one point when there was a misunderstanding. That time, devotions started with tears and ended with hugs and forgiveness.

Everyone especially relished getting on a tour bus and watching people marvel at all twenty-one of them. It thrilled Will to see that his kids and grandkids loved this time together as much as he hoped they would. They all realized it was more than just being in a beautiful, warm place in the middle of winter—although that helped—it was more about being together and sharing family love. They all knew these special times would always be cherished.

Will looked forward to planning more of these adventures for his family. He prayed God would open the door to make it possible.

# CHAPTER 29
## More of Life and Love

It was now 2003, and Aaron and Christine were expecting their first child while Steven and Brooke were expecting their fourth. They were both due in September, a common month for DeVee babies to be born.

Will and Vesta were always nearby when their grandchildren were born. This year, however, looked to be the exception since their due dates coincided with their cattle shipping trip to Idaho. Thankfully, when September came, both babies were due to arrive after the shipping time in Idaho was over. In fact, Will and Vesta were packing up to head home when they got the call.

"Hi, Mom. We're going to the hospital in a bit. Brooke's water broke, but she isn't having a lot of pain yet. The doctor figures it will start soon," Steven told his mom.

"Oh, that's so exciting! Please call us, even if it starts in the middle of the night. If I don't pick up, leave a message." Vesta was excited and sad at the same time. This would be the first of her grandchildren that she wouldn't see at the hospital right after birth.

Vesta slept fitfully waiting for Steven's call. The longer she waited, the more she prayed, trying hard not to worry that something was wrong. Finally, at about 5:30 a.m., she woke with Will and said, "I can't stand to wait. It's a long time for a fourth child to be born. Do you think I should call Steven?"

Will replied, "Yes, I'm surprised too. Steven hasn't called yet. Go ahead. Let's find out what's happening."

Vesta quickly dialed Steven's number, "Hi, Mom. It's another girl. She's beautiful and looks like Brooke. She was born around 1:00 a.m. Brooke did great and is doing awesome except we're tired since we've been up all night. Thankfully, her mom's staying with her so I can go home and get some sleep."

With relief in her voice, Vesta replied, "That's wonderful. Give Brooke our love and give your little Ariel lots of kisses for us. I can't wait to see her." Will and Vesta couldn't be angry their son hadn't called. They knew having babies took a lot of focus, and time could pass more quickly than anyone realized.

After two seemingly endless days of travel, Will and Vesta arrived home, quickly unpacked, and went to see their new granddaughter. Ariel was as beautiful as Steven claimed. Once again, Vesta was able to help Brooke during the day. She and Will also took the big girls home for sleepovers a couple of nights. Vesta often thanked God for the strength to help all her children this way. It wasn't always easy running after the little ones, but it gave her a heart full of joy. When the first grandchildren were born, Will gave her the go-ahead to buy a video camera. Vesta spent hours filming when she was caring for them. She knew one day the movies would be a joy to watch, just as her dad's home movies had been.

Ariel was born September 18, and on September 24, the whole family got together and celebrated Desirae, Amanda, and Vesta's birthdays. The next morning, Christine woke up in labor and asked to spend the day with Vesta while Aaron was at work. They knew first babies could take a while to be born, so they thought it would be good for Christine to have Vesta nearby just in case. The day went smoothly until late afternoon when Christine's pain level suddenly changed. Thankfully, Aaron had just arrived and drove Christine immediately to the hospital.

Katie was born on September 25 as cute as a button. Christine was in pain because her beautiful baby girl broke her mother's tailbone during the birth. Christine's injury left her entirely dependent on Vesta since her own mother worked. Vesta was thrilled to help and did everything for Katie except nurse her, which Christine handled perfectly.

Somehow, the DeVee family made it through the year with the new babies. There were lots of fun family gatherings where little Katie, who had grown to be a true social butterfly, would scream at the top of her lungs when it was time to leave. Katie's lungs helped Aaron and Christine appreciate that raising a child wasn't as easy as they imagined or hoped.

It was now late summer 2004, and Vesta was attending a Coffee Break Bible study conference for leaders in the Midwest. One of the speakers, Ray VanderLaan, had made dozens of trips to the Middle East, mostly to Israel and Turkey, where he led teaching tours of Jesus's life and the Early Church. Vesta had always dreamed of going to Israel. It was a wonderful way to get to know the Bible better and feel closer to Jesus and the life He led. Ray, or RVL, was well known for making videos of his trips through the Focus on the Family organization, and Vesta had used his videos to teach Bible study classes. She decided to introduce herself after his speech and see if he was still leading trips to Israel.

Vesta found a chance to approach Ray. "Hi, I'm Vesta DeVee, and I just wanted to tell you that I loved your talks the last couple of days. I appreciate your deep knowledge of the Bible and the way you explain Jewish history, and how it opens the door to understanding Jesus's teaching is so inspiring," Vesta said with her usual excitement.

While they talked, Vesta shared information about who she was, where she was from, and how she came to be at this convention. She also asked, "Do you still travel to Israel? So many people seem to be afraid to go there, but I've always wanted to go. Do you think it's safe to travel there?"

"Yes, I do go to Israel," Ray replied without hesitation. "In fact, next summer, I'm taking a group of Southern California teachers there. If we have room on the trip, would you and your husband like to join us?"

"Wow, that would be amazing," Vesta exclaimed, hardly able to hide her excitement. "I'll talk to my husband about it and get back to you soon."

"If you decide you want to join us, just call this number and tell the person in charge that I invited you to go on this particular trip," Ray said, handing Vesta his card.

Vesta could hardly believe what happened and couldn't wait to tell Will. They discussed it later that evening, and Will was also surprised about the invitation. Being the more practical of the two, Will suggested that they discuss it further after Vesta came home from the conference.

When they finally talked more about joining RVL's trip, they decided it was too great of an opportunity to pass by and started making calls and other plans to go on the trip. It was a volatile time in the Middle East and the Israelis recently built a wall that separated the Palestinian people in Bethlehem from those in Jerusalem. The wall made it much more difficult for a person with a bomb attached to their body to get through.

When Will and Vesta's friends heard they planned to go to Israel, they thought they were a little crazy. Many asked, "Aren't you afraid of the problems over there and potentially getting caught in the cross-fire?"

Will and Vesta talked over their friends' concerns. They trusted RVL's judgment and knew that Israel was one of the most secure places in the Middle East. They confirmed their decision to take the trip, which was called "Walking in the Dust of the Rabbi."

They also decided to use this special trip to celebrate their fortieth wedding anniversary on July 3, 2004. In addition to the trip, they were planning an anniversary party. The wedding reception-type party was held in Skylar and Tommy's backyard.

The day of the party dawned with perfect weather. As Vesta got ready for the evening, she marveled at her life and its blessings. She spent a great deal of time thanking God for the wonderful marriage and family He had given her. She remembered her wedding day and realized this day was better for the simple reason that she knew so much more about life and could appreciate everything God had given them. She was thankful that God had given her a wonderful man. Looking around at other marriages, Vesta knew she had one of the best. It made her feel so fortunate. She was aware she could be a handful at times, but Will was so patient and loving.

Will and Vesta greeted their guests in the wedding clothes they wore forty years before. Vesta was happy her wedding dress still fit, and Will even rented a tux with the same design he wore back in 1964. Vesta thought he was the most handsome man she'd ever met, and they had a fun time greeting everyone as they arrived. When dinner was ready to be served and opening prayers spoken, Will and Vesta changed into their dinner clothes, which were black, red, and white to match the colors of the decorations and for the family portraits. Their foster daughter, Terri, her husband Stan, and their family also joined the celebration, taking part in the family picture and program as well. Everyone dressed to match the décor and look great for the pictures.

For Will and Vesta, the day turned out to be more special than they imagined. Most of their siblings attended along with lots of their friends and some of Will's business associates who had become friends. Their children and grandchildren put together an outstanding program filled with music. Vesta's favorite part was listening to her cute granddaughters sing and dance to the 1964 pop hit song, "I Will Follow Him" by Little Peggy March. It was a song Vesta sang to Will when they were young. Will and Vesta were overcome with joy from everything their children and grandchildren said, sang, and performed.

Later that evening, Brooke asked Vesta, "How will we ever top this party when it's time for your fiftieth wedding anniversary?"

Vesta thought for a moment and then replied, "I have no idea! This day was so fun and special. I don't know how we could ever top it." Vesta remembered this conversation often, but nothing ever came to mind on how to celebrate their fiftieth anniversary.

CHAPTER 30

# Trip of a Lifetime: Israel

E arlier that same year, after Will gave the go-ahead, Vesta
didn't waste any time connecting with RVL's travel person
and calling the teacher's group leader in Southern California.
Will and Vesta soon realized that this wouldn't be a vacation
or tour group trip; it would be a serious learning experience.
When the pre-trip instructions arrived, they included information on how to prepare, both physically and spiritually, for
the trip. Vesta took in all the information and became more
excited about their upcoming adventure. They had almost nine
months to prepare for the trip at the end of June.

Seven months later, it was April 2005. Will and Vesta had
hiked everywhere in the Sequoia National Park area, the perfect training ground for hiking ten miles a day for twelve days
straight in Israel. They were excited by the prospect of experiencing Israel in ways most people never had, and their physical
training provided a thrilling accomplishment for both Vesta
and Will. They felt strong and would soon meet their travel
companions in a class about Israeli history and geography.
During the class, everyone was given Bible verses to memorize, which would be recited when RVL told the story connected to their verse.

The day after they arrived home from the class, Vesta noticed an email from RVL's travel person. Vesta opened it with a smile, expecting helpful last-minute travel plans. Instead, she learned that Ray VanderLaan had a heart attack and was scheduled for open-heart surgery. Vesta burst into tears as she continued to read and discovered that Ray had to take a year off for his recovery. The Israel trip was canceled, but all those signed up would be left on the list for the following year. However, if they took their names off the list, their spot could be lost.

Vesta went through so many emotions, from feeling sorry for Ray to being worried that they wouldn't go the following year. So many things could happen in a year. Vesta knew she and Will were not getting any younger, and at fifty-eight and six-ty-two, it would be hard for them to stay in shape for another year. Finally, after shedding a lot of tears, Vesta realized again that God had His perfect time for everything. After talking it over with Will, they decided to leave their names on the list.

One good thing about the trip being canceled was Aaron and Christine were expecting their second baby. This baby was the first DeVee boy who would carry on their name. The Ridders and Estradas had boys, but Steven had all girls and Aaron had a daughter as well. Even most of Will's extended family lacked boys to carry on the DeVee name. Will and Vesta had won-dered if their name would disappear.

Aaron and Christine's baby was due in the middle of July, and with the trip canceled, Vesta wouldn't suffer from jet lag and would have the energy to help Christine. Ronald Michael DeVee was born July 18, 2005, a healthy boy and another dar-ling child in every way. Will and Vesta never tired of welcoming new babies to the family. What a blessing their grandchildren were to them. Christine's tail bone was not broken during the birth, so she felt healthier this time, and Vesta helped with the usual things—preparing dinner and helping around the house a bit. Katie also came home with Vesta for a few hours each day to give Christine some free time and a chance to nap. Katie loved her grandma Vesta, and sometimes they would pick up Ariel so the cousins could play together.

The year flew by and soon it was 2006 with their new Israel trip scheduled for July. Will joked about RVL being slower after a heart operation so they'd be able to keep up. In preparation for the trip, Will and Vesta flew to Chicago a day early so they could get an extra night of sleep before traveling to Israel. The rest of the group came in that morning looking tired after their overnight flight from California. When Will and Vesta saw them, they were happy they flew in the day before.

RVL warned the group not to make jokes when being questioned before their flight to Tel Aviv. Israelis were highly skilled at profiling people and questioned Will and Vesta both as a couple and individually for about an hour. Their carry-on luggage was also inspected thoroughly. One young man in their group had a dark complexion and had grown a beard so he wouldn't need to worry about shaving during the trip. Bad idea! He was questioned significantly longer than the rest of the group because his passport picture looked quite different. Finally, after his story checked out, their group of fifty travelers boarded the beautiful Israeli airline named El Ai.

Vesta sat on the plane looking over at Will, "Can you believe we're here? I'm so excited I can hardly stand it."

They were dressed in their hiking clothes because when they arrived, they would immediately board a bus to their first hike and teaching tour. Since they arrived in the morning and it would be nighttime in California, they were told to take a sleeping pill after the meal so they would be ready for the long day ahead. The pill worked well for Vesta, and she was ready for the day. Will did not need the pill but was able to sleep on his own.

The trip was everything Will and Vesta hoped for and more. Fortunately, RVL wasn't hindered by his surgery and had more energy than ever. Will and Vesta were glad they were in good physical shape. Vesta discovered she wasn't afraid of heights when they scaled high mountains, using hand holds when there was a sheer cliff below. Mount Arbel, located on the northern shore of the Sea of Galilee, was one of the places with sheer cliffs. Somehow, they all made it to the top and enjoyed a wonderful teaching about prayer. Will and Vesta never forgot what an amazing experience that was, climbing to the place where they believe Jesus prayed all night. RVL shared with the group that the night before, he went to the top of the mountain to pray for all of them.

Vesta's eyes grew big as RVL shared his story. The group needed young lions, as Ray called the strong, young men, to help them pass on the scary cliffs and tell them where exactly to step. How in the world did RVL go in the dark? Both Will and Vesta wondered, especially Will who had turned a little white while trying to scale those same heights.

One difficult part of the trip for Vesta was when she became slightly claustrophobic in Hezekiah's water tunnel. Thankfully, at the time, she was leading a group of four through the tunnel, which kept her mind off feeling closed in. This tunnel was built during biblical times when Hezekiah, a strong, godly king, reigned after the Assyrians conquered the northern Jewish kingdom of Israel. One of Hezekiah's most impressive engineering achievements was tapping into the Gihon Spring and channeling the water underground to the City of David. Since the only year-round source of water for Jerusalem was found outside the city walls, the lack of a safeguarded freshwater supply was an ongoing area of vulnerability for Jerusalem. To address this, Hezekiah set two teams of workmen about 1,750 feet apart to dig a tunnel to channel the Gihon water supply to a collection pool within the city walls. As a result, Jerusalem had access to fresh water that was out of the army's view when the Assyrians held Jerusalem under siege.

There was so much to see and do that at the end of each day, Vesta and Will fell into bed exhausted. They spent three days near the Dead Sea, seeing where David hid from Saul. They also climbed the heights near Ein Gedi to a beautiful waterfall.

What Will and Vesta remembered most about their time in the wilderness is that God teaches us His greatest lessons in the desert of life. When things are difficult, it usually brings us closer to God because we need Him. During the trip, it was quite hot but never got to the typical highs of 120 degrees Fahrenheit in the areas they hiked. RVL kept repeating that 103 degrees was comfortable, and they were thankful for a slight wind. Will and Vesta were glad to be accustomed to the warm temperatures of the Central Valley. In fact, Israel reminded them of California's landscape and weather. It had the same familiar seas, mountains, valleys, deserts, rivers, and lakes.

The possibility of trouble breaking out during their trip was never far from Vesta's mind. She tried not to do anything foolish and did her best to stay close to the group. RVL kept everyone alert so they clearly understood what it meant to walk and follow in the dust of the Rabbi, that Jesus is the Rabbi, and one needs to follow Him so closely that one gets His dust on one's feet and person. One is to follow His lead and copy everything He does. If not, there is trouble. Will and Vesta's group experienced that trouble more than once. These experiences provided great reminders of what happens when one looks away from Christ Jesus and goes his or her own way. It always brings trouble.

One night in their Galilee hotel room, Vesta was packing for the next day, and Will was already asleep when she heard what sounded like gunshots and bombs detonating. She quickly turned off the lights and slowly peeked through the curtains. She was so relieved to see fireworks bursting in the night sky. Vesta took a deep breath and giggled to herself, thinking, *That sure sounded like bombs and gunshots.* The next day, she and Will had a good laugh over it. The interesting thing was two days after they arrived home, the Syrians attacked the area where Will and Vesta were staying. Israel soon had it under control, but it made Vesta realize that her response to the fireworks wasn't so crazy after all.

After Vesta and Will arrived home, Vesta decided to make a memory video of their trip she could share with friends and family. The video was a great way to keep their memories alive.

Vesta and Will never read the Bible the same again, and they had many new insights to share with their children and grandchildren. They also noticed how the trip made the Bible come alive when they knew exactly what the place looked like as they read about it. Will also felt it was important to help others who couldn't afford to travel to make the trip to Israel. It was especially important to him that they sponsor trips for young men and women who were interested in ministry. Vesta agreed with Will, but in her heart, she hoped to one day return.

She couldn't help but laugh at herself since so many parts of the trip were difficult. She came home with several large bruises on her legs and hips from falls on the rocky terrain. On their last day, Vesta was so exhausted that Will carried her backpack for the entire day. She even got sick on the bus one day, probably from taking medicine to keep her stomach settled. Despite these difficulties, Vesta couldn't explain it, but she knew she wanted to return. Will, on the other hand, was content to send others who might benefit more from the experience, especially if they were going into the ministry. Will also hoped to take his entire family to Hawaii again.

About a month after Will and Vesta returned from Israel, Will decided he didn't want to wait. He talked to Vesta one day and said, "Vesta, I think we ought to take our kids and grandkids to Hawaii again this Christmas. The business is doing well, and our grandkids are growing up so quickly. Before you know it, the oldest will be off to college. What do you think, are you up to it?"

Vesta, always ready for adventure, said, "Certainly! I'd love to plan another trip! Now I have some experience with planning for a large group, so that helps. I'll get right on it since it's already the end of July." As Vesta worked on the plans, she thought it might be wonderful to invite Stan and Teri, their foster daughter and her husband. She talked to Will about it later that evening. "Honey I was thinking, it feels like Teri could use some encouragement. She has had such a hard time with different things in her family. I know she wishes she could do more with us. What do you think about taking them to Hawaii with us?" Vesta thought she might be asking her dear husband for too much, so she was thrilled with his answer.

"You know, I think that is a great idea. I would love to bless them this way. Will you give her a call and see if they can get away at that time of year? Adding two more with our big family isn't going to cost that much more, so, yes, let's go for it."

For this trip, the timing worked out for everyone but Aaron and Christine. They decided instead that they would love a special four-day trip to Disneyland and to stay at the Grand California Disney Hotel. Will and Vesta planned for their trip to take place in the fall after the schools were back in session. They had a wonderful time with their little family. Will and Vesta had adjoining rooms with Aaron and Christine and their children Katie and Ronald, who were always sad when it was time to say goodnight. Every morning, Will and Vesta opened their door when they were ready for the grandkids to come in. Only a few times did they hear a little knock when the children thought their grandparents were taking a little too long to open their door. Will was very good at entertaining the children while Christine and Vesta got ready for their day.

It was a delightful time since they could enter the park directly from their hotel and return for rest anytime they were needed. Vesta was especially glad she could go back to the hotel when they went on Splash Mountain and got soaked. It was wonderful to change clothes and quickly continue their fun-filled day.

When they arrived home, it was time for Will and Vesta to get ready for the northern cattle sales on Thursday and Friday. They loved traveling, just the two of them. Vesta spent her time during the sales finishing her travel plans for Hawaii. She also took her Bible study material along so she would be ready for class on Tuesday.

The family Thanksgiving time came before they knew it. Stan and Terri always came up for Thanksgiving, and this year were extra happy to be included in the Hawaii trip planning. Stan's employer shut down during the Christmas and New Year holidays, so it worked perfectly for their schedule to come along. Vesta had an itinerary prepared for each family. This year's trip would, once again, start after Christmas and include celebrating the New Year in Hawaii. Everyone talked excitedly around the table as they went over the itinerary together.

Will and Vesta knew this was a wonderful gift to take their children, grandchildren, and foster kids on this special trip. They never grew tired of watching the children enjoy each other's company, whether they were on the beach, hiking Diamond Head, going to a Luau, snorkeling, or having a special time of praising God together. They took plenty of pictures, which they shared after arriving home again. While they looked at the pictures, everyone laughed and remembered all their crazy times trying to keep track of their children and each other.

Will had made sure each family had enough freedom to go where they wanted and enough extra cash to pay for meals or any tours they did on their own. The children laughed about how the grandchildren didn't want to separate, so once again, almost all of their meals and activities were done together. The trip ended by welcoming 2007 watching fireworks off the shore of Waikiki from the beach front room Will arranged for Steven's family to have.

## CHAPTER 31

# A Half-Marathon

W ill and Vesta marveled at how swiftly the years flew by and continued enjoying family and each other, never leaving out God. They would read devotions every evening after their dinner and were reminded how the Word of God told them to look at life. One night, Will read verses from Psalm 90, which said: "The length of our days is seventy years or eighty if we have the strength; yet their span is but trouble and sorrow, for they quickly pass, and we fly away."

"My dad often referred to these verses," Will commented. "He and my mom were always thinking that at any time, God could call them home."

"It's true, they did. It would be so hard to lose any of our family in death. But we must believe God will give us what we need at the time. I will be honest, though, Will. I really can't stand to think of losing you," Vesta said.

"Nor I, but like you said, God will help us go where He wants us to walk," Will stated. "You know, we have been so blessed. I don't want to take what God has given to us for granted. Let's make sure we always give enough away. We need to start making a list of our favorite charities, and I will help decide how we will give. I know we can never outgive what the Lord has given us, but it's time to do a little more."

"That's a good idea, Will. I'm in favor of that as well," Vesta stated sincerely.

The month of February ushered in rain and sunshine in their beautiful valley, making all the trees bloom in vibrant colors. The blossom trail was a favorite tour many came to see.

Another spot people came from the around world was the World Ag Show in Tulare. Sara and Peter decided to come that year to attend the Ag show and spend some time with Will and Vesta. They were enjoying breakfast when a phone call disturbed their happy morning. It was the skilled nursing facility their mother Johanna was living at in Southern California. Vesta was told her mother was coming close to death. They were asked if they wanted to see her before she passed. They decided together not to go as it was a four-hour drive, and they weren't sure if she would rally as she had done several times in the past. Dear Johanna no longer recognized anyone and couldn't talk or move on her own. They knew going to see her was for their own sake, not for Johanna's. Even though Vesta had recently been down to see her mother, it made her feel a little guilty and rather sad to decide to stay at home. Johanna did go home to Jesus that very day, February 14, 2007. It warmed Vesta's heart that God chose a day of love to take her sweet mom home.

Sara and Peter determined to return home and come back for the memorial service a couple of weeks later. Vesta and her family did most of the planning for the service, including any family members who were willing to take part in it. She had been able to pick everything out earlier when Frank had passed. This time was easy in a sense as all the work was done and paid for. Vesta just needed to go to the funeral home and go over the account.

Vesta made that trip by herself and stayed with friends. It felt strange to her to drive alone to Southern California. She usually had Will or a family member with her. It was good for her but a different and rather lonely feeling.

The service took place a few weeks later with a very nice group of people attending. Vesta was blessed since she knew Johanna had been ill for several years now where she did not interact with her friends. Many came and showed their love. It was a heart-warming day with Johanna's church family, her children, and grandchildren saying their goodbyes. All of Frank and Johanna's children and grandchildren went to the hotel where a room was rented for a time of sharing food and fellowship.

As a family, they were once again reminded of God's words in Psalm 39:4–5: "Show me, O Lord, my life's end and the number of my days, let me know how fleeting is my life. You have made my days a mere handbreadth; the span of my years is as nothing before you. Each man's life is but a breath."

Will and Vesta did not want to take any day for granted. They knew life was uncertain. With such a large family, anything could happen, and eventually, something always did.

Another year passed, and 2008 brought another blessing of a child, Kenneth, born to Aaron and Christine. After he was born on May 1, he grew quickly on his mother's rich milk. Although Katie and Ronald had brown hair, Kenneth was blond.

When Kenneth was almost six months old, Christine woke one day feeling ill. She thought it was just the flu, but after not being able to keep any food down, she went to the emergency room. After two days in the hospital, the doctors determined she had some kind of infection. Throughout the holiday season, Christine continued being sick, so Vesta helped with the children. When Christine first became sick, it reminded Vesta of her own trouble with her appendix. When they asked if Christine was sick with appendicitis, the doctors said it wasn't that. After a regimen of antibiotics, Christine seemed to be somewhat better.

Earlier that same year, Sienna suggested to her mom that the family should run a Disney half-marathon. Desirae laughed, saying, "Are you kidding? I've never run before, let alone a race of thirteen-plus miles."

"Well, I think it sounds fun. You even get a castle medal when you finish the race," Sienna responded.

"Do you think that helps me? I don't think I can do it, castle medal or not," Desirae replied calmly, knowing it just wasn't a possibility.

Desirae decided to talk to Vesta about Sienna's idea. Vesta wasn't running on the road anymore and, instead, ran on their treadmill in the garage. While she ran, she watched TV or memorized her scripture that she was inspired to do during the trip to Israel. When she heard Sienna's idea, Vesta thought it sounded fun.

"When is it?" Vesta asked.

"Next September on Labor Day," Desirae replied.

"So, we have plenty of time, I could help you train. What do you think, Desirae, are you ready to train with me?" Vesta challenged.

"Oh, Mom, I don't know, I'm not sure I even like running," Desirae said. She wasn't Vesta's risk-taking child. Her life was carefully planned and calm. The idea of doing this run was more than Desirae could handle at this moment.

Skylar, on the other hand, was more like Vesta. They decided, along with Sienna, to sign up for the run before it was too late. The next thing they knew, Vesta's grandsons—Joshua, Jacob, and Brody—decided to sign up too.

Will thought the run sounded great and offered to pay for the kids' entry fees. He hoped to run as well but decided to register for the race when he was sure he had time to get in shape for it.

Desirae was extremely nervous to join in, but after more encouragement from Vesta, she finally broke down. Vesta booked the Disney hotel, Paradise Pier, so everyone could get a good night's sleep before the race.

"You don't have to run fast, just at a steady pace," Vesta coached Desirae. "This run has inspired me to get back on the road. I really missed running in the open air. I'm so glad Sienna challenged us with the half-marathon," Vesta added as they ran that afternoon while the boys were in baseball practice. Vesta and Desirae usually ran six miles about three to four times a week. Skylar trained separately by running around her country home, and then, on some Saturdays, they all met up for a half-marathon run. Desirae was amazed how she grew stronger and could keep going for longer stretches of time.

In October 2008, the family continued training for their half-marathon. Vesta also received an unexpected phone call from her sister-in-law, Stephen's ex-wife, Joanie. Stephen had died suddenly of a heart attack on the morning of October 18. It was another stark reminder of the uncertainty of life.

Vesta was the closest to Stephen of her brothers. They had talked on the phone often. After his death, Vesta would catch herself thinking, *I want to talk to Stephen about that.* It was quite an adjustment to realize that he was no longer there. Their family went to Southern California to share grief with her brother's family and attend a special service at Stephen's church. Stephen was very close to his three children but had struggled in his marriage. Vesta and his ex-wife did their best to stay in touch since they had always appreciated each other's company.

Thanksgiving came and went, but Christine's health did not improve, even after more rounds of antibiotics. One evening, the pain became unbearable, and Aaron rushed Christine to the emergency room. Finally, the doctors realized that Christine had a burst appendix that had miraculously encased itself. They removed the encased appendix, but Christine's recovery was difficult, and she was left with a large scar that stretched across her abdomen. Will, Vesta, and Aaron never forgot Christine's word from God when she was so ill and believing that death was near, "This sickness will not end in death" (John 11:4).

As 2009 continued to rapidly move along, Will and Vesta sat before the Lord, knowing life was uncertain and thanking Him for sparing their daughter-in-law. They realized, once again, that doctors do their best, but their lives are always in God's hands.

Kenneth grew quickly but was a bit slow with crawling and walking. Christine and Aaron liked to say that he just loved to be waited on. Since in every other way, he was a normal baby, the doctor wasn't overly concerned. Vesta wasn't concerned either since her own son, Steven, didn't walk until he was eighteen months and didn't talk in an understandable way until he was three. She prayed for each one and left it to the Lord as to how quickly they developed.

With the race a few weeks away, Will decided he was ready to register. In total, eight members of the family signed up for the race, and everyone was excited. Desirae's family, Skylar and her boys, and Will and Vesta packed and headed for Disneyland.

Labor Day weekend, 2009, the half-marathon began early with a 5:30 a.m. line-up in the dark. They marveled at how many people were there and how much excitement was swirling around them as people kept arriving. They were also glad their hotel was nearby, so they didn't need to worry about parking their cars. During the line-up, Vesta learned that her grandsons' goal for the race was to beat their grandma's time. They knew she was a good runner, even though they were stronger, they hadn't trained much, so they were afraid she might beat them. The three boys ended up finishing before Vesta, who loved hearing them shout, "Go, Grandma!" as she neared the finish line.

They soon lost sight of Will, who started later in the line-up since he registered after the rest of the family. It occurred to them later they could have stayed together, but Will claimed to enjoy running with strangers since he could better concentrate on his pace. In the end, everyone was happy they finished, and even though the three grandsons could hardly walk the next day, they were relieved they beat Grandma.

After they showered, dressed, and enjoyed a hardy breakfast together, everyone spent time playing in the hotel pool. Will and Vesta said their goodbyes as they left for Idaho to ship the summer grass cattle. In the car that day, they had fun reliving their experiences of running a half-marathon. They also learned from their children and grandchildren how to look up online where they placed in their age group for the race. They both felt good about finishing the race without quitting and agreed it was much harder than anticipated.

Vesta told Will, "I thought if I got tired, I could walk a bit. I had no idea my legs would not let me do that," she giggled. "Now I understand how people can collapse when running a full marathon. I don't know about you, but I have no desire to do that again. I'll just stick to 5 or 10Ks from now on."

"I'm with you, honey. It was okay once, but I'll settle for other challenges," Will said.

A few weeks later, Vesta, Desirae, and Skylar used their half-marathon experience during a Coffee Break Bible study. Vesta oversaw opening the lessons, and on this day, the lesson involved persevering in a walk of faith. A passage came to Vesta's mind that would be perfect to use:

Hebrews 12:1–3

> Therefore, since we are surrounded by such a great cloud of witnesses, let us throw off everything that hinders and the sin that so easily entangles, and let us run with perseverance the race marked out for us. Let us fix our eyes on Jesus, the author, and perfecter of our faith, who for the joy set before him endured the cross, scorning its shame, and sat down at the right hand of the throne of God. Consider him who endured such opposition from sinful men, so that you will not grow weary and lose heart.

The three of them decided to run into the room with their race clothes on and share a word picture of how hard it was to run a half-marathon. They compared it to running the race of life with God and how one needs to train hard to be in shape and ready when difficult times come.

It was a time they always remembered. Vesta even included a photo from the race on the front of that year's Christmas card. The picture of the three grandsons posing as strong men, Sienna pulling a crazy face, and Will, Vesta, Desirae, and Skylar just smiling was a classic.

## CHAPTER 32
# A Year of Wonderful Memories

The year 2010 dawned with Barack Obama as president and trouble continuing in the Middle East. Will and Vesta were happy that the military continued to be respected by most people. They knew things were never perfect in the United States, but they were happy to be Americans and proud of their country.

God had been good to the DeVee Cattle Company. Will and Steven continued to grow their cattle yard and worked well together. There were always worries and risks involved, but Vesta finally learned to depend on God's care and the keeping of her family. This didn't mean they were trouble free, but it did mean she and Will could sleep well.

The family continued to be actively involved in their churches and often got together for birthdays and special events. Vesta and Will enjoyed attending all the programs and most sports events that their grandkids were involved in. Their life was rich and full, and Vesta didn't take any of it for granted. She realized every day was a gift from God.

Vesta loved her husband Will more deeply with every passing year. It amazed her how she never stopped adoring his attention, whether they were making love or just enjoying each other's company. As Will aged, Vesta thought he was the most handsome man around, and she treasured serving him in any devoted way she could.

Will adored his wife as well and never tired of lovingly touching her. He considered Vesta the most beautiful woman and had eyes for no one else. Will believed the proverb of a good woman being behind a successful man. Vesta and Will knew they had a special marriage and relationship that grew better and stronger as the years passed. As they entered their forty-sixth year of marriage, Vesta thought more about their fiftieth wedding anniversary but still couldn't come up with a great way to celebrate it. She asked Will for his ideas, but he wasn't much help at all.

His answer was generally a simple one, "I know we'll come up with something when the time comes." Vesta knew Will was right that there was no need to worry about something that was four years out.

Earlier that year, Will came to Vesta with an idea, "The grandkids are growing fast. Some of them are already in college. We should really take one more Hawaii trip with everyone before they scatter in different directions."

Vesta was in full agreement with Will's idea. Their business was doing well, and they had fifteen grandchildren. It was only a matter of time before they would start getting married. Will also suggested that "We might have to go in two groups since our business is so large that we can't all be gone at once." By this time, Steven, Aaron, and Will all had major roles in running DeVee Cattle Company. Desirae was still working in the office as well, so they all decided that Aaron would stay home since his children were the youngest. The oldest three families planned to travel over Christmas break, and Aaron's family would go in February of the following year.

Taking everyone to Hawaii was a huge undertaking for Vesta. They also decided to invite their foster daughter Terri and her husband Stan again on the trip. It was a special time for the whole family. The cousins spent all of their time together, never wanting their families to go off on their own. They went to the beach, hiked Diamond Head, visited the Polynesian Culture Center, attended the best luau on Oahu, snorkeled and boogie boarded—all as one big group. The oldest grandkids ventured out together a few times in the evening. They would go down the street to have Cold Stone ice cream and pose for silly pictures.

During the trip, Vesta assigned each family a night to be in charge of group devotions. They would read, share thoughts from the Bible or devotion book, and often sing praise songs. It was a special time for everyone.

The family welcomed in 2011 by watching beach fireworks from an oceanfront room. Tired from the day's activities, it was difficult for everyone to stay awake. Somehow, after some took naps, they made it to midnight but headed straight to bed a few minutes later so they could be ready for another fun day in the sun.

The trip flew by, and soon they were home and back to work with nice tans and happy smiles. Vesta knew that the trip would not soon be forgotten by anyone. Will and Vesta looked forward to more fun in Hawaii with Aaron's family and had a wonderful time with them as well. Swimming in the ocean and building sandcastles were some of their favorite activities with the kids. They also toured a World War II battleship.

In June 2011, Will and Vesta attended a niece's wedding in Ann Arbor, Michigan. Desirae and Skylar decided to go with them. Sara and Peter also attended the wedding with their daughters Annabelle and Denise. Since Rachel's daughter was the niece getting married, they were especially excited that all three sisters and their daughters would be together at the wedding. Vesta and Sara's daughters really liked being spoiled by their daddies, Will and Peter, who enjoyed paying for their girls. The girls said how fun it was to feel like kids again with the care and love of their dads.

It was a beautiful wedding in a lovely setting. Although Rachel's daughter, Roselan, wanted her wedding to take place outside, it rained all day. Fortunately, the large windows in the room helped everyone enjoy the beautiful garden outside.

After Will and Vesta arrived home from the wedding, Vesta heard that Elizabeth had qualified for a horse show in Chicago not far from where Rachel lived. Vesta thought it was a long shot but decided to talk to Will about traveling back to the Midwest.

"Honey, I know we can't go, but guess what?" Vesta continued, "Elizabeth is in a horse show this year in Chicago. I was thinking it would be awesome if we could go, but I know we already went twice to Hawaii and just got back from Rachel's daughter's wedding."

Will didn't take long to respond. "I think we should go. How many times will Elizabeth have this chance? Time goes by quickly, and we should take advantage of going and doing things while we can. Why don't you investigate the cost of plane tickets and some hotels? Let me know what we're looking at and then we can decide. At this point, I say let's go for it!"

Vesta was both surprised and delighted, so she quickly called Skylar for the details of Elizabeth's show and then went online for the other information they needed. A few months later, they toured Chicago for the first time in ways they never had before. Tommy and Skylar also came on the trip, and Rachel and her husband Ron joined them for the horse show and spend the rest of the day together touring the city.

"What a special day this is! The weather is perfect, and the river boat tour of the city and our walking tour were amazing," Vesta said appreciatively to Will. Vesta felt grateful that she received so much, and her life was bursting in ways she never expected it would in her sixties.

Will agreed it was a great day. He decided to treat everyone to a nice steak dinner. Will loved telling everyone he enjoyed eating what he grew. Beef is what's for dinner!

Will and Vesta arrived home a few short weeks before Joshua and Chelsey's wedding. Joshua was the first of their fifteen grandchildren to get married, and he was happy it was on a date so easy to remember: 9/10/11. It was a beautiful wedding in a gorgeous outdoor setting with delicious food, followed by fun with family and friends, a whirlwind weekend that Will and Vesta thoroughly enjoyed.

Next on the agenda was their annual cattle shipping trip to Idaho. For their side trip that year, they planned to meet up with Sara and Peter for a weekend. They also planned their usual stop at Vesta's last living aunt in Grangeville. During their visits with her, they'd go to church and take her to eat afterward.

Their first morning in Idaho, Will left early to do his cattle shipping. When he returned, they planned to take their favorite hike down to the falls and then explore the mountain trails that continued past the falls. They knew they were in good enough shape to hike a full five miles.

However, just as they crossed over the bridge by the falls, Will turned to Vesta and said, "I'm sorry, but I feel strange and dizzy. Maybe we should go back up to the car."

"I'm so sorry you feel bad! Do you need to sit down for a bit before we hike back up? Do you think you can make it?" Vesta asked. She wasn't too concerned because she knew Will had been very busy before they left Visalia. He probably just needed to take it easy and get some rest. Will made it back to the car after they stopped several times to rest on their way back up the hill.

Soon they were safely back at the Holiday Inn Express in McCall. They enjoyed staying there since it was a new hotel with large rooms, an indoor pool, and a jacuzzi. The free breakfast was another bonus, and when they tired of it, there was a delightful breakfast restaurant just across the street.

Will didn't recover as quickly as they hoped and was still feeling weak the next morning. Vesta drove Will to ship cattle and had a wonderful time watching her husband in action, and for the first time in seventeen years, helped with recording as each of the cattle was shipped.

On their way back to the hotel, Vesta said, "That was so much fun. Why didn't I help you sooner? Well, from now on, I'm going to help, next year and every year to come, whether you need me or not." Will smiled, glad to hear that Vesta enjoyed the day too and looked forward to sharing one more thing as they grew older together.

During their three weeks in Idaho, Will didn't improve much. Vesta continued helping with the shipping and bookwork. They canceled their trip to see Sara and Peter, and instead of their usual hiking and biking excursions, drove their car and took leisurely walks together.

After arriving home at the end of September, Will got more rest and was soon back to normal. Vesta wasn't surprised since he seemed to be in such good physical shape. The two of them were back to running and hiking together, and his inhaler helped him avoid getting too sick if he caught a cold.

After working in the Coffee Break Bible study for over thirty years, Vesta felt called to pass the baton to a few younger women who were ready to become program leaders. Instead, Vesta spent more time volunteering at the local Care Pregnancy Center. Although she had worked there for several years, she knew there was always more need than she was available for. Their program included training young mothers about pregnancy and motherhood. Many of these girls were in some kind of crisis pregnancy or from troubled homes. Vesta added a Bible study option for anyone who was interested. She often told her foster daughter, Terri, that she had learned so much about hurting girls when Terri lived with them. Back then, Vesta took some psychology classes, which helped her better understand people who were suffering and how it could take years for things to improve for them. It was especially hard with people who suffered abuse when they were young children.

When Will and Vesta took Terri in, she was sixteen, and they knew she had been a victim of incest in her family home. As time went by, they discovered more heartbreaking details about her past. Vesta's experience with Terri gave her the patience to help young and hurting girls make better choices. God had given both Will and Vesta love and forgiveness, and they realized it was their calling to do the same for others. They had learned how to be encouragers, not enablers. Will and Vesta also learned that they were always growing in the grace they gave since they often made mistakes.

Vesta volunteered at the center one day a week. One day, she met a young woman named Annie who seemed to want help and start Bible study right away. Annie's boyfriend had left her for another, and she came to the center to see if she was pregnant. Vesta was always thankful when the test came back negative, which Annie's did. After talking with Vesta a few times, Annie suddenly disappeared. Vesta called to check on her when she missed her Bible study appointment, but there was no answer and the line was disconnected. This type of thing had happened before, so Vesta just took it as a sign that she was no longer the one who God wanted to use in Annie's life. A few weeks later, Vesta was working at the center and felt as if God was telling her to call Annie. At the time, Vesta almost said out loud, "But God, her line is disconnected. How can I call her?" However, the feeling was so strong that Vesta finally gave into it.

When Annie answered the phone, Vesta almost fell off her chair. It turned out that Annie had been ill, and her phone was disconnected for a while. For Vesta, it was a wonderful reminder to listen when God gives a strong feeling to take action. This simple phone call was the beginning of a long and close relationship between Annie and Vesta. She had a wonderful time teaching Annie about the Word of God. When they started together, Annie didn't know the difference between chapters and verses, nor did she know what the Old and New Testament meant. Annie was eager to learn, and they both had fun discovering new things together. Annie was another person God used to teach Vesta how to be caring and understanding.

CHAPTER 33

## Challenging Days

W ill and Vesta, along with their children, knew that life was uncertain and there would always be struggles. What did Jesus say? In Mark 8:34, "Then he called the crowd to him along with his disciples and said: 'If anyone would come after me, he must deny himself and take up your cross and follow me.'" And in John 16:33, "I have told you these things, so that in me you may have peace. In this world you will have trouble but take heart I have overcome the world."

These verses reminded Will and Vesta that they should not expect a trouble-free life just because they followed God. In fact, at the end of each year, Will and Vesta reflected on who in their church became ill and died. They wondered who would pass during the next year. They didn't mean to be pessimistic; they just knew it would happen.

"We all want to stay on earth as long as possible. There is nothing wrong with hoping for a long happy life," Vesta and Will would often say as they discussed life and death. They had already buried their parents and a few siblings along with other relatives and many in their church family. They knew that one day death could come to their core family but were so grateful for their forty-seven years of marriage, fifteen healthy grandchildren, and having four children in happy marriages. Their first grandchild was happily married, not to mention foster children and foster grandchildren with good marriages. Will and Vesta were extremely thankful for every way God had blessed them.

It was now the end of October 2011. Almost a month had passed since Will and Vesta returned from their Idaho trip, and Will decided he needed some new cowboy boots. His favorite type was soft leather alligator skin. He bought a pair that fit perfectly, but when his legs and feet started to bother him, he guessed the pain might be caused by the new boots.

One night, Will woke up, and his legs hurt so much that he needed to crawl to the bathroom. The next day, the pain seemed to have disappeared, so he and Vesta were not overly concerned. They continued running together and looked forward to celebrating Thanksgiving, which was about a month away. Thanksgiving was a favorite time of year for their family. They celebrated other holidays together either before or after the actual day, but Vesta insisted that the entire family save this one holiday to celebrate together.

The family traditionally ran the three-mile fun run for Visalia Emergency Aid, which took place on Thanksgiving morning. Will and Vesta were training for the run one morning when Will said, "I feel more winded than usual. You go ahead." Vesta ran on, shouting back at him, "Okay, I think I can win a medal this year in my age group if I just step it up a bit. I'm sixty-five now, and I think that puts me in a new age group."

Will encouraged her, "Go for it! I'm just going to head home."

After the morning run, Will headed to work and mentioned to his son that his feet and legs were sporadically hurting. He blamed his new boots, so he would occasionally wear his old ones. Will also noticed he wasn't running as well during their training runs. He was already sixty-eight, so he just assumed this was due to getting older.

Thanksgiving was a week away, and Vesta was planning for the big day. Once again, their kids, grandkids, Terri, her husband, and their son would be with them. After the morning's fun run, everyone would go home to get ready and come back for salad and hors d'oeuvres before the big meal. They shared devotion time and sang praise songs as they ate their salads. Afterward, everyone did their part in carving the turkey, making gravy, getting all the hot food in bowls for the family-style, sit-down dinner.

When dinner was over, they each shared what they were thankful for. Tissues were passed as tears flowed when they shared their many blessings from the past year and how God took them through trials. Next came a quick clean up and then everyone headed out for bowling. After bowling, they would go back for pies and turkey or beef buns, along with leftover salad to finish off their joy-filled day.

On Monday of Thanksgiving week, Will woke feeling strange again. This time, he thought it was a flu bug. By Monday evening, he started noticing odd red spots on his arms and legs.

When Vesta saw the spots, she said, "Now I know what's been bothering you. You have shingles. Remember a few years back when I had pain on the side of my leg, and it finally broke out into red spots? I'm sure that's what you have, honey. That must be why your legs keep hurting. Let's call the doctor first thing in the morning to get a prescription for it. It will go away quickly; you just need the medication."

The next morning, Will was feeling a bit better. He had a slight fever, which convinced Vesta that it was probably shingles. Fortunately, the doctor was able to see Will at 9 a.m.

Vesta was happy and said, "I'll go with you, and afterward, drop you off at home and then get the Thanksgiving Day groceries. You'll probably need some medication, and I should be able to pick that up too."

"Great, sounds good to me," Will replied.

The doctor came in, and Will explained how he was feeling and showed the spots on his arms and legs.

"I want to run some blood tests," the doctor said.

Vesta tried to hide her impatience, saying as calmly as she could, "Isn't this shingles? Doesn't that need to be treated quickly so it doesn't spread?"

"I don't think it's shingles. We need blood tests so we know for sure what we need to treat," Dr. Bailey answered.

As they left the doctor's office, Vesta told Will how annoyed she was about the tests. Will did his best to reassure Vesta. "I'm sure he knows what he's doing. Let's not worry about it. We should find out something soon."

After dropping Will at home, Vesta hurried off to the grocery store. When she was halfway done with her shopping, her cell phone rang. It was Will. She was sure he was going to ask her to pick up some medication.

"Hi, honey. I'm sorry I'm calling you while you're shopping. I just needed you. The doctor called and told me to call a cancer doctor immediately. I need to make an appointment today or first thing in the morning," Will said with a tremor in his voice.

"What! Oh no! I'll come home right now. Should I just leave the cart?" Vesta said, trying to keep her head.

"No, why don't you finish your shopping and come home as soon as you can."

Vesta hung up and finished shopping. She managed to hold back her tears and prayed she wouldn't run into anyone she knew because she would burst out crying. When she finished, she hurried home and had no idea how she managed to get all the shopping done.

Will and Vesta cried together before deciding to tell their children. Their daughter Skylar knew a cancer doctor. They called him immediately, and he was able to see them first thing the next morning.

Lying in bed that evening after they said goodnight, Vesta tried to hold in her tears. Although she was numb with pain, she managed to cry quietly until her sweet husband slept. She tried not to worry but realized this was the worst she had ever felt in her life and knew that she never wanted to feel this bad again. Finally, Vesta recited scripture in her head to help her fall asleep. She happened to be memorizing John 8. The beginning starts with the story of a woman caught in adultery and how Jesus lovingly handles the situation. Vesta loved that story and even did a drama depicting the scene at one time. The end of the chapter goes into Jesus's claims of who He is and anyone believing in Him and keeping His Word will never see death. Those words were so comforting and had a soothing effect on her.

The next morning, both Will and Vesta woke with a black cloud hanging over their heads. They shared devotions together and quickly got ready for their 10 a.m. appointment. As they were leaving the house, much to their surprise, all of their children were at their door. The girls planned to cook what Vesta usually prepared in advance for Thanksgiving dinner. They sent their parents off to learn what kind of cancer their dad had, and when Will and Vesta came home, they would be there to hear about the appointment.

Dr. Havard was a caring man in addition to being one of the best oncologists in town. He drew more of Will's blood, and since the results came back right away, he immediately shared his diagnosis with Will and Vesta.

"It looks like you have chronic leukemia, Will. This is something we can treat here in town, and you can live with it for at least ten years, maybe longer, depending on how you respond to treatments," Dr. Havard stated. "Go home and enjoy Thanksgiving with your family. We'll see you next Tuesday and begin treatment. In the meantime, here is a prescription you should fill immediately and take as directed. See you on Tuesday."

Will and Vesta returned home rejoicing and thanking God! It was such a relief that Will had so much more life to live. After they shared the good news with their children, the boys headed to work while the girls continued cooking. Everyone was laughing and talking when the phone rang.

Will answered, and after he hung up, he told everyone, "That was Dr. Havard. He said he was sorry, but I need to go immediately to the emergency room. He would check me in there for observation and care until they find a bed for me at either the Stanford or UCLA hospital. He said that, based on additional blood tests, I actually have acute leukemia, which can progress rapidly, so I need to get treatment as soon as possible."

As a person who could handle stress well, Vesta stayed strong for Will and her family. She packed bags for them both and made sure they ate something before leaving for the hospital. Will was put in the emergency room of the hospital where Will's grandniece, Isaak's granddaughter, worked. She was the one who secured the ambulance to take Will to Stanford. Their children and several friends were in and out during the afternoon to pray and wish them well. They appreciated their pastor who was very caring and sad over hearing the news. Pastor Joel prayed with them and spent time talking with them and their children while they waited.

It was a long day, but they finally made it to Stanford around midnight. They immediately met with a doctor who told them Will had a rare form of leukemia, and at his age, it probably could not be cured. Will told the doctor that he was willing to try the first month of treatment.

"It's a good idea to try and see how you respond. I'm sorry this happened on this holiday weekend, but you'll receive good care here. In fact, tonight and for the next couple of days, you'll get an IV of treatment that should help you feel better right away," the doctor told him.

Vesta was grateful they had a private room where she was able to stay with Will for the month. The nurses showed her where to find blankets for her cot. Will and Vesta settled in quickly with Vesta keeping everything clean and helping take care of Will's needs.

On Thanksgiving, all of the children and grandchildren, along with Terri, Stan, and their son Craig, surprised them by showing up at the hospital with the entire Thanksgiving dinner. They ate in a large atrium that had couches and chairs. Since the area had signs that said no food or drink, the hospital staff looked the other way as they brought in the food. They sang their praise songs while other visitors on the stairs looked down and watched. The music flowed with such emotion and beauty that many people thought their family was brought in by the hospital as special entertainment. Vesta and Will were glad they could bless others with their beautiful family as they knew they were not the only ones suffering on this Thanksgiving Day.

Most of the family stayed overnight in nearby hotels so they could hear the doctor's report the next day. All the adult children and grandchildren joined Will and Vesta to meet with the doctors. Even though none of the test results were encouraging, Will was still determined to go through the first month of treatment.

"I think I should try it; otherwise, I won't know if I can beat this." Everyone agreed with him. After the doctors left, they talked about how many people were praying for his recovery and believed completely that God could always grant healing.

With this decision made, Will and Vesta began their cancer journey. The first week seemed straightforward as they walked the hospital halls to help Will's treatment move faster through his body. Side effects started during the second week, and soon Will couldn't eat or barely get out of bed. With every new test, the diagnosis seemed to get worse.

Vesta kept a journal on a care page for the many people praying and wanting to know how Will was doing. Being a humble man, Will didn't really think the journal was necessary until Steven told him, "Dad, people are constantly calling me. Please let Mom write the journal. I'm too busy to answer all the calls."

"I didn't think of that," Will replied. After that conversation, Vesta started reading the comments to Will and asking if there was anything he wanted to say in reply.

They received so many cards that Vesta finally asked the nurses for tape to hang them up in the room. Since many people didn't have a huge family of God surrounding them, the cards spoke volumes about their faith and community to the doctors, nurses, and even other patients. Vesta started making friends with other patients' family members and soon learned where to go for runs and even shop nearby. For Vesta, the hardest thing to do was shop. It was Christmas season, and although she needed gifts for her family, her heart wasn't in it. When she did go shopping, she would often see couples together, which would make her cry. Vesta ended up only buying more comfy clothes for Will on her shopping excursions as that was all she could handle.

As Will grew weaker, he encouraged Vesta to get out whenever she could. He especially wanted her to do her running. She would go, but it often turned into a time when she cried and prayed for strength. She knew God answered her prayers because, even in the hospital, both she and Will could sleep through the night. Then, every morning, Vesta would climb into Will's bed so they could share devotions, read their Bibles together, and pray.

During this long month, Skylar came twice to relieve Vesta at the hospital so she could go home overnight to take care of things. Before each drive, Vesta thought the trip home would refresh her, but she found that she only ached to return to Will. After her second trip home, she decided not to leave again without him.

A month after first arriving, on Christmas Eve 2011, Will's final treatment, a chemo shot into his spine, was scheduled. He was so weak that Vesta didn't want him to get the shot; she was afraid he wouldn't survive. After talking to the doctors, they agreed to forgo the shot and released him to go home.

Desirae and Brock arrived at the hospital to help Vesta drive Will home. They were surprised to find that he had lost thirty pounds and could barely walk. After arriving home, Will was so confused with all the medication and chemo in his system that he couldn't think clearly. Vesta realized she needed help for Will and called a nurse friend who became their angel by helping Will calm down and take the required medicine.

As Will and Vesta tried to sleep, they discovered that having the hospital bed in their room wasn't working at all. Will was most comfortable in his own bed beside Vesta. After he joined Vesta, Will was still restless, so Vesta began to pray aloud. The prayer gave them both peace and praying aloud in bed became a habit for Vesta. Prayer became the best medicine for both of them to relax and sleep.

The following day, Christmas Day, all their children came to their house for dinner. Tommy barbequed a delicious prime rib, and the kids brought along all the trimmings to go with it. It was a bittersweet time, but they were thankful to have their parents back home. Will rested in a special place on the couch that soon became his favorite spot. Since chemo had compromised Will's immune system, no one got too close to avoid spreading any germs to him.

A few days later, Will and Vesta visited his cancer doctor in Visalia. He took one look at Will and apologized for sending him to Stanford. Will went from being a healthy-looking, sixty-eight-year-old man to looking like a frail, hairless eighty-year-old. The doctor sensed that Will wasn't interested in any more treatments. In fact, Will and Vesta had talked it over and asked about hospice care. The doctor explained it to them and agreed it was probably their best course of action.

Will and Vesta were glad to be home and content to leave their lives and the time they had left in God's hands. They would often hug and cry together but also believed in miracles and knew that God could heal Will if that was His plan. Many relatives and friends made their way to visit. Pastor Joel was also at their side with prayer and encouragement.

Since time was precious, the family decided to have dinner together once a week. Terri and her family came up often as well to spend as much time with Will as possible. During their dinners, they also shared devotions and sang praise songs. It blessed Vesta's heart to hear everyone sing together. One of their favorites was, "Bless the Lord" by Matt Redman, along with a few of Chris Tomlin's songs, "I will Rise" and "Our God." The singing always made Will cry, which brought tears to everyone's eyes.

One morning, Will and Vesta were enjoying a devotion that was about being "Expected" by Christ in heaven. It reminded Vesta of when she was a young wife and her mother-in-law would invite them for Sunday lunch after church. She never actually invited them but would simply call Vesta and say, "I expect you tomorrow for lunch." Vesta remembered being annoyed by these invitations that she felt she couldn't decline. Of course, there were times when they did turn down the invitation, but it was always difficult.

As she thought back on the lunch invitations, Vesta realized she wasn't being caring by being annoyed. Her mother-in-law loved them so much and just wanted to have them nearby. To be expected was a wonderful thing that Vesta hadn't appreciated at the time.

During their next devotion with their children and grandchildren, they shared this story, and Vesta ended by saying, "Grandpa and I will most likely die and go to heaven before you, but we want you to always remember we 'expect you.' We expect you because we love you and want to spend eternity with you."

Will and Vesta hoped their children and grandchildren would always remember they were expected that Jesus also expected them and hoped to spend eternity with all. After all, that's why He died and rose again.

A few days later, Vesta and Will were talking, and Vesta asked, "Do you think everyone understood the whole 'we expect you' concept? Sometimes it's hard to explain something and make it meaningful for the grandchildren. I guess I won't worry about it. God will lay on their hearts what He wants them to remember. Anyway, it's not about us; it's about God."

That same afternoon, Skylar and Sharyl came for a visit. As they entered through the back door, Skylar announced, "Sharyl wants to show you the new cute baseball cap she had specially made."

Vesta started to cry as she read the words "Expected in Heaven" on Sharyl's hat. *Wow, they really understood after all*, Vesta thought.

After seeing Sharyl's hat, they decided to make t-shirts with "Expected In Heaven" on the front and "RU–2 Corinthians 5:1–10" on the back. They made pink ones for the girls and blue ones for the boys. Everyone in the family and foster family got a t-shirt and, of course, a group picture was taken.

## CHAPTER 34
# Expected in Heaven

As their cancer journey continued, Will and Vesta learned from the hospice nurse that their oncologist gave Will about three weeks to live. After they were told this news, a pastor friend, Peter Holwerda, said he wanted to visit and pray with Will. This man had become a dear friend since he was a pastor for Home Missions and served the West Coast. During that time, he and his family lived in the Lakewood area of California. When he traveled to Northern California for his work, he would spend a night or two with Will and Vesta. They told him he was their Elisha as he was God's servant, and they had a room and meal for him anytime he needed it. Will and Vesta loved visiting with Peter and hearing about his latest ministry endeavors.

Sometime later, Peter, his wife, and his family moved to Colorado as he felt called to another area of ministry. When he heard about Will's sudden illness, he called and told Vesta he was coming right over. He asked Will and Vesta to assemble their family to pray together for healing. They gathered their adult children and spouses together for the prayer time led by Peter and alerted others through Vesta's care page to mark the day and time to join in prayer.

When the prayer day arrived, the gates of heaven must have shaken. Although they didn't know exactly how many people prayed, they knew there were many. People across the country and locally let them know they were praying. Will and Vesta would always remember how cherished they felt that day by God and others.

After the prayer day, Will and Vesta went on with their lives, the days becoming weeks and the weeks becoming months. By May 2012, Will was feeling so good that, with encouragement from their hospice nurse, they planned a trip to the coast with some of their kids.

Upon returning, Will knew he needed to get his blood levels tested again. This meant that they had to sign off hospice and visit their cancer doctor. The cancer doctor told them that Will's blood test came back normal. He was excited for them and told them to enjoy the life God gave. Will and Vesta were thrilled and immediately told their children who celebrated the great news with them.

Even though Will was able to do more and more, he still used a cane to walk and knew in his heart that he wasn't fully back to normal. He walked with Vesta to strengthen his legs and improve his balance. They began cautiously by walking inside the house, holding hands, and going through the living room and family room in a large circle. Next, they ventured outside to walk a dirt path in the field across the road. Will even went alone to a cattle sale one day.

For another enjoyable outing, Will and Vesta went on a trip to Disneyland with Aaron's family. Their youngest grandson, Kenneth had turned five in May. It was a tradition to take the grandkids to Disney on or close to their fifth birthday.

One day, Will said, "I think we need to take Aaron's family to Disneyland for Kenneth's birthday."

"That's quite an outing. Do you think you are up to it?" Vesta asked with a little trepidation in her heart. She liked the idea, but it required a whole lot of walking with a cane.

"Yes, I was thinking about it, and why don't you check on getting me a motorized wheelchair for the day. I bet we could rent one at Disney," Will replied.

They worked it out and off they went. Staying in the Grand Californian offered easy access to the parks, and when needed, Will could go rest. Will stayed strong and treated his youngest children and grandchildren to days of wonderful memories.

On July 3, 2012, their forty-eighth wedding anniversary, Will suggested they visit his cancer doctor. He could tell his body didn't feel perfect. After another blood test sadly revealed his white cell counts had gone up again, Will got his first chemo treatment since his time at Stanford. Fortunately, it was a milder form of chemo that his doctor felt would give Will more time.

During the months of feeling somewhat stronger, Will and Vesta took five short trips. One trip was for a special cattle auction in Northern California honoring Will as Cattleman of the Year. It was a wonderful weekend with part of the family attending and hearing their father give a speech in front of a large crowd of people. Vesta stood beside him on the stage and was filled with pride for her dear man.

Another trip, this one to Southern California, was to take part in a grandchild's wedding. The July wedding was for their foster daughter Terri's youngest son. Her son Craig was marrying a wonderful woman named Candice. Stan and Terri were excited for him but were also sad that their baby was leaving home. Their daughters, Janie and Bonnie, were already happily married to Andy and Charlie and had two children each. Terri loved to tell Vesta that her grandchildren, Anya, Danny, Cara, and Davie, were the apples of her eye. Terri appreciated everything she'd learned from Vesta and Will because it helped her family stay grounded, especially when it came to following God. Will and Vesta's entire family was excited to attend Craig's wedding and knew it was a gift from God to have Will along.

In August, they attended their oldest granddaughter Sienna's wedding in Visalia. As Will and Vesta entered the church sanctuary and were seated, they looked at each other and tears flowed from their eyes. They both wondered, "Who would have thought ten months ago that we would have the privilege of attending this wedding together?" The night was wonderful with Skylar and Tommy hosting the reception in their yard. Desirae was so grateful to her sister for helping create such a perfect wedding for Sienna and Anthony. Will and Vesta both enjoyed the evening, not leaving until the most important wedding events were over.

Sienna and Anthony had a beautiful courtship that began shortly after Will's diagnosis. They seemed perfect for each other. Will and Vesta were thankful to have another couple in their family begin their lives together resting on God and His direction for them. Will and Vesta were incredibly pleased to have witnessed Sienna and Anthony's marriage and attending Joshua and Chelsey's wedding the year before.

*God is so good, even when we have sorrow*, Vesta thought.

September came, and the doctor shared the bad news with Will and Vesta. His white blood cell counts were sky high, and his only options were returning to hospice or stronger chemo treatments at Stanford. Will chose hospice. The hospice nurse encouragingly told them, "I just know you'll be healed again and have a lot more time to enjoy life."

One evening, Will shared with Vesta, "You know I am thankful that I don't have pain. I have some weakness at times but can't say I have pain. I am thankful for that."

"Oh, honey, I agree. What a blessing. My dad suffered from so much pain, especially during his last several months. You barely needed pain meds at all in comparison to many others," Vesta said. With that thought, they said their evening prayers together, claiming all the promises of God as they walked in this difficult place.

One morning, Will woke with tears in his eyes. "What's wrong," Vesta asked with alarm in her voice.

"I just had a dream. You know I rarely dream. This was so very real. I could see through what seemed like a portal. It was a beautiful green open meadow. There was a large crowd of people standing around. I only recognized one who was waving at me with a big smile. It was my sister Henrietta's husband, Case. He's so tall, and he stood a head above everyone." Will choked up as he explained his dream.

"It sounds like it was a vision more than a dream. It sounds like you are getting a glimpse of heaven," Vesta whispered back, fighting her own tears. She knew Case had died in 2006, and Will and Vesta pondered together about who else might be there to greet them in heaven someday.

A few days later, Terri called and asked if her son-in-law, Charlie, could join her and Stan to visit Will and Vesta. Charlie wanted to interview Will for a documentary he was working on about Christian men who had endured heavy trials.

"I feel there isn't much time left for Will, so you may want to make plans to come soon," Vesta sadly stated.

They arrived the following Saturday. Charlie brought all the equipment needed to record and film both Will and Vesta as they answered his many questions. Even though tears flowed heavily from time to time, they all persevered, knowing the interview would be something everyone would cherish for years to come.

On Monday evening, Will and Vesta shared their thoughts about God's Word and teaching. Vesta remembered that Will's father Dirk worried he wasn't good enough to be saved when he was near death and wanted to know how Will was feeling. "Honey, I know how I feel about the fact I may lose you, but I can't imagine how it feels to be in your place. I hope you don't mind me asking. Remember when your dad came close to his death and he was worried he wasn't good enough to be saved? Well, how about you? How are you feeling?"

"That is a good question and easy to answer, especially since I had my dream. I am not at all afraid of death. I do not worry about where I'm going or if I'm saved. I know I am," Will answered with deep assurance and conviction. Speaking again with tears in his eyes, Will said sadly, "My main sorrow is having to leave you . . ." Then they both broke into tears and embraced, letting their grief out freely.

A few days later, on Thursday, Vesta was out getting her hair done in the morning. Skylar stayed with Will while Vesta was gone, and Desirae was coming in the afternoon to be with Will while Vesta worked at Care Pregnancy Center. Desirae stayed a little longer that afternoon to work with Will on solving an issue with selling her home. She was so grateful to her dad. She appreciated his keen business mind, love, and how willing he was to help whenever he could.

After Desirae left. Will and Vesta shared a nice dinner together. They talked about their day until it was almost time for Will to go to bed. He mentioned that he felt a little strange, so Vesta felt his forehead and said, "Oh goodness, you are warm. Let me take your temperature."

Sure enough, Will's temperature was 101. Will looked at Vesta and said, "I don't think this is good. What do you think we should do?"

"Let's get you ready for bed and give you some medicine for the temperature. I'll also call the hospice nurse to see if she wants me to do anything else." The hospice nurse agreed with Vesta and with the medicine she had given Will. She also told Vesta to call her back if she needed more help.

That night was the longest of Vesta's life. The last normal conversation between Vesta and Will occurred just before she helped him to bed. After that, he was never fully coherent again. She finally decided to call hospice for help. They came and set up a hospital bed for Will. They helped Will get comfortable and showed Vesta how to administer morphine to him. Knowing she was an early riser, Vesta called Skylar around 5:30. Skylar called her siblings and then rushed right over. Skylar took over caring for her dad and giving him morphine since Vesta felt uncertain what to do. Fortunately, Skyler had checked with Tommy's niece (a nurse) who knew exactly how to help keep Will comfortable.

Everyone else took turns answering phone calls and calling the pastor. They tried hard to convince Vesta to get some rest and eat a little. She ate but found sleeping difficult, so she stayed awake. She wanted to keep vigil.

On this last day of his life, the entire family crowded around Will's bed to be with him. He left for heaven around 6 p.m. on September 28, 2012. Everyone mourned loudly as he left his body while Vesta looked up, tears streaming, and waved goodbye. She had told Will that if he left for heaven before she did, he should look back to see her wave.

Vesta stood by Will with Pastor Joel and let more tears flow. She couldn't believe he was gone since his body looked so normal. She would never forget how earlier in the day, he squeezed her hand tightly as if saying goodbye. He had lost weight, but his skin was still pink. His face had a blueish tint, but the rest of him looked natural. It occurred to her that death is so final, and eternity so far away. It was almost impossible to believe in heaven when seeing death up close and personal. At that moment, Vesta felt so alone and helpless. She realized she would need to lean hard on God to get through all of her emotions.

Vesta's daughters insisted on staying the night and sleeping in her bedroom with her. Even though she believed she could manage alone, Vesta loved having them so close. As Vesta thought about the next phase of her life, she concluded that she would spend it alone since there was no one like her Will and no man could possibly replace him. However, when she had talked to Will about this, he told her, "You are a beautiful woman. You should marry again when I'm gone."

She remembered telling him, "No, because I love you and I can't imagine living with or loving anyone but you." They never discussed the matter again. It was all they could do to handle what was left of their life together.

Will's memorial service was a whirlwind but would always be remembered by Vesta. Steven insisted on using a large church as his father had been well known in the business community and greatly loved and respected. Steven was right, and over one thousand people attended the service. Pastor Joel shared a wonderful eulogy full of encouragement while Skylar put together a beautiful slide show tribute to Will. The grandchildren joined with a praise band to lead everyone in song. In the weeks to come, singing "Bless the Lord" brought tears to their family's eyes as it reminded them of Will, their beloved husband, father, foster father, and grandfather. Vesta was most surprised at how she was able to make it through the service. She thought she would have trouble talking to the people who came without breaking down in tears. Thankfully, God gave her the strength to persevere. Her children, grandchildren, and foster family showered her with love and encouragement.

Another dear friend, Scott Elgersma, who was a pastor, shared some of the thoughts and memories of Tom from the family. Vesta wrote a special goodbye letter that she asked Scott to read:

*To my beloved husband, Will,*

*How do I say goodbye? This is the hardest thing I've ever done! I love you so MUCH! I want to hang onto you! You were so good to me, loving me and being a wonderful example to our children of what Christ-like love looks like. Truth is, I could hardly believe we would be separated BEFORE fifty years of marriage. Your strength helped me face it, as you reminded me of all the good years we had together. God has been so faithful in giving us His care throughout life. I believe we will both think on those God-guided events throughout eternity!*

*I admit I'm a little jealous you beat me to heaven! But we both knew God had the timing under His perfect control. We also knew you would have been a mess without me and on your own!*

*Thank you for leaving me with a mantle of wisdom on how to handle the practical, material side of life! I will work hard on going slow, not rushing headlong, as I tend to do when making important decisions. Thank you, too, for always encouraging me to get involved in the things you felt I was gifted in. You've challenged me with your great listening skills, common sense, and how you ALWAYS think of others before yourself! I love you, honey, and know that one day we will dance together again, and you will know how! Smile. I know you'll be expecting me in heaven one day!*

*LOVE YOU ALWAYS,*
*Your wife Vesta*

Scott thought reading the memories, especially Vesta's letter, would be a great way for him to bless the family. He didn't realize how hard it would be and confessed to the audience that it was difficult, but he would do his best. When he finished, there were not many dry eyes in the church, including Scott's, but the family was grateful he helped them through this time by sharing their thoughts at the service.

Another family friend and pastor, George Vink, took part in the graveside service. He led it with thoughtful words and many encouraging reminders of God's promises in the Bible about the life to come, one day for us all.

Vesta's sisters both attended the service with Sara coming with Peter from Washington and Rachel with Ron from Chicago. Her brothers, Matthew and Tommy, came together, and several nieces and nephews attended as well. After the service, Vesta's home was filled with family, many of whom stayed the night. It was comforting for Vesta to have the family so close.

One morning before everyone returned home, the girls decided it would be good to take Vesta on a shopping trip. Her sisters really wanted to buy her a belated birthday gift, and Will had given her money to buy some clothes as soon as she had a chance to shop. It felt like a good way to have some fun things after all the sadness. Off to Fresno, they went, shopping at Vesta's favorite store, Chico's, and eating lunch at a great restaurant. When they arrived home, it hit Vesta hard that Will was gone and she had no husband to show her purchases to. After shedding more tears, Vesta enjoyed more time with her family before they left.

After all the relatives went home, Vesta sat alone, knowing the road ahead without Will would be challenging. She woke up every morning feeling her life just dragging on. She wanted at least five years to pass by. She didn't know why five years sounded good, but she guessed it was because she wanted time to pass.

As time passed, Vesta got more involved with people and caring for others. Once a month, she invited other widows to dinner at her home. She made plans for the holidays so they wouldn't feel lonely. She stayed involved with her ministry to the young women at the Care Pregnancy Center, and of course, she never stopped spending time with God. Many dear people called on her to check on how she was doing. Pastor Joel also continued to call or visit with encouragement and concern. Her church became such a comfort and picture of God's grace. She knew that her time with God was what kept her sane. God helped her when she felt a black cloud come over her and she couldn't hold back the tears. Letting them flow was difficult, but to her relief, the crying often subsided, and she would regain her strength to carry on. She knew crying was good, so she would listen to her emotions and cry as needed.

Whenever Vesta fought the temptation of thinking heaven wasn't real, she often thought of words a pastor had once shared, "When doubts attack you, do what you know to be right and stay in God's Word. Eventually, the head knowledge of the truth will penetrate the heart as well." Vesta knew that it took time for emotions to catch up with understanding, so she took her time and didn't give up on God, even when she didn't feel He was close by.

In those early days of learning to be alone, Vesta also realized that she was never afraid. She was often sad but not afraid. When Will was alive, she feared being alone but now she knew that God was giving her strength to face each day. As she gave in and cried for as long as she needed, Vesta discovered that she felt much better and continued to take her tears to God.

Before Will died, Vesta feared that she might not feel comfortable attending her church or would be so sad it would be unbearable to attend. However, just the opposite happened. She still loved to be at her church and never wanted to miss a service. Over time, she found she wasn't afraid to share her tears with others. All these things and reading good books helped her through the grieving process.

Although life appeared ominous at times, Vesta still felt young at sixty-six. She ran three to six miles without much effort. She loved babysitting her grandchildren, playing games, and traveling. Vesta trusted God to help her decide each day what was important. She realized life could be a spiritual adventure, no matter what came her way—difficult or easy. The most important thing, after all, was to be sure one was "Expected in Heaven."

# Postscript

The same year Will died, his brother Isaak lost his wife, Margot, rather suddenly from a fall. After living close by for over thirty-five years, Vesta and her family rushed to help Isaak and his family in their grief. It was only a matter of time before Isaak and Vesta realized they enjoyed spending time together and decided to marry. It gave both their pastors, Steve and Joel, great joy to marry Isaak and Vesta. They had shared the sadness and now were a part of their joy.

This was when Vesta learned that it was possible to love again. She was surprised by how needy she was after losing Will and struggled with guilt before marrying Isaak. She realized she needed to decide what she wanted, or she would lose him. In the end, Vesta knew that Isaac was a gift from God to help her through her untold grief.

Together they enjoyed trips to his beautiful Marriott time-shares in various places while Isaak continued working at his real estate business. Vesta also continued her ministry at the Care Pregnancy Center and worked to help women discover God's Word. After two years together, they welcomed seven great-grandchildren between them, and Vesta welcomed another grandchild, Abigail, the daughter of Christine and Aaron. Abigail was another darling little blonde, blue-eyed child.

At this point, Vesta had sixteen grandchildren with her four children each having four children of their own. Vesta and her daughters had a great time posing for photos together. Vesta would hold her newborn granddaughter while her two daughters, Desirae and Skylar, held their new grandsons, Will and Samuel, all of the babies just a few months apart. Vesta's daughters were both grandmothers to baby boys Will, Sienna and Anthony's son, and Samuel, Joshua and Chelsey's son. Will had been named after his great grandfather. When they told Vesta his name, she couldn't help but cry; it touched her so.

During their second year of marriage, in summer 2015, Vesta talked to Isaak about selling the country home that she and Will had built together. He soon found a home to purchase nearby that was perfect for them both. Vesta needed to work through more grief from leaving the country home because it came with wonderful memories of her life with Will and her children. Even her grandchildren were upset about the sale. There were many happy memories of parties and celebrations in the house, not to mention all the hours they played together in the big backyard and the swimming pool.

Desirae helped her siblings accept the decision by asking, "Who wants to buy the house from Mom?" The replies were clear. "We can't buy the house. It's too much work and costs a lot of money to care for." "If none of us is willing to buy it, then how can we expect Mom and Isaak to take care of it and everything that entails?"

Vesta was grateful for Desirae's wise counsel, but signing the final papers was still difficult.

Isaak was patient and understanding through the entire process, and the moment they moved into their new home, Vesta knew it was a perfect spot for them. It was in a quiet, gated community filled with wonderful neighbors. It was also close enough to her old home that she could still run in the same fields she had been running in for the last thirty years. This meant a great deal to Vesta. As she ran in the same open fields, she felt her closeness to God and how He cared for her.

Not long after they moved, Isaak decided to sell his real estate business. Since Isaak had such a strong reputation in the community, it only took a few weeks to find a buyer. Isaak and Vesta were both thrilled to have extra time to spend together and looked forward to discovering what God had in mind for them in the future.

However, God doesn't promise that we will not have trouble in this world. After a short two-and-a-half years of marriage and living in their new home for only six months, Isaak was diagnosed with cancer and a heart condition that took his life in five short weeks.

For so many reasons, Vesta was thankful God gave her Isaak to love. He was a wonderful man and helped her through the difficult work of selling her country home with his real estate knowledge. She now lived in a place that felt reassuring after another unbelievable loss. Vesta knew why God brought her here for such a time as this. There were two other ladies in her neighborhood that had recently lost their husbands. It was very consoling to be surrounded by a loving community who knew exactly what she was going through.

A wonderful (if such things can be called wonderful) Celebration of Life service was held for Isaak. It took place at his home church in Tulare. It felt right to have Pastor Joel and Pastor Steve, who had married them and walked so much of the journey of life and death with them, to be a part of this ceremony. His children and grandchildren put most of the service together, but since they were all cousins of Vesta's children, they all took part in the service. Skylar made a beautiful slide show while Desirae read a letter to Isaak from Vesta and shared her and her siblings' memories of Isaak. Isaak's three children shared their thoughts and warm memories of their father. They also sang some of Isaak's favorite songs and enjoyed lunch for everyone who attended.

For the next two months, Vesta invited her granddaughters to take turns spending the night with her. Having them with her helped her tremendously. After Isaak's death, Vesta mourned deeply, but life was full and helped fill her days. She had so much to be thankful for. During this time, two more grandchildren married, Jacob to a wonderful girl named Lisa, and his sister, Elizabeth, to a great guy, Tanner. Two more darling great grandsons were born as well; Jack came to Joshua and Chelsey and Alex to Sienna and Anthony. Her children and stepchildren were often by her side, encouraging Vesta. Vesta also spent a great deal of time crying out to God. He was the answer to what she needed most, and it seemed that the more she needed, the more He gave.

One and a half years later, a friend encouraged Vesta to go out on a date with a widower, Joseph VaBrea. In many ways, Vesta knew she was ready to open her heart to marriage again. She wasn't exactly sure why but was certain the biggest reason was that her marriages to both Will and Isaak had been so good. Vesta loved being married, so she wasn't against what God might have in store for her. On one hand, it was a hard decision, but on the other hand, it would be a joy to share love and attention with a kind man. Vesta realized she was ready to take that risk.

Any man Vesta would consider had to love God as much as she did and attend church every Sunday. It was also important that he have a great reputation in the community of God and anyone else who knew him. Joseph had it all, so when he called for a date, she said yes. After some ups and downs, they became serious and decided to marry in April 2018. They were happy to have Pastor Joel and Pastor Steve be part of their ceremony of marriage. It was a happy time for them both. They loved the same food and entertainment. They also loved to travel, run, hike, and ride bikes. Most importantly, they loved each other's families.

Later that year, Joseph started feeling ill. On October 31, they found out he had stage-four lung cancer. They cried together, and Joseph kept apologizing for doing this to Vesta a third time. Although Vesta knew it wasn't Joseph's fault, she struggled at times and wondered why her again. She knew she had had an amazing life, and God always had good reasons to ask people to walk down certain paths. She knew this was God's calling for her, and she must continue to stay close to Him and His Word so she could do what was right. The night would usually challenge her determination and her tears would be difficult to stop.

Joseph continued his cancer treatments for the next seven months when they celebrated their first wedding anniversary on April 7, 2019. They knew their God was not limited and miracles happen, so they lived one day at a time to see what God would give. No matter how many tears fell or joys shared, they knew they were "Expected in Heaven," so they remained hopeful.

As the months passed, Joseph's cancer pill seemed to help. They were able to attend some programs for their grandchildren, a graduation, and a party for another grandchild. They felt blessed for every special day that they lived a somewhat normal life. One thing that seemed particularly difficult for

Joseph was how the food tasted. Vesta did her best to cook all varieties of food to help keep Joseph eating.

In July 2019, they planned a vacation with Joseph's family, one they hoped Joseph would be well enough for. It was an Alaskan cruise for all seventeen of them. As Joseph and Vesta boarded the plane to Seattle, they had a hard time keeping the tears of joy at bay. They spent the night in Seattle and boarded the ship the following day. During the trip, Joseph did quite well with breakfast and lunch, but dinner was difficult. His stomach would get upset, and although he tried to stay with Vesta at the table, he only managed to enjoy two dinners with the family during the ten-day cruise. Despite this, Joseph and Vesta counted their blessings for being with the family and witnessing the beauty of God's creation from their ship.

After arriving home, Joseph worked hard to stay strong, but each week produced new problems. His doctors did their best, but with every new test or medicine, nothing improved. Vesta could feel the clock was ticking against her and Joseph.

Many days Vesta wanted to cry but knew she had to cherish every moment she had left with Joseph. She needed to love and care for him and not get angry with God or even blame poor Joseph for being sick. It took effort, but as she enjoyed each day talking during their devotion time in the morning or watching favorite movies or shows at night, she was so glad he was there and part of her life. She didn't have any regrets. A few times she did become frustrated with Joseph and his lack of energy. She couldn't seem to help herself and would apologize later.

During this time, many friends and loved ones visited, praying for healing. Pastor Joel and Pastor Steve were regulars in visits and offering prayers. They had become more than pastors;

they were close friends. Joseph and Vesta appreciated everyone's tender care and concern. They never stopped hoping in their Lord and had thankfulness for friends and family.

As fall arrived, Joseph and Vesta started hoping they could celebrate another Christmas with their families. Sadly, Joseph started getting sores on his body and his appetite grew worse. It was a difficult time when Joseph realized he needed to change the way he was living. He knew he needed to ask the doctor about hospice. The doctor looked at Joseph, noticing his low energy and slow steps. He asked Joseph what he wanted. Joseph was honest and said he couldn't take any more cancer pills and was relieved when the doctor told him that it was time for hospice. Both Vesta and Joseph were relieved when the hospice nurse told Joseph that he didn't need to eat if he didn't want to.

During the last few days of his life, the families took turns to visit and spend some quality time with Joseph. With lots of tears, the families said their goodbyes and let Joseph go home to his Lord and Savior on October 14, 2019. Vesta never forgot how Joseph rubbed her back as she knelt by his bedside weeping. She knew he was on the brink of death, yet he seemed to be saying goodbye in such a tender, giving way.

Vesta couldn't believe she was burying her third husband. Tears and grief followed a beautiful service at the Christian school chapel that Joseph helped build during his time as school superintendent. Pastor Steve Duyst and Pastor Joel Renkema took part in this service once again. To Vesta, it only seemed right for them to be a part. The children and grandchildren in both families added to the service by sharing memories in beautiful ways.

All three of her husbands are buried in the Visalia cemetery. Although she rarely goes there, she grieves deeply for each of them. At times, Vesta wonders why she doesn't visit their graves. She has come to understand it's because she doesn't think of them as being there. In fact, she knows they're in heaven, waiting for all their loved ones to join them, including her, and worshiping God in a beautiful place.

Vesta still grieves and cries over her losses, but her hope remains in God and His Word. When she breaks down and cries, asking God "Why?" she often opens her Bible to Hebrews 12:1. This verse reminds her that all those who have gone before are cheering her on and that she is expected in heaven. She believes that these three men, who finished their earthly lives with grace and strength, are cheering her on to finish what God calls her to do each day. She is comforted, knowing that there's a heaven waiting and believing that she's "Expected."

A few weeks after this difficult experience, Vesta received an email from Joseph's nephew, Steve Laman, who was very close to Joseph. Though Steve, having been born with cerebral palsy, can neither walk nor talk without help from a computer, he is a great writer and often wrote devotionals for their church's magazine. It strengthened Vesta to go back and read the copy she made of the email. She knew it applied to everyone waiting for their meeting with God.

Steve's letter said:

> *Let us fix our eyes on Jesus, the author and perfecter of our faith, who for the joy set before him endured the cross, scorning its shame, and sat down at the right hand of the throne of God (Heb. 12:2).*

*The evening before my Uncle Joseph died, my sister-in-law and I attended a worship concert featuring two very popular contemporary worship composers. In the midst of their original songs, one of them grabbed an acoustical guitar and began to sing the hymn "Turn Your Eyes Upon Jesus." Everyone in the arena joined him in singing, "Turn your eyes upon Jesus, look full in His wonderful face, and the things of earth will grow strangely dim, in the light of His glory and grace." As I listened to the words of this great hymn, I thought of my uncle. I realized that the song was describing what Joseph was going to experience.*

*I imagined Joseph's view of this earth growing dimmer and dimmer as his new home with his Savior was growing clearer and clearer. This thought put a smile on my face because I knew the stress and worries of cancer would melt away as his eternal home was coming into view.*

*In Hebrews 12:2, the biblical writer is encouraging us to fix our eyes on Jesus and think about how much He sacrificed on the cross for us. When we do, we find the cares of this earth will temporarily seem to disappear. In doing this, maybe we can have just a taste on this earth of what Joseph has already experienced.*

*Steve*

Vesta's prayer continued as she read this to keep focused on her Lord and Savior Jesus and rest in His strength to get through all the uncertainties of life. A few short months after losing Joseph, the world was brought to its knees by the coronavirus. That battle continues, and Vesta continues to rest in her God and His Word, the Bible. To her, it is the only answer for all the struggles of life. She is certain her only comfort in life and death is to belong to her faithful Savior Jesus Christ and knowing that she is "Expected in Heaven."

CPSIA information can be obtained
at www.ICGtesting.com
Printed in the USA
BVHW031052250222
630078BV00001B/6